CRITICAL INSIGHTS

To Kill a Mockingbird

CRITICAL INSIGHTS

To Kill a Mockingbird

by Harper Lee

Editor
Don Noble
University of Alabama

Salem Press
Pasadena, California   Hackensack, New Jersey

Library of Congress Cataloging-in-Publication Data

To kill a mockingbird, by Harper Lee / editor, Don Noble.
    p. cm. — (Critical insights)
  Includes bibliographical references and index.
  ISBN 978-1-58765-618-7 (alk. paper)
  1. Lee, Harper. To kill a mockingbird. I. Noble, Donald R.
PS3562.E353T66 2010
813'.54—dc22
                                            2009026311

Contents

The Book and Author

Critical Contexts

Critical Readings

Resources

About This Volume

Don Noble

Commentators on *To Kill a Mockingbird* often refer to what may be a singular paradox. This 1960 American novel is one of the most popular books of all time, but it has attracted relatively little critical commentary. Although there is no doubt the 1962 award-winning movie propelled sales even higher, the book had won the Pulitzer and was a best seller before there was any movie, so success cannot be attributed to Horton Foote, screenwriter, and the performance of Gregory Peck. The novel famously stands for and by itself. In fact, Ms. Lee refused to write even a brief introduction to the thirty-fifth anniversary edition, stating that "*Mockingbird* still says what it has to say; it has managed to survive without preamble."

It has survived indeed. *Mockingbird* sales have probably exceeded forty million copies, selling about a million a year in recent years, and half of that million is sold abroad, in one of the approximately forty languages into which the novel has been translated.

In this volume of commentary on *Mockingbird*, there are two related points to make about *To Kill a Mockingbird* and its lack of commentary. First, the fact that it is an American best seller, a popular book, weighs against it. The best-seller list is so laden with thrillers, genre fiction, mysteries, fantasies, and romances that it has, understandably, become a commonplace to associate popularity with the second-rate, following the logic that "If that many people like it, it can't be any good." The indisputably authoritative *The History of Southern Literature*, edited by Louis D. Rubin, Jr., et al., has only one paragraph about *Mockingbird,* with three brief mentions given to Lee in the section on Truman Capote. Margaret Mitchell's *Gone with the Wind* is discussed in two pages of text, and in a section entitled "Popular Fiction, 1920-1950."

What these two novels share, besides having been given short shrift in this 1985 literary history, is that both have since risen in critics' estimations and both are now upgraded, as it were, from popular fiction to literary fiction, and are, more and more often, written about, interpreted, understood from a variety of points of view.

The second reason one might offer for the lack of commentary on *Mockingbird* is that at a basic level of reader response, it does not seem to need much. *Mockingbird* is, to put it mildly, not like James Joyce's *Ulysses* or *Finnegans Wake* or William Faulkner's *The Sound and the Fury* or, more recently, Thomas Pynchon's *Gravity's Rainbow*. Readers, over forty-eight years in forty-some countries, believe quite rightly that they understand the novel. They feel that they "get it" without the interpretive help needed for more intellectually complex works such as Joyce's or Faulkner's or Pynchon's. *Mockingbird* needs little "unpacking."

I think it could be successfully wagered that the sales-to-essay ratio of *To Kill a Mockingbird* is the highest of any well-known American novel. It may even be a million to one.

But a work of such huge popularity will generate a different kind of interest and curiosity—what is it about *Mockingbird* that causes it to resonate so? And, since it is in fact a sophisticated work of art, when carefully examined, depths and dimensions not previously suspected are revealed. Also, a success of this magnitude, by an author who has remained a very private person, generates a good deal of curiosity about the publishing history of the book and the biography of the author.

Several of the essays in this volume take up the general questions of author biography and publishing/sales history. Edythe M. McGovern offers such an overview of the author and novel, as does, very briefly, Sasha Weiss of *The Paris Review*. An extended essay by Nancy Grisham Anderson, "Successes and Myths," does a clear and reliable job of outlining the history of the book, its dramatizations, its worldwide success and the much misunderstood life of the author, including laughable errors such as the dedication to "Mr. Lee and Slice" being misunderstood as Ms. Lee's husband and child, when she has neither, and the myth that Ms. Lee is in fact deceased. Not true. You can ask her.

Readers who want what is at present the most authoritative and complete study of Harper Lee and her novel are advised to go to *Mockingbird: A Portrait of Harper Lee*, a full-length biography by Charles J. Shields (Henry Holt, 2006). Ms. Lee did not authorize or cooperate in the creation of this book, but Shields, through diligent research and many interviews, was able to do an excellent job nevertheless.

Another essay which attempts an overview of the novel's history and major themes is "*Mockingbird* in Context," by Gurdip Panesar. Panesar explores some of the autobiographical elements in *Mockingbird* and points out a number of places the novel has received negative critical attention—in the depiction of African-Americans, for example, and in what are sometimes perceived as lawyer Finch's personal and professional shortcomings.

Neil Heims, in "'Were You Ever a Turtle?': *To Kill a Mockingbird*—Casting the Self as the Other," elaborates at some length on a central tenet of Atticus Finch's philosophy and of the novel in general, namely, that the road to dignity and justice may wind through empathy. If a person will pause, listen to others' arguments, attempt to see matters from others' points of view, strife and prejudice will be reduced, understanding enhanced.

Another essay in the "Critical Contexts" section, one I think worthy of special notice, is "*To Kill a Mockingbird* as an Introduction to Faulkner." Here Matthew Bolton pursues what at first seems to be a very arbitrary line of reasoning, that a fairly straightforward novel set in 1936 might serve as a gateway to the much more complex novel *The Sound and the Fury*, published thirty-one years earlier, in 1929. This is not an influence study, nor is *S&F* to be thought of as a prequel. Bolton demonstrates how most of the Deep South themes, character types, family dynamics, social, racial, class, and cultural issues of *The Sound and the Fury* are also taken up in a very accessible manner in *Mockingbird* and, if properly understood in that novel, can be better understood in Faulkner's masterwork.

In the essays which constitute the second half of this volume we have two main groupings. One grouping might properly be considered close examinations of Atticus Finch, as man and lawyer.

Christopher Metress sums up the new discussions of Finch. Atticus, while deemed heroic for thirty or so years, is now found by many to be complicit in the segregation/racism of Maycomb, Alabama. Atticus, as Metress points out, is faulted by many for failing to be a civil rights activist, for defending Tom out of noblesse oblige rather than pure, righteous passion, for failing to demand changes in the law from the state legislature. Metress asks, sensibly, where this line of reasoning will end.

Tim Dare likewise summarizes the debate on Atticus's claim to hero status but focuses on the issue of character-based ethics. He points out that Atticus is eloquent in his defense of legal procedures, as they apply fairly to everyone, but then "takes the law into his own hands," in his agreeing, with Sheriff Tate, that Boo Radley should not be arrested and tried for the killing of Bob Ewell, even though it is a certainty Boo would be acquitted. Most readers admire Atticus's character, to be sure, but procedures of law must be followed, in every case, to keep us from those situations where the person making the extra-legal decision does not possess a character we are confident would yield the right decision. No man's heart is pure enough to trust to not circumvent the legal process.

Ethics is also the subject of Thomas L. Shaffer's "Growing Up Good in Maycomb." Scout and Jem are "good" children and are taught the virtues, as expressed by their father, their neighbors, their aunt, and the community at large. More specifically, Scout must learn to one day be a white, Southern lady, and that is a complicated business indeed.

Readers of *Mockingbird* usually find the scene in which peaceful, mild-mannered Atticus shoots the mad dog a memorable one. Carolyn Jones uses this emblematic scene to discuss Finch's confrontations with the lynch mob and, to extend the metaphor further, the mad dog mentality that is racism.

As the years passed and *To Kill a Mockingbird* achieved the status of something like a sacred text, it is only natural that this would provoke reactions to it. Several essays discuss the flaws and inadequacies of this novel and lament that absence of what should have been in *Mockingbird*.

Teresa Godwin Phelps takes on the question of social class and castes. As readers are told explicitly in the novel, there are people like us (the Finches) and folks like the Cunninghams. There are also the Ewells and the African Americans. To some degree all are marginalized except the people like "us."

Theodore R. Hovet and Grace-Ann Hovet also explore the question of class in *Mockingbird*. The narrative voice of this novel is "middle-class," they argue, but finally readers become aware of the range of other voices, including Mayella's, Calpurnia's, and the adult female voice of Scout as the novel's narrator.

Diann L. Baecker writes of "The Importance of the Africanist Presence in *To Kill a Mockingbird*." Not only is the African-American presence smaller than one would wish, but also readers and critics tend to give it too little attention, focusing instead on the gothic element provided by Boo Radley or the "white trash" issues raised by the Ewells.

Dean Shackelford wishes to raise awareness of gender and the female voice in the novel and, to a lesser extent, the film. Scout's narration of the novel is, of necessity, much diminished in the film, where it is an occasional voice-over. This is largely due to the greater percentage of the film taken up by the obviously dramatic trial of Tom Robinson.

Laurie Champion, expanding a concept from Ralph Waldo Emerson, writes of the "Unconquered Eye" in *Mockingbird*. She demonstrates how someone with poor actual vision, like Atticus himself, sees moral and social issues pretty clearly indeed, and the eye of the child is more likely to see without bias and prejudice.

Gary Richards, writing of what he calls "The Destabilization of Heterosexuality," examines the domestic arrangements of Maycomb and finds almost no successfully married couples. This essay will provoke considerable discussion, I imagine, on subjects like why Atticus never remarried, why his brother Jack never married at all, is Scout in "drag" wearing overalls under her dress, and to what extent Boo's long years inside the Radley house might be considered "closeted." He suggests that "without ever being fully conscious of the fact," Lee presents Maycomb as "already distinctly queer."

To whatever degree any given reader is convinced by this or any other essay in this volume, one thing seems clear. The critical examination of *Mockingbird* has only just begun in earnest, and the ratio of sales to essays will be falling steadily in the coming years.

THE BOOK
AND
AUTHOR

On *To Kill a Mockingbird*

Don Noble

Although the novel *To Kill a Mockingbird* was published more than forty-eight years ago in far-off New York City, it is not a dead, historical document to citizens of Alabama, and the author, Nelle Harper Lee, is not a writer from the past, like Mark Twain or, now, Faulkner. Nelle Harper Lee lives today in Monroeville, Alabama, spends a good deal of her time with her older sister, the attorney Alice Lee, and can be seen, if one really needs to establish a sighting, eating lunch occasionally at a restaurant called Boo Radley's.

There seems to be a desire to classify Miss Lee in the same category as Thomas Pynchon, who has not in fact been seen or photographed for many years and gives no interviews, or J. D. Salinger, who is described as a recluse but in fact has friends and neighbors in to dinner when he pleases. She is closer to Salinger or to Cormac McCarthy, who lives a pretty regular life in a gated community in El Paso, Texas, with his wife and daughter but, like Salinger, refuses interviews, television shows, and reporters of all kinds. Miss Lee was supersaturated with journalists' attention in the early sixties, becoming especially irritated when reporters persisted in asking where her next novel was. When she began refusing interviews, some reporters commenced making things up, and Miss Lee was then really finished. Because Miss Lee was seldom photographed, she was actually able to live in Manhattan, take buses and cabs and go to plays, movies, museums, and restaurants without attracting attention. In Monroeville, she is so revered that if a visitor should attempt to take her picture FROM ACROSS THE STREET, a Monroeville native, if present, might ask him to refrain, out of courtesy to Miss Lee's privacy.

Monroeville, Alabama, is now, in many ways, to Miss Lee what Oxford, Mississippi, is to Faulkner—both hometown and cottage industry. Monroeville in fact has gone farther than Oxford, since it is arguably the "hometown" of Truman Capote; the novelist Mark Childress, author of *Crazy in Alabama*, among other books; the Pulitzer Prize-winning editorial writer for the *Atlanta Journal-Constitution*, Cynthia Tucker; and a dozen other successful prose writers. Yes, one can actually buy Monroeville "Inspirational" bottled water, if water is what you believe does it.

Monroeville has even been declared by the Alabama State Legislature to be, officially, the "Literary Capital of Alabama."

At the center of Monroeville is the courthouse square with THE courthouse. Gregory Peck and the advance party came to Monroeville to scout the place out and the director, Robert Mulligan, decided, for ease in shooting and to control the lighting, to build an exact replica of the courtroom on a soundstage in Hollywood. Most moviegoers never knew the difference.

Inside the courthouse are extensive exhibits of *Mockingbird* memorabilia and Capote memorabilia and a bookstore with many Monroeville titles.

Every spring, in late April and early May, local amateurs perform a stage version of *Mockingbird* to sold-out houses. The play is in two acts. The first is performed on the lawn outside—the scenes with the rabid dog, Jem's destruction of Mrs. Dubose's flowers, and the scene in which Atticus, alone at night reading by a single bulb, is accosted by the would-be lynch mob that rolls up to the door in a vintage car, with rednecks clinging to the running board. With Scout's unexpected help, he faces the gang down, and they retreat.

The second act is performed in the courtroom itself, and the setting could not be more realistic and effective. In fact, before the performance each evening, twelve jurors are chosen as part of the cast. Every year, women volunteer to sit on the jury, on stage, and are surprised that they cannot be chosen. African Americans, of course, likewise. In fact, the jury of twelve white men, on which I have served more than once, is taken backstage and advised to play their parts correctly, believe Mayella if possible, and, most important, vote to convict. Some modern jurors are reluctant to convict, just as women are astounded they cannot serve. There can be no clearer signs of progress than a situation in which individuals can hardly believe that things really were the way they were.

This production of *Mockingbird* has been presented for a number of years now and is so appealing it has been produced at the Kennedy Center in Washington, D.C., in Jerusalem, and in England.

The *Mockingbird* play was also produced a couple of years ago by two high schools in the Birmingham, Alabama, area. This production was a collaboration between a very affluent, predominantly white suburban school, Mountain Brook High School, and the predominantly black Fairfield High Preparatory School, both in the Birmingham area. This production received a great deal of attention, including coverage on the evening national news, and is regarded as a triumph of interracial cooperation and goodwill. And it was. The cast had a most powerful experience and in many ways the audience did as well. What almost everyone declined to dwell upon, however, was the disturbing fact that there were no white students at Fairfield Prep and too few black students at Mountain Brook to cast the play using the students of only one school. Out-and-out racism and cruelty are hugely diminished, but the integration so sorely lacking in Maycomb, Alabama, in 1936 has not yet been achieved as we move toward the end of decade one in the twenty-first century.

It is useful to remember, however, that *To Kill A Mockingbird* is a novel, a work of art, and was never meant to be a document of the kind written by, say, Upton Sinclair in *The Jungle*, the novel about the meat-packing industry that led to the passage of the Pure Food and Drug Act. It is not and never was agitprop, meant to accomplish social or legal aims or legislation. The novel is not in fact about integration; it is about respect, decency, fair treatment under the law. It is a novel that intrinsically urges people to empathize with one another, be kind to one another, understand one another, think about things from someone else's point of view, to, as Atticus famously says, try to get into someone else's skin, to walk around in someone else's shoes.

There is a good deal of amazement at the enduring and global popularity of *Mockingbird*, but there need not be. To begin with, children—especially bright, attractive, nice little children—are always appealing, and Jem, Scout and tow-headed Dill are fetching youngsters. They are not saints but are mischievous enough to step over the line in tormenting Boo Radley and with emotion enough, in Jem's case, to behead Mrs. Dubose's camellias. Readers in forty languages have shared the delight of watching the phenomenon of maturation and understanding in these children as Jem moves to young manhood and Scout, albeit reluctantly, moves toward female adolescence.

The novel's appeal can also be attributed to what most people take as an accurate piece of social realism. Few commentators argue that Lee gets it wrong in her portrait of small-town Alabama in 1936. The argument most often proffered is that she leaves out slices of the society that surely existed. But this is not a rural novel of a cotton plantation, nor a novel about the Jewish dry goods store, nor a novel of African American or poor white life in Maycomb. This novel, the one Lee actually wrote, is about Atticus Finch, small-town lawyer and father of two, and the case he undertook on behalf of the wrongly accused Tom Robinson. *Mockingbird* is primarily about a white family of modest means but long established in the community where they will continue to live when the action is ended.

One should also remember that *Mockingbird* is also a humorous novel that contains a certain amount of social satire. Aunt Alexandra and her kind, especially the Missionary Society, are supposed to be amusing to the reader. They offer a kind of comic relief.

Most of all, the novel is about Atticus Finch himself, as seen mostly through the eyes of his daughter. Finch is a good man. Sometimes critics seem to demand that he be a saint, a real saint. But he is not. Atticus is an idealist, perhaps, but he is not a self-deluded dreamer. On the very last page of the novel, after Scout has escorted Boo Radley back to his house, she says to her dad, "Atticus, he was real nice. . . ." Atticus replies, "Most people are, Scout, when you finally see them." He does not say everyone is. He does not suggest Bob Ewell is, deep down, nice and has been misunderstood. Right and wrong are pretty clear in this novel.

A human being who is, by definition, flawed and a person of his time, Atticus goes as far in defending Tom as he possibly can within the constraints of local and contemporary law. As it is, he so publicly humiliates Bob Ewell that Ewell tries to murder his children. No, Atticus, a state representative, does not offer bills to the state legislature outlawing segregation. That would have been out of character, and Atticus would have had no better results than Galileo did arguing before the Pope. Segregation in 1936 Alabama had, in the minds of 99 percent of the white population, the same force as the law of gravity, inconceivable to repeal.

It is true Atticus "takes the law into his own hands" in deciding Boo Radley should not be forced to stand trial, but Atticus knows children, and Boo is essentially a child and has become the mockingbird of the story.

Most readers, over these intervening years, have not expected sainthood from Atticus and thus have not been miffed at his flaws. Most readers, in fact, understand the novel pretty well. Atticus is a decent man trying to do the right thing, and when we evaluate Atticus and his behavior in the privacy of our own hearts it might be good to remember what many mothers have told their children over the years. What if everyone did that? What if everyone behaved that way? Well, just imagine if everyone did behave like Atticus Finch in Alabama, or anywhere for that matter, in 1936. It would be a better world, I think.

Biography of Harper Lee

Edythe M. McGovern

Achievements

Based entirely on her first and only novel, Lee's success has been phenomenal. According to a survey of reading habits conducted in 1991 by the Book-of-the-Month Club and the Library of Congress's Center for the Book, researchers found that *To Kill a Mockingbird* was "most often cited as making a difference in people's lives, second only to the Bible." In 1961, *To Kill a Mockingbird* won a Pulitzer Prize for fiction, the Brotherhood Award of the National Conference of Christians and Jews, the Alabama Library Association Award, and the British Book Society Award. By 1962 it had become a Literary Guild selection and a Book-of-the-Month-Club choice, it had won the Bestsellers' Magazine Paperback of the Year award, and it was featured in the *Reader's Digest* series of condensed books. In the same year Lee was given an honorary doctorate by Mount Holyoke College. She would receive another honorary doctorate in 1990 from the University of Alabama.

Initially enjoying seventy-three weeks on the national bestseller lists, *To Kill a Mockingbird* has been translated into numerous languages. In 1962 it was made into a motion picture starring Gregory Peck, which won several Academy Awards. President Lyndon Johnson appointed Lee to the National Council on the Arts in 1966, on which she served for five years. In 1970 playwright Christopher Sergel published a stage version of Lee's novel, *Harper Lee's "To Kill a Mockingbird": A Full-Length Play*, with Dramatic Publications. The play was professionally performed on both sides of the Atlantic Ocean during the 1980s and 1990s.

Biography

The third daughter and youngest child of Amasa Coleman Lee, an attorney and newspaper publisher, and Frances Finch Lee, reportedly a somewhat eccentric pianist, Nelle Harper Lee grew up in Monroeville, Alabama, attended public school there, then went to Huntingdon College for Women in Montgomery for a year before transferring to the University of Alabama in 1945. Lee edited the college humor magazine, the *Rammer Jammer*, and spent a summer term in a study-abroad program at Oxford University.

In 1950, she entered law school, no doubt with the intention of following in her father's footsteps. However, after one year she decided to abandon the study of law and go to New York City to pursue a career in writing. Throughout the early 1950s, Lee worked by day as a reservation clerk for Eastern Airlines and British Overseas Airways, living in a cramped flat with no hot water, and writing in her free time. During this period, she also made many trips to Monroeville to be with her ailing father, who died in 1962. Happily, Amasa Lee did live long enough to see *To Kill a Mockingbird* become a hugely successful book.

In a short article published in *McCall's* in December, 1961, called "Christmas to Me," Lee recounted how she missed her home and family during this time, contrasting New York City with memories of Monroeville during the Christmas season. However, she had made some very close friends in her adopted home, and she spent Christmas with one of these families, who surprised her with a monetary gift. On the accompanying card were the words, "You have one year off from your job to write whatever you please. Merry Christmas." She was overwhelmed, but her benefactors felt that their faith in Lee's ability was well founded.

Lee used this time carefully: A methodical writer, she composed a few pages each day and revised them carefully, completing three short fictional sketches by 1957. After being advised that she must do more to transform this work into a novel, she continued to write for two and a half years until *To Kill a Mockingbird* went to press in 1960, dedicated to her father and to her older sister, Alice, a partner in the family law firm.

Writer Truman Capote spent a great part of his childhood in Monroeville, staying each summer with relatives whose house was in close proximity to the Lees'. The character of Charles Baker Harris, nick-named Dill, in *To Kill a Mockingbird* is an accurate portrait of the young Capote, who remained in touch with Lee throughout his life. In the early 1960s, Lee went with Capote to Kansas to help him research *In Cold Blood* (1966), which chronicles the murders of the Clutter family in Holcomb, Kansas; Capote dedicated the book to Lee and another lifelong friend, Jack Dunphy.

Lee was invited to write the screenplay for the film version of *To Kill a Mockingbird*, but she declined. She was, however, very pleased with screenwriter Horton Foote's script, about which she said, "If the integrity of a film adaptation is measured by the degree to which the novelist's intent is preserved, Mr. Foote's screenplay should be studied as a classic." She was so delighted by Gregory Peck's portrayal of Atticus Finch that she honored his performance and resemblance to her father by giving him Amasa Lee's gold pocket watch, which was in-scribed, "To Gregory from Harper, 1962."

Although *To Kill a Mockingbird* has sold more than fifteen million copies, Harper Lee never produced another book. As she told her cousin Richard Williams, when he questioned her about this, "When you have a hit like that, you can't go anywhere but down." Although known in her hometown as a friendly and jovial woman, Lee has con-sistently refused all attempts to interview her. In 1995, when Harper-Collins released the thirty-fifth anniversary edition of *To Kill a Mock-ingbird*, Lee declined to write an introduction, stating, "The book still says what it has to say: it has managed to survive the years without pre-amble." She now lives in Monroeville, Alabama.

Analysis

To Kill a Mockingbird has gained stature over the years, becoming thought of as more than merely a skillful depiction of small-town Southern life during the 1930s with a coming-of-age theme. Claudia

Durst Johnson, who has published two books of analysis on *To Kill a Mockingbird*, suggests that the novel is universally compelling because Lee's overall theme of "threatening boundaries" covers a wide spectrum, from law to social standing, from childhood innocence to racism.

The narrator of the book is Jean Louise (Scout) Finch, who is discussing childhood events with her adult brother, Jem, as the story begins. She then slips effortlessly into the role of the six-year-old tomboy who matures over the three years of the book's action. In the first half of the novel, Scout and Jem, along with their childhood companion, Dill, are fascinated by their mysterious neighbor, Arthur (Boo) Radley. Because no one has seen Boo in many years, the youngsters construct a gothic stereotype of him, imagining him as huge and ugly, a monster who dines on raw squirrels, sports a jagged scar, and has rotten yellowing teeth and bulging eyes. They make plans to lure Boo from his "castle" (in reality the dark, shuttered Radley house), but in the course of their attempts to breach the boundaries of his life, they begin to discover the real Boo, an extremely shy man who has attempted to reach out to the children in a number of ways, and who, in the final chapters of the book, saves their lives.

The second half of the book is principally concerned with the trial of Tom Robinson, a young African American unjustly accused of raping a white woman. Racial tensions in the neighborhood explode; Scout and Jem are shocked to find that not only their peers but also adults they have known their whole lives are harshly critical of their father, Atticus, who provides the legal defense for the innocent man.

Throughout both sections of *To Kill a Mockingbird* Lee skillfully shows other divisions among people and how these barriers are threatened. Obviously, it is not a matter of race alone that sets societal patterns in this provincial Alabama town. For example, when Atticus's sister, Alexandra, visits the family, she makes it clear that she is displeased by Scout's tomboyish appearance, since she feels a future "Southern belle" should be interested in more ladylike clothing and more feminine behavior. Furthermore, as Jem tells Scout later, there is a strict caste system in Maycomb, with each group threatened by any possible abridgements of the social order. As Jem suggests, there are the "old" families—the gentry, who are usually educated, frequently professional, but, given the era, often cash-poor. On the next level down are the "poor but proud" people, such as the Cunninghams. They are country folk who pay their bills with crops and adamantly refuse all charity. Beneath them is the group commonly called "poor white trash," amply represented by Bob Ewell, "the only man ever fired by the WPA for laziness," and his pitiful daughter Mayella, the supposed victim of the rape. At the lowest rung of the social ladder are African Americans, although many are clearly superior to some of the poor white trash, who have only their skin color as their badge of superiority. They are represented by Tom Robinson, the accused rapist, and Calpurnia, the housekeeper for the motherless Finch family.

In addition to the clearly defined social castes, there are deviants, such as Dolphus Raymond, a white man involved in a long relationship with a black woman. He pretends to be an alcoholic to "give himself an excuse with the community" for his lifestyle. There is Mrs. Henry Lafayette Dubose, a member of the upper class who became a morphine addict and whose one desire is to overcome her habit before her death. Also featured is Miss Maudie, the friendly neighbor who seems to represent, along with Atticus, the best hope for change in the community.

Lee uses many symbols in the book, none more pervasive than the mockingbird of the title. The bird is characterized as an innocent singer who lives only to give pleasure to others. Early in the novel, when Atticus gives Jem and Scout air rifles, he makes it clear that it would be a sin to harm a mockingbird, a theme reiterated by Miss Maudie. Two of the main characters are subtly equated with the birds: Boo Radley and Tom Robinson, both innocents "caged for crimes they never committed." Atticus himself is a symbol of conscience. Unlike his sister, he is a nonconformist, an atypical Southerner, a thoughtful, bookish man at odds with his environment. He constantly tells his children that they can understand other people only by walking in their shoes. He is mindful of the majority opinion but asserts, "The one thing that doesn't abide by majority rule is a person's conscience."

Sometimes, of course, violent action is necessary to alter boundaries. This is foreshadowed early in the novel when Atticus finds it necessary to shoot a rabid dog. However, later, when he faces the mob from Old Sarum that is intent on lynching Tom Robinson, he simply sits in front of the jail, ostensibly reading a newspaper. Atticus seems very calm, upset only by the appearance of the children and Jem's refusal to take Dill and Scout home, not by the men who threaten violence. After Scout recognizes Mr. Cunningham and mentions Walter, his son, as her school friend, the group leaves. Braxton Underwood, owner of the *Maycomb Tribune*, leans out of his window above the office holding a double-barreled shotgun, saying, "I had you covered all the time, Atticus," suggesting that there may well be occasions in which force is appropriate.

Tried before a jury of white men, in an echo of the 1931 Scottsboro Nine case, which convicted nine innocent black men of raping two white women, Tom Robinson is found guilty in spite of proof that he could not have committed the crime. Yet even here there is a bit of hope for change to come, because the jury does not reach a quick decision, deliberating for three hours in a case involving the strongest taboo in the South, a black man sexually molesting a white woman. Tom, however, does not believe that Atticus's legal appeals will save him, and again violence erupts when he is shot and killed while trying to escape from the prison exercise yard.

Although Lee set her novel in a very isolated locale, which she calls Maycomb, in an era when her notion of crossing racial and social boundaries did not always seem imminently attainable, the world of 1960, when *To Kill a Mockingbird* appeared, was radically different. The Civil Rights movement had begun; the United States Supreme Court had ruled against school segregation in the 1954 *Brown v. Board of Education* decision; and there had been a successful bus boycott in

Montgomery, Alabama, in 1955-1956, which brought activist Martin Luther King, Jr., to public attention. Finally, people who believed in the importance of applying the law fairly (as Atticus Finch did) were being heard.

There was some criticism of the melodramatic ending of the novel, in which Bob Ewell attacks the Finch children, who are in costume returning from a school Halloween pageant. Jem's arm is broken in the scuffle, and Scout is saved from the attacker by Boo Radley, who kills Ewell with his own knife. However, in addition to providing closure for the plot, Lee uses this ending to confirm her view of Atticus and his moral character. At first, when Sheriff Heck Tate comes to the Finch home to learn the details of the evening's happenings, Atticus mistakenly assumes that Jem has killed Bob while defending Scout. Heck tries to reassure Atticus, saying, "Bob Ewell fell on his knife. He killed himself." Atticus believes that the sheriff is suggesting a cover-up for Jem, which he refuses, saying, "I can't live one way in town and another way in my home." Finally he realizes that it was Boo Radley who had stabbed Bob with a kitchen knife, not Jem. Atticus then agrees out of kindness to the reclusive Boo to go along with the sheriff's version of the death. When he tells Scout that Mr. Tate was right, she says, "Well, it'd be sort of like shootin' a mockingbird, wouldn't it?"

Most literary critics have written of *To Kill a Mockingbird* in glowing terms. One critic has suggested that Atticus is the symbol of the future, of the "new" South that will arise when it takes into account all human experience, discarding the old romantic notions of an isolated regionalism in favor of a wider Emersonian view of the world.

From *Critical Survey of Long Fiction, Second Revised Edition* (Pasadena, CA: Salem Press, 2000): 1900-1904. Copyright © 2000 by Salem Press, Inc.

Bibliography

Betts, Doris. Introduction. *Southern Women Writers: The New Generation*. Ed. Tonette Bond Inge. Tuscaloosa: University of Alabama Press, 1990.

Bloom, Harold, ed. *To Kill a Mockingbird*. Philadelphia: Chelsea House, 1999. Part of the Modern Critical Interpretations series, this volume includes a number of critical essays concerning the novel.

Johnson, Claudia Durst. *To Kill a Mockingbird: Threatening Boundaries*. New York: Twayne, 1994. A thesis regarding Lee's feelings about the South.

_____. "The Secret Courts of Men's Hearts: Code and Law in Harper Lee's *To Kill a Mockingbird*." *Studies in American Fiction* 19, no. 2 (Autumn, 1991): 129-139.

_____. *Understanding "To Kill a Mockingbird": A Casebook to Issues, Sources and Historical Documents*. Westport, CT: Greenwood Press, 1994. Useful for those doing in-depth studies of the novel.

Moates, Marianne M. *A Bridge of Childhood: Truman Capote's Southern Years*. New York: Henry Holt, 1989. Clearly shows Capote as character Dill Harris, re-iterating childhood episodes which Lee used in the book.

O'Neill, Terry. *Readings on "To Kill a Mockingbird."* San Diego, CA: Greenhaven Press, 2000. A collection of essays useful for students.

Shields, Charles J. *Mockingbird: A Portrait of Harper Lee*. New York: Henry Holt, 2006. This biography tells of the events that led to Lee's writing of *To Kill a Mockingbird*, as well as her decision to shun the spotlight that shone on her after its publication.

The *Paris Review* Perspective

Sasha Weiss for *The Paris Review*

Mention *To Kill a Mockingbird* to almost anyone who grew up in the United States after 1960, and he or she will smile discreetly, seeming to recall an old pleasure. As with most events that imprint us as children, people often remember where they were when they first encountered this novel. Scout Finch, the boisterous, sly narrator; Jem Finch, her sometimes imperious, sometimes heroic older brother; the impish Dill Harris; the shut-in Boo Radley; Atticus Finch, their gentleman father; and the town of Maycomb, Alabama, itself, drawling, cozy, and sinister: these figures have drawn around them a fellowship of readers.

When Nelle Harper Lee submitted the manuscript for *To Kill a Mockingbird* to publishers, she was told to keep her expectations low. Lee was almost preternaturally shy, known more as Truman Capote's sidekick (Capote was a childhood friend and a possible model for Dill Harris) than for her writing. But the book quickly became a best seller and has sold over thirty million copies since it first appeared. Lee was awarded the Pulitzer Prize, but the novel marked the beginning of her withdrawal from public life. After a few years, she returned to her hometown in Alabama and never published another book. *To Kill a Mockingbird* is all we have from Harper Lee; thank goodness it's more than enough.

The novel opens the way that it closes: with Jem's broken arm—the violent end to a series of events that roil the town of Maycomb and push the Finch children into uneasy adulthood. Scout, nine years old, has a fresh and quick eye, unencumbered by convention. The habits and manners of the adult world are mysterious to her, and in simply recounting the conversations of the bigoted adults around her, their foolishness is exposed. At the same time, her life is relatively sheltered:

> When I was six and Jem was ten, our summertime boundaries . . . were Mrs. Henry Lafayette Dubose's house two doors to the north of us, and the Radley place three doors to the south. We were never tempted to break them.

Home is a neatly protected place, a place from which Scout has no desire to stray. But by the end of the novel, after Scout has watched the jury disgrace itself at Tom Robinson's trial, her sense of home is reconfigured. She has become a subversive, infiltrating backyards and black churches with a shambolic glee. Her world, which until now had been broken up into component parts that fit together, becomes a blended abstraction: she sees that "A steaming summer night was no different from a winter morning." The seasons themselves have become intermingled; the most basic of boundaries have dissolved.

During the years that Lee was writing, two events catalyzed the rapid rise of the Civil Rights movement: Emmett Till, a fourteen-year-old black boy accused of a crime similar to Tom's, was brutally killed in Mississippi; and Rosa Parks refused to cede her seat to a white passenger on a bus in Alabama. Harper Lee's achievement was to capture—with infinite gentleness, as a child might trap a lightning bug—that moment in American life when the familiar world had become unrecognizably strange, when the discrepancy between vaunted ideals and base reality was exposed. When we read *To Kill a Mockingbird*, we are asked again to take the measure of where we are—and where we might yet go. Speaking of William Faulkner in a 1964 interview, Lee pinpoints his greatness in his "vision of enlargement, of using the novel to encompass something much broader." It is a capacity for expansiveness that she admired, and that she shared.

Bibliography

Lee, Harper. *To Kill a Mockingbird*. New York: HarperPerennial, 2005.

Newquist, Roy. *Counterpoint*. London: G. Allen & Unwin, 1965.

Shields, Charles J. *Mockingbird: A Portrait of Harper Lee*. New York: Henry Holt, 2003.

CRITICAL CONTEXTS

To Kill a Mockingbird:
Successes and Myths_____

Nancy Grisham Anderson

In the opening scene of *To Kill a Mockingbird*, Scout and Jem wonder about the origins of the events in their lives between the summer of 1932 and the fall of 1935. So readers might question the origins of this novel. If they want "to take a broad view of the thing," as Scout suggests, readers might trace Harper Lee's writing back to some storytelling gene in the Lee and Finch families. Regardless of that genetic heritage, readers can agree that the lives of the two Finch children and their friend Dill began in the small-town life of Monroeville, Alabama, a life experienced by the novel's author.

Born on April 28, 1926, Nelle Harper Lee is the youngest child of Amasa Coleman Lee and Frances Cunningham Finch Lee, with two sisters, Alice and Louise, and a brother, Edward. During the hardships of the Depression, the young Nelle attended school and played with her friends and siblings under the watchful eyes of family and neighbors in the small community. Even in the early years of her schooling, Nelle Lee was interested in writing, and she worked on her skills in high school and college. After graduation from high school in Monroeville in 1944, Lee attended Huntingdon College (Montgomery, Alabama) during 1944-1945. English and history professors at the college acknowledged and encouraged her writing abilities and fondly recalled her presence in their classes. Margaret Gillis Figh, a Huntingdon English professor who stayed in touch with her former student, saved some of Lee's early papers as well as copies of a caricature Lee drew after she transferred to the University of Alabama, which she attended from 1945 to 1949. There she continued to write, editing the *Rammer Jammer*, the university's humor magazine, and writing features and columns for university publications. She was pursuing a law degree to follow in the profession of her father and her older sister, Alice, but never completed law school. After a summer in Oxford, England, she moved to New York City in 1949.

The story of Lee's life in New York as an airline reservation clerk, among other jobs, and her struggles to begin her writing career is best told in her essay "Christmas to Me." After the day at work, Lee returned to her cold-water flat to write the short stories that enabled her to attract an agent. As she writes in "Christmas to Me," in December, 1956, she received a generous gift from friends Michael and Joy Williams Brown: money that would to allow her to write full time. The note accompanying the gift read: "You have one year off from your job to write whatever you please. Merry Christmas" (63). Working with Tay Hohoff, an editor at J. B. Lippincott, Lee turned her short stories into the novel *To Kill a Mockingbird*, completing it in the summer of 1959. The published novel was released on July 11, 1960, marking the beginning of a "summer storm," a phrase used to describe the immediate success of the novel.

No one seemed to expect the initial reactions to Lee's first novel, least of all the author herself. In an interview with Roy Newquist on *Counterpoint* (for WQXR in New York in March of 1964), she said, "I sort of hoped that maybe someone would like it enough to give me encouragement. Public encouragement. I hoped for a little." Certainly she received the "public encouragement," with more than two million copies sold in the first year and more than five million in the first two years. *To Kill a Mockingbird* spent one hundred weeks on best-seller lists and was chosen by Book-of-the-Club, Literary Guild, and Reader's Digest Condensed Books. One British book club also made it a selection. Translations have been numerous, perhaps into more than forty different languages: Hebrew, Chinese (at least two editions), Magyar, German, Italian, Spanish, Dutch, French, and dozens of others. The dust jackets of these translations are also fascinating studies in cultures, from the German stylized silhouette of leaves and an orange-brown bird on a tree limb to one Chinese edition featuring a young Victorian woman reading a book on the cover or a scene of Scout and Atticus reading together in a scene from the movie on a Hebrew paperback edition.

In 1961 the first literary prizes were announced. In April Harper Lee received the Alabama Library Association's literary award, followed in May by the announcement that *To Kill a Mockingbird* was receiving the 1961 Pulitzer Prize for Fiction. It also received the Brotherhood Award of the National Conference of Christians and Jews in 1961 and the *Bestsellers* Paperback of the Year Award in 1962. Through the years, Lee has continued to receive recognition, honorary degrees, and awards, including the 2002 Alabama Humanities Award and the Presidential Medal of Freedom in 2007.

Sales figures for the novel attracted interest from Hollywood. Rights ultimately were sold to Alan Pakula and Robert Mulligan, who became partners to produce the film that Mulligan directed. Gregory Peck was cast to play Atticus Finch, after consideration of a number of actors including Rock Hudson. Horton Foote adapted the script, which condensed the three years of the novel into one summer and fall in the movie. After its release on December 25, 1962, the movie was nominated for eight Academy Awards: best picture, best director, best actor, best screenplay adaptation, best cinematography, best musical score, best art direction/set design in black and white, and best supporting actress. Peck won for best actor, Foote won for best screenplay adaptation, and the movie won for best black and white art direction/set design. Just as the novel has had an ongoing success, so the movie has continued to draw a following and critical praise. A review of the movie in 2002 describes the movie as "a faithful adaptation of one of the 20th century's most important American works of literature" that resulted in "An astonishing motion picture by any standards" (Berardinelli).

The success of *To Kill a Mockingbird* has, in no way, been restricted to the decade of the 1960s. By 1977 the novel had sold twelve million copies, and by the late 1990s about thirty million. It continues to sell about one million copies a year worldwide. According to the author's sister Alice Lee, sales are even stronger outside the United States than within the fifty states. It has never been out of print. It appeared on several of the lists of 100 best books published at the end of the twentieth century, including the one from the New York Public Library. The American Library Association named it the best book of the twentieth century. In a 1991 survey conducted by the Library of Congress, it was second only to the Bible as the book that had made the most difference in individuals' lives. It has been chosen more than any other book for One Book One Community reading programs. Harper Lee even wrote a blurb for One Book, One Chicago:

> When the people of Chicago assemble in various parts of the city to read and discuss *To Kill a Mockingbird*, there is no greater honor the novel could receive. People of all backgrounds and cultures coming together to put their critical skills to work? Nothing could be more exciting! Or fruitful: when people speak their minds and bring to discussion their own varieties of experience, when they receive respect for their opinions and the good will of their fellows, things change. It is as if life itself takes on a new compelling clarity, and good things get done.

Now, in the twenty-first century, *To Kill a Mockingbird* is one of the novels featured in The Big Read, a community reading initiative sponsored by the National Endowment for the Arts. This program has moved the One Book One Community idea to a national level, with communities—large and small—all over the country reading this novel, or one of the others featured, and then meeting to discuss it and its historical, cultural, and thematic implications. NEA has produced numerous supplemental materials to support the program—reading guides, booklets, bookmarks, DVDs, discussion guides, and program formats. Such an initiative is aimed at readers of all ages and backgrounds.

Rare book prices may or may not be indications of success, but a full-page advertisement from Bauman Rare Books in *The New York Times Book Review* of November 6, 2005, contains a listing for *To Kill a Mockingbird:*

Harper Lee
To Kill a Mockingbird
1960.
Rare first edition of the Pulitzer-winning classic, in lovely bright original
dust jacket, *inscribed by Harper Lee.* $33,000.

In the April 30, 2006, issue of the *NYTBR*, the same company adver-
tised a signed copy of the "1999 anniversary edition" for $950.

With such a consistently strong following, the novel has become a
standard reading assignment in classrooms all over the world, certainly accounting for some of the ongoing sales. Teachers at all levels—K-12 and undergraduate and graduate classes—have found the
novel very accessible for storytelling and for study of literature, history, cultures, values, and themes such as race, coming of age, and
gender. Depending on the survey, the percentages of public, private,
and parochial schools teaching the novel range from 60 to 75 percent
in the United States. This classroom use has resulted in a publication phenomenon all its own: at least sixteen versions of "notes," the
shortcuts to reading the novel such as Cliff's Notes, Barron's Outline
Series, Passnotes, and Monarch's. In addition, numerous teachers'
guides have been published—more than thirty-five listed on Ama-
zon.com on one day, including one for teaching the book to children
ages 4-8.

Dramatic adaptations also appear with some frequency. One of the
best known is the production in Harper Lee's hometown of Monroeville, performed on weekends each April and May. The performances
take place in the courthouse square with act one outside on a set of the
house fronts and act two inside the Monroe County Court House. The
actors are members of the community. This production has also gone to
Jerusalem, England, and the Kennedy Center in Washington, D.C.
Since the jury is chosen from men in the audience during the intermis-
sions, the foreign performances have resulted in some unusual situations when the members of the jury, not familiar with the original story,

have to be convinced to read the line announcing the guilt of Tom Robinson, the defendant.

Another Alabama production of the play that has received widespread attention is the unique collaboration of two high schools in Birmingham. Mountain Brook High School, a predominantly white school in the affluent suburb of Birmingham, joined the all-black Fairfield High Preparatory School to produce the play in October of 2006. The production attracted the attention of the NBC *Today Show* and NBC *Nightly News* as well as the attention of Harper Lee, who met with the cast and attended a performance held in Montgomery hosted by Alabama Governor Bob Riley.

Productions of the stage adaptation are not limited by geography or time. From the mid-1990s through 2008 the play has been staged at professional theaters throughout the country, in Washington State, Kansas, Missouri, California, Kentucky, New York, Montana, and Alabama, among other locations.

The initial success of *To Kill a Mockingbird* attracted considerable media attention for the novel and its unassuming southern author and for the movie. In addition to the numerous reviews of the book and the movie in newspapers on the East and West coasts and in national magazines, the novel and its author were the subjects of newspaper articles and features across the country. Harper Lee was a popular subject for interviews, appearing in such diverse media as on *Counterpoint* with Roy Newquist and in *Rogue*, in which Bob Ellison published his account of "the flood of questions the noted writer must endure all in the name of publicity."

Not surprisingly, given the sales records of the novel, the interest in the novel and its author has persisted through the decades. A survey of *The New York Times* reveals its ongoing coverage, beginning with the early reviews and articles and continuing through the latter part of the century and into the twenty-first century. Similar patterns appear in newspapers in Atlanta; Myrtle Beach, South Carolina; and predictably in Birmingham, Mobile, and Montgomery, Alabama. Periodically through the 1980s and into the twentieth-first century, newspaper features have continued to appear throughout the country, often reporters' accounts of their visits to Monroeville, Alabama, or their brief encounters with the elusive author or their totally failed attempts to meet her and interview her.

As might be expected, Harper Lee soon tired of the demands of public life and became reluctant to give interviews. She agreed to what she called a "visit" with Don Keith in 1966, a session during which the interviewer uses the word "recluse" in connection with Harper Lee's name. As biographer Charles Shields acknowledges, it was a negative statement: "Harper Lee is no recluse" (Shields, 248). Over the years, however, the word has begun to be used to describe the author, reversing the original statement. Since she continues to appear in public to speak, to attend special programs, to eat out with friends, and to accept awards, the label is inappropriate. For example, one special event that she attends most years is to meet with the young writers of the Harper Lee essay competition at the University of Alabama, and newspapers like *The New York Times* publish a story about this meeting, accompanied by a photograph. "Discriminating" is a more accurate description than "reclusive."

Media attention has persisted into the twenty-first century. Boston filmmaker Sandy Jaffe, who grew up in Birmingham, produced a one-hour documentary entitled *Our Mockingbird*, in 2009. The film includes interviews with academics, lawyers, teachers, and actors who have performed in professional productions of the staged versions, coverage of the collaborative production by the Birmingham high schools, and footage of sites around Alabama central to the story of Scout and Jem.

With the popularity of the novel and the movie continuing to grow, the legal world turned to the novel for careful study of its portrayal of that field. Many lawyers practicing today confess that they became interested in pursuing legal careers after reading the story of Atticus Finch. Over the years law reviews have published articles analyzing the stand taken by this southern lawyer in the 1930s, with interpretations changing as the times change. In her bibliography of secondary sources in her groundbreaking work, *To Kill a Mockingbird: Threatening Boundaries*, Claudia Durst Johnson lists legal articles published in journals of law schools in New Jersey, Pittsburgh, Mercer (Georgia), and Los Angeles and articles with legal subjects published in the *American Bar Association Journal, Legal Times*, and *The New York Times*. Earlier articles have portrayed him as a strong man of principle standing against the beliefs and practices of his time. Later, in more politically correct times, some analyses have portrayed him as paternalistic and weak and even condescending in the stands that he takes. Two titles and their publication dates illustrate this diversity of interpretation: Claudia A. Carver's 1988 "Lawyers as Heroes: The Compassionate Activism of a Fictional Attorney Is a Model We Can Emulate" and David Margolick's "Chipping at Atticus Finch's Pedestal," in 1992.

Even with the popular readership, the success of the movie, the extensive use of *To Kill a Mockingbird* in classrooms around the world, and some legal analyses, the academic world has been slower to give the novel careful and thorough critical attention. Among the earliest works of critical analysis was Fred Erisman's "The Romantic Regionalism of Harper Lee" in the 1973 *Alabama Review,* followed closely by R. A. Dave's essay in *Indian Studies in American Fiction* in 1974. William T. Going's "*Store* and *Mockingbird*: Two Pulitzer Novels about Alabama" appeared in *Essays on Alabama Literature* in 1975. Through the 1980s and early 1990s, literary criticism appeared sporadically in academic journals. Johnson's book devoted to the novel published in the Twayne series in 1994 has provided a foundation—and perhaps a stimulus—for additional critical analyses in academia.

In its Literary Companion to American Literature, Greenhaven Press published *Readings on "To Kill a Mockingbird"* in 2000, edited by Terry O'Neill. The four sections of reprinted articles consider "The Critical Reception," "Literary Techniques . . . ," "Social Issues . . . ," and "The Character of Atticus Finch." In 2007 the University of Tennessee Press published a collection edited by Alice Hall Petry. Though it could be more aptly entitled "On *To Kill a Mockingbird*" than *On Harper Lee*, it is a collection of eleven original essays, three of which are "personal reflections" by creative writers Doris Betts, Gerald Early, and Nichell D. Tramble, in addition to the Foreword by William T. Going, one of the early scholars to write about *To Kill a Mockingbird*. The critical studies in Petry's collection consider religion, Gothicism, southern code, humor, and race among other subjects. Bibliographies in books devoted to studies of the novel are beginning to show more recent dates of publications, so perhaps academic attention is growing.

In 2006, Charles J. Shields's unauthorized biography of Harper Lee was released by Henry Holt—*Mockingbird: A Portrait of Harper Lee*. Shields did an impressive amount of research including hundreds of interviews and exchanges of letters with individuals who had known Lee, especially in schools in Monroeville, Montgomery, or Tuscaloosa. The result is a compilation of important verifiable and documented information about Lee and some puzzling, even annoying, commentary about Lee's looks, clothing, and sexual orientation. Two years later Henry Holt also released Shields's adaptation of the biography for younger readers: *I Am Scout: The Biography of Harper Lee*. Another biography of Lee for young readers ages 9 to 12 is young-adult author Kerry Madden's *Harper Lee: A Twentieth-Century Life*; published in 2009 as part of the Up Close series, it is also a heavily researched study.

Despite the continuing popularity of the novel, the popular and critical success of the movie, and attention—however slight—in legal and academic publications, myths swirl around the novel and its author. There could be a number of explanations for these myths, rumors, errors: Harper Lee has been out of the limelight for more than forty years; no second novel followed the successful *To Kill a Mockingbird*; the lack of extensive attention in academic and legal journals has left a void for the myths to fill.

One myth—"error" would be a more accurate label—is in a reference book and provides an excellent example of how myths start. Lee dedicated her novel to her father and sister:

> Dedication:
> for Mr. Lee and Alice
> in consideration of Love & Affection

Tuttle Dictionary of Dedications, however, prints this version:

> For Mr. Lee and Slice
> in consideration of Love & Affection

Not satisfied with the typographical error, the editor added an explanatory note: "The American author's first and award winning novel presumably dedicated to her husband and child, the latter called by a nickname."

Less amusing—and probably more disturbing, at least to the author—is the myth that Harper Lee is dead. She has responded to this one herself in her objection to writing an introduction to the thirty-fifth anniversary edition of the novel:

Please spare *Mockingbird* an introduction. As a reader I loathe Introductions. To novels, I associate Introductions with long-gone authors and works that are being brought back into print after decades of internment. Although *Mockingbird* will be 33 this year, it has never been out of print and I am still alive, although very quiet. Introductions inhibit pleasure, they kill the joy of anticipation, they frustrate curiosity. The only good thing about Introductions is that in some cases they delay the dose to come. *Mockingbird* still says what it has to say; it has managed to survive without preamble.

Harper Lee, 12 February 1993

This "introduction" was printed as the foreword to both the thirty-fifth and fortieth anniversary editions.

Another error that has become part of the mythology is that this novel is the only thing Harper Lee ever published—or even ever wrote. Any complete bibliography of primary sources will refute that error. She has published five magazine articles since the novel was released, not counting the earlier works published during college days. In addition to the "introduction" to the anniversary editions and the blurb for One Book, One Chicago, there are a number of short selections published in a variety of sources. One delightful example of Lee's wry wit comes as a result of a banning of *Mockingbird* by the Hanover (Virginia) County Board of Education for immoral subject matter. After publishing a flurry of letters praising the school board and condemning "the controversial book" and the "diabolical movie," the *Richmond News-Leader* printed this letter on January 15, 1966:

Editor, *News-Leader:*

Recently I have received echoes down this way of the Hanover County School Board's activities, and what I've heard makes me wonder if any of its members can read.

Surely it is plain to the simplest intelligence that "To Kill a Mockingbird" spells out in words of seldom more than two syllables a code of honor and conduct, Christian in its ethic, that is the heritage of all Southerners. To hear that the novel is "immoral" has made me count the years between now and 1984, for I have yet to come across a better example of doublethink.

I feel, however that the problem is one of illiteracy, not Marxism. Therefore I enclose a small contribution to the Beadle Bumble [Charles Dickens' character responsible for the orphanage and workhouse in *Oliver Twist*] Fund that I hope will be used to enroll the Hanover County School Board in any first grade of its choice.

Harper Lee
Monroeville, Ala.

The editor of the newspaper added the following italicized comment:

In most controversies, the lady is expected to have the last word. In this particular discussion, it seems especially fitting that the last word should come from the lady who wrote "To Kill a Mockingbird." With Miss Lee's letter, we call a halt, at least temporarily, to the publication of letters commenting on the book-banning in Hanover County.
Editor

Probably the most persistent myth is that Harper Lee did not write the novel attributed to her. The name that usually fills that void is Truman Capote. With so many ways to refute that claim, the fact that it continues to surface is the puzzle. We have the writings of Harper Lee's editor, Tay Hohoff—"We Get a New Author" and "About the Author"—telling of her work with the author. We have Lee's account in "Christmas to Me." We have Capote's own testimony about his friend's novel in a July 9, 1959, letter to an aunt: "she [Nelle] showed me as much of the book as she'd written and I liked it very much. She has real talent" (qtd. in Marshall 1A). And, if readers could ignore these facts, can they really believe that Capote's personality would have allowed him to remain silent in the face of the success of his friend's novel and the movie based on it, remarkable success that continued to elude him? Does a comparison of the styles of the two authors allow serious consideration of his authorship? Indeed, a much stronger case exists for Lee's coauthorship of Capote's *In Cold Blood*. After all, there are hundreds of pages of notes that she took while working with Capote in Kansas, when they were researching material for his nonfiction novel. These notes are now with Capote's papers in the New York Public Library. Occasionally other candidates are suggested for authorship, but these myths cannot persist after careful scrutiny of the facts.

With the sales figures of the novel and its presence in classrooms, it would be easy to believe that acceptance of the novel has been universally positive throughout its history. A survey of reviews at the time of the novel's release easily contradicts that myth. Titles at the time included phrases like "good but flawed novel," "*TKAM* lacks realistic characters," and "questionable portrayals of women." Some reviewers attacked the novel for a flawed point of view, arguing that the insights are too mature for a child narrator. These reviewers had obviously overlooked wording like "When enough years had gone by to enable us to look back on them . . . ," which appears in the second paragraph of the novel. As the story unfolds, Lee reminds readers with phrases like "a tired old town when I first knew it" or "not until many years later" that the older Jean Louise is recalling her childhood with insights gained as she matured. One dramatic production reminds audiences of this double point of view with the constant presence of the older Jean Louise on stage, overseeing the actions of the children. The movie uses a voice-over to provide the same reminder.

Some of the reviewers argued that the two plots—the children's efforts to draw Boo Radley out of the house and Tom Robinson's trial—are never integrated. Such a conclusion ignores the climactic scene where Bob Ewell tries to avenge his embarrassment in the courtroom by attacking Atticus's children, only to have Boo come out to save the children he has watched over through their childhood. Other early reviews claim that the novel is bound by time and place and cannot possibly endure or move beyond its small geographical setting. The continuing worldwide readership of the novel and the praise for the black-and-white movie clearly contradict these theories.

Weak characterization is the focus of some reviews—stereotypical characters who are all good or evil. Even Atticus is attacked as being too nearly perfect. Careful readings, however, reveal Lee's subtlety in creating her characters. Mayella plants flowers to bring beauty to her house near the junkyard. Atticus admits that he wishes he did not have to take this case and ultimately compromises his commitment to truth by accepting the sheriff's plan to protect Boo from public scrutiny. Lee's complexity and subtlety of characterization are particular strengths of the novel.

The classification of *To Kill a Mockingbird* as simply autobiography denies Lee's creativity. Certainly the story and its setting grow directly out of Lee's home and her childhood, and there are obvious autobiographical details: her father was a lawyer, Finch was her mother's maiden name, Maycomb is a small town similar to Monroeville, Dill is based on Truman Capote and his visits to Monroeville (a claim he made with some frequency), and the list can go on. In the interview printed in *Rogue*, Lee wryly answers the question about whether characters are based on real people: "No, but the people at home think so. The beauty of it, though, is that no two people come up with the same identification. They never think of themselves as being portrayed in the book. They try to identify others whom they know as characters" (Ellison, 24). After all, the artistry and creativity come from the ways in which things develop, the details invented to bring the children and their stories to life, and the sensitive observations about people, races, education, life in a small town with the complex classes of people that inhabit it, and the portrayals of human nature. A 1962 Gadsden (Alabama) newspaper article quoted Harper Lee's view of the novel: "It portrays an aspect of civilization—not necessarily Southern civilization. I tried to show the conflict of the human soul—reduced to its simplest terms" (qtd. in Petry xxi).

Some critics want to argue that the novel's popularity exists because it is such a "sweet," "feel-good" novel where everything ends happily. Another reviewer claims that it is "pleasant, undemanding reading" (Adams, 98-99). Certainly there are some emotionally satisfying qualities, but to draw such simple conclusions is to overlook the darker elements of the novel: dysfunctional, even abusive families (Ewells, Radleys, and even Dill's neglectful parents); conviction and eventual death of an innocent man; brutal attack on two children to get even with their father; a lynch mob; bigotry, racism, hypocrisy; and the list can continue. Does the novel really end happily? Tom is dead, Jem's arm is seriously damaged, Boo has killed a man, the two children are traumatized by a vicious attack, and Atticus has compromised his commitment to truth—and perhaps violated the law—by becoming part of the cover-up to protect Boo.

The most persistent myth will be proved—or disproved—only in time: the possibility, or probability, of a second novel by Harper Lee. There is strong evidence from reliable sources that Harper Lee lived in Alexander City, Alabama, for at least six months researching the case of the Reverend Maxwell, the alleged murderer of several people close to him; Rev. Maxwell was the beneficiary of their life insurance policies. He was never found guilty of any wrongdoing in any trial. However, at the funeral of one of his supposed victims, a member of the family stood up and shot Rev. Maxwell in front of the hundreds of people attending the funeral. The shooter was found not guilty, despite the many witnesses. According to some sources, Lee, using the skills she developed while working with Capote in Kansas as he wrote his nonfiction novel, *In Cold Blood*, researched the Maxwell case with the intent of developing it into her own nonfiction novel, theoretically entitled "The Reverend." One member of her family has been quoted as saying she has read it and believes that it is better than Lee's first novel. The myth continues with the detail that the novel will be posthumously published because *To Kill a Mockingbird* consumed Lee's life—and the lives of her family—and she does not intend for that to happen again. And so anticipation continues to build.

Whatever the myths, rumors, and critical views that come and go as new audiences come to the novel and to the movie, *To Kill a Mockingbird* endures as a work of art that has made significant differences in peoples' lives around the world. It tells the stories of engaging characters, especially the narrator, and effectively incorporates lessons about right and wrong, tolerance, and courage without heavy-handed didacticism or moralizing or preaching. Harper Lee has on a number of occasions described the novel as a "love story pure and simple"—embodying a love of the South, a love of small towns, a father's love for his children, and the children's love for their father.

Alabama historian Wayne Flynt, who has spoken about Harper Lee and her novel throughout the United States and abroad, sums up the power of novel in one sentence: "*TKAM* is the single most unifying literary experience in American education and probably the most important single source of American values derived solely from literature" (Flynt email).

Selected Bibliography

Primary Sources

"Christmas To Me." *McCall's* (December, 1961): 63.

"Dear Oprah . . . [A Letter to Oprah from Harper Lee]." *O, The Oprah Magazine* (July, 2006): 151-53.

"Love—In Other Words." *Vogue* (April 15, 1961): 64-65.

"Romance and High Adventure." In *Clearings in the Thicket: An Alabama Humanities Reader*, edited by Jerry Elijah Brown. Macon, Ga.: Mercer UP, 1985, pp. 13-20.

"When Children Discover America." *McCall's* (August, 1965): 76-79.

Secondary Sources

Adams, Phoebe. Review of *To Kill a Mockingbird* by Harper Lee. *Atlantic Monthly* (August, 1960): 98-99.

Anderson, Nancy G. "Nelle Harper Lee." <http://www.encyclopediaofalabama .org/face/Article.jsp?id+h-1126>.

"Author Harper Lee Comments on Book-Banning." *Richmond News-Leader* (January 15, 1966): 10.

Berardinelli, James. "*To Kill a Mockingbird*: A Film Review." <http:// www.reelviews.net/movies/t/to_kill_mockingbird.html>.

Carver, Claudia A. "Lawyers as Heroes: The Compassionate Activism of a Fictional Attorney Is a Model We Can Emulate." *Los Angeles Lawyer* (July-August, 1988): 13.

Dave, R. A. "*To Kill a Mockingbird:* Harper Lee's Tragic Vision." In *Indian Studies in American Fiction*, edited by M. K. Naik, S. K. Desai, and S. Mokashi-Punekar. Dharwar: Karnatak University and The Macmillan Company of India, 1974, pp. 321-23.

Ellison, Bob. "Three Best-Selling Authors: Conversations [Harper Lee]." *Rogue* (December, 1963): 20-24, 78.

Erisman, Fred. "The Romantic Regionalism of Harper Lee. *The Alabama Review* 26, no. 2 (April, 1973): 122-136.

Flynt, Wayne. Email to Nancy Grisham Anderson. March 1, 2006.

_____. "*To Kill a Mockingbird*." <http://www.encyclopediaofalabama .org/face/Article.jsp?id+h-1140>.

Going, William T.. "*Store* and *Mockingbird*: Two Pulitzer Novels about Alabama." In *Essays on Alabama Literature*. Tuscaloosa: University of Alabama Press, 1975, pp. 9-31.

Johnson, Claudia Durst. *"To Kill a Mockingbird": Threatening Boundaries*. New York: Twayne, 1994.

Margolick, David. "Chipping at Atticus Finch's Pedestal." *The New York Times* (February 28, 1992): B1.

Marshall, Mike. "Note Voids Myth Capote Wrote 'Mockingbird.'" *The Birmingham News* (March 2, 2006): 1A, 2A.

Newquist, Roy. "Harper Lee." In *Counterpoint*. Chicago: Rand McNally, 1964, pp. 403-412.

O'Neill, Terry, ed. *Readings on "To Kill a Mockingbird."* San Diego: Greenhaven, 2000.

Petry, Alice Hall, ed. *On Harper Lee: Essays and Reflections*. Knoxville: University of Tennessee Press, 2007.

Shields, Charles J. *I Am Scout: The Biography of Harper Lee*. New York: Henry Holt, 2008.

_____. *Mockingbird: A Portrait of Harper Lee*. New York: Henry Holt, 2006.

Mockingbird in Context_____

Gurdip Panesar

Nearly half a century after its first publication, the status of Harper Lee's novel *To Kill a Mockingbird* as one of the most esteemed and well-known literary works of modern times remains assured. It has never been out of print, it has been translated into several languages, and it has become a part of literary curricula around the world. Moreover, it continues to figure prominently in literature surveys and polls. In 1999, for instance, it was voted the best novel of the twentieth century by the readers of the *Library Journal*. Even more recently, it came in at number one in a survey conducted online to find the fifty best novels of all time.[1] Furthermore, Lee has received numerous honors since her novel was first published, including the Pulitzer Prize in 1961 and culminating in the highly prestigious Presidential Medal of Freedom in November, 2007. It is entirely in keeping with this that the 1962 film adaptation of the same name has become almost as famous as the original novel, garnering a string of Oscars including Best Actor for Gregory Peck in the role of Atticus Finch.[2]

Yet, for all this, the novel itself has not been the object of much literary criticism and analysis over the years, as Claudia Johnson, among others, has remarked (*Boundaries*, 20). Johnson made this observation in the early nineties, but the number of literary studies concerning this novel has not increased markedly since then. Similarly, there are few full-length biographies of Harper Lee. Of course there is an obvious reason for this; like J. D. Salinger, author of another celebrated twentieth century American novel, *The Catcher in the Rye*, Lee is thought of as being reclusive. Even more intriguingly, and unlike Salinger, she has produced virtually no other literature of any note. However, the impact of her one novel has never been in doubt, as Johnson recognizes. "*To Kill a Mockingbird* is unquestionably one of the most widely read, best-selling, and influential books in American literature. It has made a significant difference in the lives of individuals and in the culture as a whole" (*Casebook*, 9). Johnson goes on to note that the novel came in second only to the Bible in one readers' list of books that were felt to contribute most significantly to individual people's lives (*Casebook*, 9). *Mockingbird* is one of those relatively rare single works of literature that can truly be said to have attained a mythical status; it is ultimately lauded less for its brilliance in terms of literary art than for the way in which it seems to impress people on a deeply human level. Of course in the simplest sense it is an appealing tale of the fight against injustice, a play on the age-old theme of good versus evil.

Although the book is seen to have such a universal and lasting appeal, it does of course have a special historical significance. Lee's native state of Alabama, where the story is set, provided one of the flashpoints for the burgeoning American Civil Rights movement of the 1950s, with such momentous events as the Montgomery bus boycott which began in 1955, five years before the book's publication. Given its overriding theme of racial oppression in the South, Lee's novel, not unlike Harriet Beecher Stowe's *Uncle Tom's Cabin* in the previous century, has taken on strong political dimensions. This, in turn, has led to the common but misleading association between Lee and the Civil Rights struggle—despite the fact that she took no actual part in it (*Boundaries*, xi-xiv). Of course, she drew on the current climate of racial tension and unrest for her material, as well as incorporating her own memories of growing up in Monroeville during the thirties. It has been suggested that Tom Robinson's plight was inspired by the real-life, protracted case of the Scottsboro Boys, who in 1931 were falsely accused of rape by two white women (*Boundaries*, 7-11). Patrick Chura has also closely examined the highly emotive case of Emmett Till, who was brutally murdered by a gang in Mississippi for flirting with a white woman. In addition, Charles Shields recounts in his biography of Lee how Lee's own father, an attorney, unsuccessfully defended two black men in 1919 and thereafter never tried another criminal case (120-121). It might be said that the book takes much of its potency from the way in which it fuses together autobiographical elements with high-profile cases of injustice and brutality which were continuing to fuel racial tensions at the time of its publication. Certainly there was something opportune about its timing. As Fred Erisman's analysis makes clear, this work, with its portrayal of small-town Southern life and its host of quirky characters, can be viewed as being primarily a "regional" novel, something in the so-called "Southern Gothic" tradition.[3] It might be characterized therefore as a regional novel that, by reason of its temporal and geographical proximity to the Civil Rights movement, became elevated to a position of national importance. As already remarked, however, its influence continues to be felt many years later and in different countries; it has transcended its original contexts.

For all its fame, however, *To Kill a Mockingbird* has not had a unanimously favorable reception. For one thing, as Johnson has discussed at length, it has frequently fallen afoul of the censors for such reasons as its use of slang, reference to sexual activity, and "expression of anti-establishment attitudes" (*Casebook*, 197). In fact, objections continue to be raised even at the turn of the twenty-first century—for example, by Isaac Saney—which is a measure of its lasting impact. Most of the issues raised by the censors probably have never much troubled the majority of readers. However, the portrayal of black characters in the novel has attracted a fair bit of criticism. For instance Roslyn Siegel takes issue with the fact that Tom Robinson, in the tradition of many writings by Southern whites, is seen to be abjectly helpless and wholly reliant on whites. It is true that he can be viewed as a flat character, who really appears only in the capacity of victim—a role which is of course necessitated by the book's plot. Other blacks appear in much the same light, endowed with "Biblical patience" (Lee, 228), full of humble gratitude toward Atticus for fighting their cause and delivering masses of food to the Finch household in return "although times are . . . hard" (Lee, 232). There is undoubtedly truth in the assertion that Lee does not engage as fully with the black characters in the story as she does with the white (with the notable exception of Calpurnia, the Finches' housekeeper); and there is an undeniable note of condescension at times toward blacks, as when Atticus blasts whites who would "take advantage of a Negro's *ignorance*" (Lee, 241, emphasis added). An even more striking instance of this comes from Miss Maudie, who points out that, despite appearances to the contrary, there are white people in Maycomb with some humility—"enough humility to think, when they look at a Negro, there but for the Lord's kindness am I" (Lee, 257). Such remarks do seem to provide fair ammunition for those who feel that Lee's depiction of black characters is decidedly limited and—for all the book's themes of tolerance and understanding—inherently racist.

To Kill a Mockingbird, then, is not a radical call to arms; it seems to stop well short of depicting, or even really advocating, proper racial integration. Even Calpurnia, who is the most individualized black character, is said to lead "a modest double life," an existence outside of the Finch household which is entirely "separate" (Lee, 136); when she takes the children to the Negro church, they notice that she even speaks in an entirely different way than usual, in the black people's idiom (Lee, 129). Of course, she makes the point that "it's the same God" (Lee, 129) in reply to one of the black women who complains about her bringing white children to the Negro church; but the sense of division remains. All the same, it is worthwhile remembering that the only time the book ever descends to the level of crude caricature of blacks is in Mrs. Merriweather's comments at the missionary meeting following the trial, about her servant girl Sophy (Lee, 252-253); and these comments are deliberately meant to reflect back upon the speaker. In fact all the members of the white missionary circle unconsciously reveal themselves to be the most narrow-minded "hypocrites" (Lee, 254) through their supposedly genteel conversation around the tea table. And while it is true that Lee does generally keep a certain distance from the black section of Maycomb society, it might be pointed out that she is merely reflecting the world in which she grew up, where social divisions along racial lines remained rigid. In this way the novel gives readers today a vivid picture of what everyday life really was like in the American South in that era. Overall, although Lee's portrayal of blacks has attracted complaints, it is neither an unduly negative nor over-sentimentalized picture that she gives, and generally speaking, readers do not seem to feel that it pulls the book down very sharply.

In any case, it is important to bear in mind that Lee's portrayal of race and race issues is not the whole story. Edgar Schuster states the case as follows:

> The achievement of Harper Lee is not that she has written another novel about race prejudice, but rather that she has placed race prejudice in a perspective which allows us to see it as an aspect of a larger thing; as something that arises from phantom contacts, from fear and lack of knowledge; and finally as something that disappears with the kind of knowledge or "education" that one gains through learning what people are really like when you "finally see them."

Tom Robinson's trial, which highlights the racism endemic in Maycomb, is the most dramatic and emotionally charged element of the novel, but it forms only a small part of the larger theme of prejudice in general. It is therefore a tad misleading to describe the novel (as it often is) as dealing predominantly with the issue of racial injustice. Atticus's oft-repeated maxim illuminates the wider purpose of the story: "You never really understand a person until you . . . climb into his skin and walk around in it" (Lee, 31). He constantly exhorts his children to put themselves in other people's shoes in order to see things from different perspectives. This is salutary advice in a community as riddled with prejudices as Maycomb, which harbors fixed ideas about how people behave (or ought to behave) according to their race, gender, and class; and Maycomb can be taken as a microcosm of the world at large. For Scout, narrator of the story, this lesson begins and ends with Boo Radley, the mysterious and reclusive neighbor about whom she and her brother Jem and friend Dill spin wild fantasies. But as the novel progresses, her understanding and compassion grow, and she gradually realizes that far from the "malevolent phantom" (Lee, 13) that she once imagined him to be, he is actually an eminently decent human being—despite the strange conditions of his life—and she is finally able to recognize him as being a true "gentleman" (Lee, 304). She comes to see the world, quite literally, from his point of view by standing on the Radley porch (Lee, 305)—a place that finally loses the sense of terror it once caused her.

Atticus's injunction to walk around in another person's shoes in order to understand them extends even to the likes of Bob Ewell, the villain of the piece, as when Atticus explains to his children why Ewell feels the need to threaten him in the aftermath of the trial; Atticus fully understands that, despite the positive outcome of the trial for Ewell, any "credibility" Ewell ever had was destroyed by Atticus's rigorous cross-examination (Lee, 238). In a similar way, and much more poignantly, a stark comprehension of Mayella Ewell's position suddenly dawns on Scout during the trial. Living among the lowest of the low in the white community, at the mercy of her brutal father, ostracized by white people as "trash," and shunned by blacks because she is white, Mayella, as Scout realizes, "must have been the loneliest person in the world. She was even lonelier than Boo Radley, who had not been out of the house in twenty-five years" (Lee, 209). At this point Scout, for a few moments at least, is able to empathize very clearly with Mayella and to understand the basis of her actions in helping to convict an innocent man. The book is nothing if not a call for the enlightenment of empathy, a plea not to judge too quickly and certainly not on the basis of unreasoning prejudice. At the same time it does not take this to maudlin extremes; the Finches display a measure of understanding for the Ewells but do not harbor any particular compassion for them as they are willfully responsible for the great wrong done to Tom Robinson (and Bob Ewell, at least, is seen to be beyond redemption if he can do something as cowardly as attacking children in the dark). *Mockingbird* simply suggests that people should try to live by a basically decent set of values. There are no unrealistic hopes or expectations that radical changes can take place in people or that miraculous events—like Tom Robinson being acquitted—can happen, but simply an appeal for people to try and understand each other as far as possible. This is the message that continues to resonate with readers worldwide. On one of the rare occasions on which she has broken her silence on the novel, in a 1966 letter to the *Richmond News-Leader,* Lee herself remarked that "Surely it is plain to the simplest intelligence that *To Kill a Mockingbird* spells out in words of seldom more than two syllables a code of honor and conduct, Christian in its ethic, that is the heritage of all Southerners." It is interesting to note that she puts a distinctly "regional" slant on things here, and invokes a broadly Western (Christian) moral framework for her story; but the novel's relevance certainly does not appear to be limited to any one time or place, or to people of any one particular religious or social background. As Shields says, its "lessons of human dignity and respect for others remains fundamental and universal" (1).

Atticus is not the only enlightened adult figure in the book: there are others, like the straight-talking Miss Maudie (who refuses to conform to ladylike notions by spending most of her time outdoors working in her garden and wearing overalls). Mr. Underwood, the editor of the local paper, is another example; he denounces the shooting of the physically disabled Tom Robinson during an escape attempt simply on the grounds that it is "a sin to kill cripples, be they sitting, standing or escaping" (Lee, 262). It is Atticus who absorbs much of the character interest in this regard, however. He has become one of the best-known fictional characters in modern times and functions as a moral exemplar, not least for members of the legal profession, as Alice Petry notes: "Atticus has become something of a folk hero in legal circles and is treated almost as if he were an actual person" (xxiii). Yet at first glance he does not appear as a typical hero. His physical shortcomings are carefully enumerated; his children chafe against the fact that he is older than their classmates' parents so that he is unable to play football with

Jem, nor does he hunt, drink, play poker, or do anything else glamorous in their eyes; he simply "(sits) in the living room and read(s)" (Lee, 97). Furthermore—in a wry twist on his sister Alexandra's "preoccupation with heredity" (Lee, 141)—he is virtually half-blind, apparently owing to the fact that "left eyes (are) the tribal curse of the Finches" (Lee, 97). He is deliberately conceived as a foil to the popular image of the macho, gun-toting type of American hero—although ironically, for all his expressed antipathy to guns,[4] he proves to be a deadly shot in the incident of the mad dog (Lee, 104). Unfortunately he is not so successful in fighting the "mad dog" of racism;[5] as Scout waits for the trial verdict to be announced she feels as though she is watching him walk into the street to shoot the dog all over again "but this time knowing that the gun was empty" (Lee, 230). Of course, his attempt to fight for what he knows is a lost cause is admirable, although it is only the most visible part of his work as lawyer. He also deals with more routine and mundane tasks such as sorting out tax matters (Lee, 126) or "making a will so airtight can't anyone meddle with it" (Lee, 98). On the face of it there is actually nothing very remarkable about his character; it is simply his principles of hard work, honesty, humility and tolerance, which he always tries to put into practice and also to inculcate in his children, that make him noteworthy. It is precisely because he is, essentially, such an ordinary person that readers identify with him and look to him as a role model; he is manifestly not superhuman.

Some might argue, however, that Atticus appears altogether too good and noble, occupying too much of the moral high ground as a man "who does (his) best to love everybody" and who disregards insults from others as it is only a sign of "how poor they are" (Lee, 118). Certainly he has appeared in a less positive light in some revisionist readings of the novel. A notable case of this was an Alabama editorial in 1992 that opined he should not be looked up to because, for all his good points, he still served a racist and sexist legal system. This editorial provoked many replies from lawyers who vehemently disagreed (Petry, xxv-xxvii). Another and more recent example is a critical article by Steven Lubet in the *Michigan Law Review*; again, the strength of the response to Lubet in defense of Atticus illustrates how the character continues to fulfill an important role outside of merely literary discussion. He has come to be accepted as an embodiment of basic decent values which anyone, both in legal work or in day-to-day living, can strive to emulate.

The stalwart character of Atticus Finch, then, remains a prime reason for the lasting success and cultural significance of *To Kill a Mockingbird*. Another is the novel's style. The issues it deals with are serious, so much so that R. A. Dave has likened it to classical tragedy or epic in its depiction of the defeat of innocence, for which the mockingbird functions as a symbol. Tom Robinson's death (Lee, 262) and the treatment of Boo Radley (Lee, 202) are both explicitly compared to the shooting of mockingbirds—"which don't do one thing but sing their hearts out for us," as Miss Maudie remarks (Lee, 98). The story is also about the loss of innocence in the sense that the children—Scout, Jem, and Dill—come to recognize the nature and the power of evil active in the world as they grow older. However, the book is not weighed down with these themes. Instead it opts for a lively and frequently very humorous mode of narration, from Scout's perspective as a small child. In using a child-narrator to explore themes of adult prejudices and hypocrisy and racial oppression, the book is comparable to *The Adventures of Huckleberry Finn*, and, like Twain's celebrated novel, its style has proved a hit with readers. It is a refreshing and easy-to-read narrative which is also quite subtly done, as Scout's child-view is aided by the reflections of her older self. And, in fact, we do not get just Scout's double perspective but also that of her older brother Jem, to whom she constantly refers; his point of view is more developed than that of the young Scout but still immature compared to that of adults. Therefore the novel meshes together child, adolescent and adult perspectives, which makes for a certain richness in the storytelling and much amusement as the children struggle to come to terms with the adult world. Scout's tomboyish ways—beating up Dill and other schoolmates,

swearing, and rebelling at the prospect of living in "a pink-cotton peni-
tentiary" (Lee, 148-149)—provide plenty of scope for humor, particularly in the face of the constant disapproval of her prim-and-proper Aunt
Alexandra and other ladies in the neighborhood. All three of the children also spend much of their time speculating about the adults who inhabit their small world, which, as Theodore and Grace-Ann Hovet
have discussed, provides the reader with entertaining glimpses into a
varied and fascinating gallery of characters in a small Southern town.

More pertinent to the central purpose of the novel is the way in
which the straightforwardness of a child's perspective shows up the irrationality of adult prejudices and preconceptions. Scout is perpetually
bemused by her aunt's ideas on background and class: "Somewhere, I
had received the impression that Fine Folks were people who did the
best they could with the sense they had, but Aunt Alexandra was of the
opinion, obliquely expressed, that the longer a family had been squat-
ting on one patch of land the finer it was" (Lee, 141). This is made to
look ridiculous by Jem who points out that, by this definition, the
Ewells are also "fine folks" as they have been living in the same dump
for generations (Lee, 141). Such an approach allows Lee to use humor
to make some valid points about the essential superficiality of many
social distinctions. The tone becomes more serious, though, when
Scout wonders how her teacher Miss Gates can speak out against Hitler
for persecuting Jews and at the same time persist in her animosity toward blacks in her own neighborhood: "how can you hate Hitler so bad
and then turn around and be so ugly about folks right at home?" (Lee,
268). Indeed, to the young Scout, the adult world sometimes appears
utterly incomprehensible: "I came to the conclusion that people were
just peculiar. I withdrew from them and never thought about them unless I was forced to" (Lee, 264). Lee therefore turns a sharp eye on virtually every aspect of Maycomb society; she targets notions on race,
gender, class, and also criticizes social institutions—not just the judi-
ciary (which is obviously gravely at fault in a case like Tom Robinson's) but also organized religion (the missionary circle, as seen above)

and education.[6] However, the humor of the book, although often ironic and verging on the satirical, never becomes too uncomfortable or sardonic; the tone generally remains warm and pleasant, which is why it continues to hold so much appeal for readers. Scout, Jem and Dill simply have to learn to come to terms with the adult world, the world of Maycomb, for all its follies and inconsistencies. This does not mean that they should tamely submit to it; they can continue to view it critically, as the older Scout obviously does—but they do not repudiate it altogether.

At the core of the novel appears to lie a belief in the innate goodness of human beings; as Atticus tells his daughter at the end, "Most people are [nice] Scout, when you finally see them" (Lee, 307). The book therefore concludes on a positive note. Although it provides a thoroughgoing critique of society, it does not do so in an angry and confrontational way, making it easier to assimilate for the majority of readers. It does not surrender human ideals or despair either of society or of individuals. It is moralistic but does not preach at its readers, instead making its observations in a generally sly and humorous manner. It is a novel that combines humor and social comment with a strong and stirring plot, a hero (and villain), and moments of genuine pathos. These are the ingredients of its continuing widespread significance well into the twenty-first century.

Notes

1. Reported in *The Telegraph* newspaper.

2. There have, however, been no other really well-known adaptations, excepting the play by Christopher Sergel that has been performed annually in Lee's hometown of Monroeville since 1990, and which had become a tourist draw.

3. The novel can also be considered a bildungsroman as it charts the moral and emotional development of its central character, Scout Finch.

4. Atticus impresses upon his children that "having a gun is an invitation for someone to shoot you" (Lee, 237). He also mentions guns when he tells them that Mrs. Dubose, the fierce and dying old lady who attempts to cure herself of her morphine addiction, is an example of true courage as opposed to the "idea that courage is a man with a gun in his hand" (Lee, 121).

5. See Carolyn Jones for a full discussion of the mad dog as a symbol of racism in the novel.

6. Having been taught to read by Atticus at home, Scout finds it difficult to adjust to her school's teaching methods, with the comic result that she is not allowed to read there at all to begin with, so that her official education leaves her with "the prospect of spending nine months refraining from reading and writing" (Lee, 30).

Works Cited

Chura, Patrick. "Prolepsis and Anachronism: Emmett Till and the Historicity of *To Kill a Mockingbird.*" *Southern Literary Journal* 32, no. 2 (Spring, 2000): 1-26.

Dave, R. A. "Harper Lee's Tragic Vision." In *Indian Studies in American Fiction,* edited by by M. K. Naik. Dharwar: Karnatak University and The Macmillan Company of India, 1974, pp. 311-323.

Erisman, Fred. "The Romantic Regionalism of Harper Lee." *The Alabama Review* 26, no. 2 (April, 1973): 122-136.

"Harper Lee Twits School Board in Virginia for Ban on Her Novel." *The New York Times* (January 16, 1966): 82.

Hovet, Theodore R., and Grace-Ann Hovet. "'Fine Fancy Gentlemen' and 'Yappy Folk': Contending Voices in *To Kill a Mockingbird.*" *Southern Quarterly* 40, no.1 (Fall, 2001): 67-78

Johnson, Claudia. *"To Kill a Mockingbird": Threatening Boundaries.* Twayne: New York, 1994.

_____. *Understanding "To Kill a Mockingbird": A Student Casebook to Issues, Sources, and Historical Documents.* Westport, Conn.: Greenwood Press, 1994.

Jones, Carolyn. "Atticus Finch and the Mad Dog: Harper Lee's *To Kill a Mockingbird.*" *Southern Quarterly* 34, no. 4 (Summer, 1996): 53-63.

Khan, Urmee. "*To Kill a Mockingbird* Voted Greatest Novel of all Time." *The Telegraph,* June 16, 2008.

Lee, Harper. *To Kill a Mockingbird.* 1960. London: Vintage, 2004.

Lubet, Steven. "Reconstructing Atticus Finch." *Michigan Law Review* 97, no. 6 (1999): 1339-1362.

Petry, Alice, ed. *On Harper Lee: Essays and Reflections.* Knoxville: University of Tennessee Press, 1994.

Saney, Isaac. "The Case against *To Kill a Mockingbird.*" *Race & Class* 45, no. 1 (July-September, 2003): 99-110.

Schuster, Edgar. "Discovering Theme and Structure in the Novel." *English Journal* 52 (October, 1963): 506-511.

Shields, Charles J. *Mockingbird: A Portrait of Harper Lee.* Henry Holt: New York, 2006.

Siegel, Roslyn. "The Black Man and the Macabre in American Literature." *Black American Literature Forum* 10 (1976): 133-136.

"Were You Ever a Turtle?":
To Kill a Mockingbird—
Casting the Self as the Other_____

Neil Heims

1.

To Kill a Mockingbird is part bildungsroman,[1] part wisdom literature,[2] and modeled on early twentieth-century boys' mystery, adventure, and character-building books, particularly *The Gray Ghost*, from which Atticus reads to Scout at the very end of *To Kill a Mockingbird*. The twin subjects of *To Kill a Mockingbird* are racism and growing up. Its narrator's tone suggests that she is guided by a desire to define, by the story, and by the attitudes of the central characters, fostering in her readers a sense of decency. Perhaps it is even something more: decency elevated to the eminence of wisdom. Decency becomes wisdom in *To Kill a Mockingbird* because when decency is exercised in the world of the book, it is exercised in a world governed by the fundamental indecency of pervasive, inhumane racism. The two subjects of the novel, racism and growth, and the narrative tone of transparent and ingratiating wisdom, are brought together, and the action of the novel can be seen as the process of growing up decent, virtuous, and wise inside a racist, bigoted, and hidebound society. The model of wisdom that the book offers is Atticus, the narrator's father. In him, Harper Lee provides a vision of what the soul of a decent person living inside an indecent world ought to be like.

The themes of the novel are introduced in its first paragraphs. "When he was nearly thirteen, my brother Jem got his arm badly broken at the elbow." That first sentence, with its awareness of and precision regarding age, signals that a novel about growing up, a chronicle of formative experience, is beginning. Something, as yet a mystery, happened that caused Jem to get his arm broken. It signaled a rite of passage for him and for his sister, Scout, the narrator, whose growth is guided by his. The sentence does not say he broke his arm. It says he *got his arm broken*. Something painful happened to him with which he had to cope. Must pain accompany growth? Is it essential for growth, the cause of growth? In *To Kill a Mockingbird*, it seems to be. How must we live when we live inside a world defined by indecency and pain but which encourages the pretense that it is politely free of both? How can we survive with integrity when our values place us outside a society we must nevertheless live within? This quiet, winningly narrated novel about the nature and triumph of decency in an indecent world and about the nature of wisdom in a world that thwarts goodness, sets the pain of inhumanity and the defeat of the good and, nevertheless, the triumph of virtue, at its center, and it takes on the task of responding to problems like these for the reader's edification.

When Jem's arm healed, "his left arm was somewhat shorter than his right," but, "he couldn't have cared less, so long as he could pass and punt." The body is less important than the *acts* the body performs. Ability trumps appearance. These are lessons, it is generally acknowledged, that are worthwhile to learn. They constitute the wisdom that comes with growth, the wisdom that is the result of reflection upon experience. They teach that perspective plays a major part in seeing and in achieving wisdom. Wisdom comes from having a sense of something beyond oneself to which one is devoted, as Jem is, whether to playing football, to being a gentleman, or to seeing justice prevail; as Atticus is to right action and fairness; as Scout is, also, to fairness, and to making sense of and mapping the world around her. Yet that something beyond oneself must in itself be worthy. What makes it worthy is that self-transcendence and the good of others are at its heart, as suggested by the accumulated events of *To Kill a Mockingbird*.

The importance of a sense of perspective in the attitude of the narrative is introduced in the lead sentence of the second paragraph: "When enough years had gone by to enable us to look back on them, we sometimes discussed the events leading to his [Jem's] accident." There is a flow of experience and then there needs to follow upon experience the disposition to examine it and to reflect upon it. This disposition signifies the process of growth and the beginning of wisdom, the practice of the Socratic injunction to pursue knowledge, of oneself, of the nature of the world, of what is right. The conjunction of connection and detachment required for the exercise of perspective is fittingly represented in *To Kill a Mockingbird* by the duality of the narrative voice. The adult Scout narrates the events of the novel, but frequently she assumes the point of view and the voice of her younger self, the girl in the book. "I maintain that the Ewells started it all," the narrator says. "But Jem," her brother, "who was four years my senior," and whose experiences teach him that there is an uncanny, intangible attachment that can join people to each other, "said it started long before that . . . when Dill . . . gave us the idea of making Boo Radley come out."

"Perspectives vary" is the lesson of the third paragraph. But differences in point of view, in the conflicting way individuals see something, can cause conflicts. Scout admits that fighting is one way to settle conflicts. But she relegates that method to childhood, accepting that it must be left behind to be supplanted by a better means. That means is by consulting the wisdom of her father. He embodies thought, examination of facts, and self-suppression in the service of fairness, rectitude and respectful deference to the authenticity of the otherness of others. Consequently, in order to settle the argument, Jem and Scout take their dispute to Atticus.

Atticus is tellingly named. He is, in some sort, an allegorical figure, a man representing a quality. The name "Atticus" suggests the classical restraint and firmness of temper, the intelligence and faith in reason associated with the culture of ancient, democratic Athens, the wellspring of Socratic wisdom. Athens is also the place where that wisdom met its severest test when it encountered its citizens' aversion to Socratic teaching. They put Socrates to death. Even then, Socrates retained his equanimity, just as Atticus does despite the attacks upon him and his family and the martyrdom of Tom Robinson. Atticus is a Socratic figure and an ironist. He sees deeply and speaks modestly. He is characteristically aware of the limitations of his ability to see. In fact, he has a bad left eye and he wears glasses. He is upright to a fault, intellectually dedicated to what is right, and emotionally solid. He projects the sense of a deeply chastened yet compassionate spirit that, like Boo Radley, shuns the light of day but comes to the rescue when danger threatens. He is content to be withdrawn and ready to be engaged. He is aware that he will lose the battle for Tom Robinson's life and freedom even as he, nevertheless, addresses it. Regarding the origins of the story Scout tells in *To Kill a Mockingbird* Atticus says, aware of shifting perspectives, that they "were both right."

These three paragraphs serve as an overture to the book. All the major themes and principle characters that are developed in *To Kill a Mockingbird* are introduced. Scout has found the origin of the story in "the Ewells." Jem sees it "when Dill first gave us the idea of making Boo Radley come out." The Ewells, Jem, Atticus, Dill, Boo Radley, Jem's broken arm are then left for several pages as Scout leads the reader through the history of Maycomb, the town in which the action of *To Kill a Mockingbird* is set. She describes Maycomb and its inhabitants before she returns to the microcosm of her world with Jem and Dill and their fascination with the Radley house, its famous recluse, Boo Radley, and their efforts to draw him out, see him, and befriend him.

Maycomb, Alabama, is "a tired old town." Its inhabitants "moved slowly . . . ambled across the square . . . shuffled in and out of the stores . . . took their time about everything." The time is the 1930s. It is summer. Scout and Jem's mother has been dead since Scout was two and Jem six. Atticus is a lawyer. The children have always been cared for by Calpurnia, Atticus's devoted housekeeper, a black woman. She is wise, literate, and steady, firm but gentle, one of the few in her church who can read. She taught Scout to write. She instructs her in the graces of being social and comforts her when she needs comforting. It is Cal, along with Atticus, who teaches Scout the importance of taking the good of others as the central concern that must govern behavior. The lesson is introduced in a simple domestic context, at lunch, when Scout erupts at the way Walter Cunningham, whom Jem and Scout have brought home from school to eat with them because his family is too poor for him to buy lunch, pours syrup thickly on everything in his plate. Scout is taken with astonishment, but not with ill will. But Walter Cunningham reacts with mortification. Atticus shakes his head at her in admonition. She tries to explain her outburst: "But he's gone and drowned his dinner in syrup." "It was then," the narrator continues,

that Calpurnia requested my presence in the kitchen.

She was furious. . . . "There's some folks who don't eat like us," she whispered fiercely, "but you ain't called on to contradict 'em at the table when they don't. That boy's yo' comp'ny and if he wants to eat up the table cloth you let him."

2.

The parameters of the novel once established, Scout begins the narrative anew, drawing back three years into the past. The first eight chapters of *To Kill a Mockingbird* are not only *modeled* on a boys' adventure mystery, they construct a narrative concerned with children's adventures and a childish mystery. "When I was almost six and Jem was nearly ten," she begins, "our summertime boundaries . . . were Mrs. Henry Lafayette Dubose's house two doors north of us, and the Radley Place three doors to the south." These boundaries were self-imposed and touched the edge of childish terror. Passing Mrs. Dubose's house was odious because Mrs. Dubose was herself odious. She tormented the children with insults and stinging vituperation. Their obligation to behave in a mannerly way to adults obliged them to listen politely and respectfully to her insults. The Radley Place—which they had to pass in the winter on their way to school, running in fear of an unknown that they had endowed with mysterious and ghastly powers—had assumed the dimension of a haunted house in their imagination. It was the home of a living ghost, Boo Radley, whom they had never seen but who loomed for them as a fascinating, mysterious demon whom they wished to conjure with a terrified longing.

Until the ninth chapter, nearly a third of the way through, the narrator of *To Kill a Mockingbird* tells a pastoral story of children playing in the summer, going to school in the winter, being mischievous, and becoming integrated into their society. She shows them building an emblematic snowman of muddled race and mixed gender. A layer of white snow coats a body of brown mud; a woman's hat sits on a male torso. The distinctions that govern Maycomb merge and then melt in this creation, as they will not in reality. They see a fire burn down the house across the street, and always they are obsessed with the mystery of Boo Radley. They make up plays about his family, venture with fear and bravery to approach his house, and continuously devise unsuccessful ways to draw him out so that they might see him and befriend him. Through Scout's narration, Harper Lee shows them in school, at home, and with their father. She presents the class, cultural, racial, and economic conditions of the Southern town during the Great Depression. In the ninth chapter, a new element enters the story, forces the children to reconsider the nature of their world, and introduces the major plot, the story of racial segregation that drives Part Two of *To Kill a Mockingbird*.

The sense of the segregated South is already pervasive in the first eight chapters. It is a given of the place and the time the adult Scout is remembering, in the late 1950s, as she describes her adventures as a girl growing into a world of arbitrary racial and gender demands in the mid-1930s. In those first eight chapters, neither the ideology of the surrounding environment nor its class structure is a particularly troublesome matter to the children. The racial injustice that is the foundation of their society does not become the focus of the novel or a disturbing element in their lives until in the first sentence of chapter nine, without narrative introduction, a voice, which is only afterward identified as Scout's, demands, "You can just take that back, boy!" The boy is a schoolmate, Cecil Jacobs. What he said that has made Scout clench her fists ready to fight, despite her father's injunction against fighting, was "that Scout Finch's daddy defended niggers." From this point on, Tom Robinson becomes a mighty force in Scout and Jem's world, and, because of him, the themes of racism and sexual disorder demand a reader's attention.

When Scout asks Atticus if he "defend[s] niggers," he answers, "Of course I do," and immediately corrects her, adding "Don't say nigger, Scout. That's common." "Common!" It seems like such a quaint rebuke to a word that carries such an odious weight of injustice and disrespect. The way Scout defends having used it, ironically, relies, indeed, on the fact that its use is widespread. But she is referring to the homonym of "common." "'s what everybody at school says," she says. "From now on," Atticus says wryly, "it'll be everybody less one—." When she hears the word "common," she thinks of it as a word indicating numbers. When Atticus uses it he is referring to the character of a person with an undeveloped sense of humanity, to a person who has not achieved himself or herself truly as a person.

It becomes clear with this turn of the plot that the structure of *To Kill a Mockingbird* relies on a number of contrasts that parallel each other. Most obvious is the contrast between black and white, the injustice of racial disparity that pulsates at the heart of the novel. But *To Kill a Mockingbird* is also a story whose morality is defined in black and white terms. Right and wrong, virtue and vice do not blend into each other in *To Kill a Mockingbird* and are not relative. They are absolute and absolutely distinct from each other, as are the persons of the book who represent virtue and vice or certain of their aspects.

Atticus and Bob Ewell, for example, the two great adversaries in *To Kill a Mockingbird*, represent the contrast of wisdom and ignorance, of fairness and bigotry, of generosity and crabbedness. Their relationships with their daughters, Atticus's with Scout and Ewell's with Mayella, represent a contrast in the possibilities of father/daughter relationships and, by extension, of the human disposition. The former one is generous and nurturing; the latter, selfish, exploitative, and abusive.

Tom Robinson's case does not merely introduce the problem of racial injustice. It also introduces the consequent problems of how to live a virtuous life in a world governed by injustice and of how to live a life guided by tolerance among intolerant people. *To Kill a Mockingbird* addresses the problem of how to remain unprovoked by evil and how not to succumb to evil action in response, while struggling to overcome evil. The episode that Scout narrates after the encounter with Cecil Jacobs recapitulates the episode with him and amplifies it; it combines the issue of racist aggression and the problem of self-discipline. And always, because Scout is the "tomboy," she is at a time and in a culture that demands that girls learn to behave as "ladies," the issue of how she copes with compelled gender identity is present, and, at the trial, in the person of Mayella Ewell, it is bound up with racial bigotry. Scout, in the episode at Finch's landing when she confronts Francis Hancock, who taunts her by calling Atticus a "nigger-lover" and a disgrace to the family—and Jem, in the story of his encounter with Mrs. Dubose that follows soon after—must both acquire the strength and the moral character to be able to resist retaliation against persons and, with her brother, to remain themselves even as they restrain themselves. This is the strength that characterizes Atticus, the ability to absorb and tolerate unjust aggression without rancor even as he remains dedicated to fighting injustice and endeavors to do so.

3.

Scout first experiences a miscarriage of justice and identifies it as such after she "split[s her] knuckle to the bone on [her cousin Francis's] front teeth" after he repeats the taunt that her father is a "nigger-lover." She tells her Uncle Jack, after he punishes her for cussing and fighting, that his punishment was not "fair." When he reproaches her for her lingering resentment because, he says, she "had [it] coming and you know it," using a formula she has recently learned from Atticus, when he told her that her Aunt Alexandra "didn't understand girls much," Scout tells her uncle that he does not "understand children much." He begins to repeat her infractions in justification of his behavior, but Scout respectfully interrupts him.

> You gonna give me a chance to tell you? she says. You never stopped to gimme a chance to tell you my side of it—you just lit right into me. When Jem an' I fuss Atticus doesn't ever just listen to Jem's side of it, he hears mine, too.

Scout explains that Francis had called Atticus a "nigger-lover" and that she had, therefore the "extreme provocation" that Jack had earlier told her was necessary to justify outbursts of temper or the use of unacceptable words like "hell" and "damn."

Jack is chastened, humbled, and enlightened by Scout's explanation. But Scout has more to show him about what constitutes real character as she has learned it from her father. When he hears what Francis's "extreme provocations" have been, Jack is ready to drive back to Finch's landing, make the matter public, and see that Francis is properly reprimanded. Scout begs him not to. Since Atticus "asked me one time not to let anything I heard about him make me mad . . . I'd ruther him think we were fightin' about somethin' else." Jack does keep her secret in a conversation later with Atticus that Scout overhears. That conversation serves as one of the preludes to the ensuing action, Tom Robinson's trial. And through his conversation with Jack, Atticus, who knows Scout is eavesdropping, and who knows without having to be told what the cause of Scout's fight was, indirectly lets Scout know what difficulties await her and how he expects her to behave.

The lesson that Atticus must teach and which Scout and Jem must master in order to weather the events of Part Two of *To Kill a Mockingbird*, the virtues of suppressing pride and of cultivating modesty and humility without betraying one's own integrity, and the capacity to recognize the humanity of people who do not recognize one's own humanity or the humanity of others, is developed in the last chapters, ten and eleven, of Part One of *To Kill a Mockingbird*. In chapter nine, much to the children's amazement, Atticus shoots a rabid dog dead, head-on, with one cool and perfect shot. They are astonished because Atticus seems old to them and, unlike the other fathers in Maycomb, Atticus "didn't do anything." His work was not colorful or even, really, visible. "He worked in an office, not in a drugstore." He was not a dump-truck driver, a sheriff, a farmer, or a garage mechanic. He did not hunt, play poker, fish, drink, or smoke. "He sat in the livingroom and read." He did not, in their estimation, "do anything that could arouse the admiration of anyone." Consequently his shooting the mad dog is a revelation to them, but not just of his prowess. What is more impressive is that he never spoke of his marksmanship and never went hunting. Their neighbor, Maudie Atkinson, explains to the children that Atticus is "civilized in his heart." She explains that because he knows he "has an unfair advantage over most living things," he refrained from shooting "till he had to." When Scout ventures that Atticus ought to be proud of his gift, Maudie responds, "People in their right minds never take pride in their talents." When Scout tells Jem a little later that they'd "really have something to talk about at school," he tells her that they ought to say nothing. "If he'd wanted us to know it, he'da told us. If he was proud of it, he'da told us." Jem finds a quality in his father that he senses is worthy of emulation. "Atticus is a gentleman," he says, "just like me." But Jem is premature. There is one more trial that he must undergo on his path to enlightenment before the final encounter with evil. His encounter with Mrs. Dubose provides not only a lesson in self-control, self-suppression, or bearing insults without yielding to rage but also something more even than what Atticus intended. After Mrs. Dubose's death, Atticus tells Jem that even if Jem had not destroyed Mrs. Dubose's camellias in a rage, he would "have made you go read to her anyway," not only because he wanted to distract her from the suffering of withdrawal from morphine, but also because

I wanted you to see what real courage is, instead of getting the idea that courage is a man with a gun in his hand. It's when you're licked before you begin but you begin anyway and see it through no matter what. You rarely win, but sometimes you do.

Atticus is challenging the strong-man ethos of courage. He is also providing the philosophical underpinning of his own action in Part Two when he undertakes the defense of Tom Robinson with complete determination despite his strong sense of almost-sure defeat. But there is something more than a lesson about discrediting machismo for Jem in the encounter with Mrs. Dubose. He learns to return good for evil, to feel no animosity for one who uses him badly, to see the soul beneath the slime. That is what it means to be a gentleman.

Although there is never a scene of direct reconciliation between Mrs. Dubose and Jem, there is a deep, albeit indirect, encounter between them. Scout sees Jem "fingering the . . . petals" of the camellia Mrs. Dubose sent him before she died, accepting as a gift what he had first tried to destroy. The flower represents that buried part of Mrs. Dubose's nature, her soul, the essence she could only show in her garden but not, until this gift to Jem, in herself. Thus are the opposite sensibilities of the story demarcated, as were the "summer boundaries." On the one side, there is reconciliation and a human connection that can be too deep for words, as represented by the communion Mrs. Dubose forges with Jem and, at the end of the novel, by Boo Radley's action; and on the other, there is self-consuming, prideful revenge, the force that Bob Ewell serves and in whose clutches he lives and dies.

4.

Tom Robinson serves a complex and disturbing function in *To Kill a Mockingbird*. He is at the moral center of the novel, not because of anything he has done to secure such a place but because of what is done to him. His story is not, really, about him but about white reactions to him and his story. By definition, as a black man in Alabama in the mid-1930s, he is constituted not by his own self-presentation but by the way others represent him. Consequently, others are morally defined by their response to him. What happens on the witness stand in his trial for the rape of Mayella Ewell is that Atticus fights to deconstruct Bob and Mayella Ewell's representation of him and Mr. Gilmer, the opposing lawyer, leads Tom into presenting himself in a way that a black man must not, that violates other people's expectation of him. The fault that glares in the courtroom is not that Tom is guilty of raping and beating Mayella Ewell. Atticus's defense is strong and convincing. The crime that defines Tom on the witness stand is his remark that he felt sorry for Mayella. The audacious presumption of a black man to feel sorry for a white woman's troubles has nearly the weight of a rape.

Although Lee draws Tom with compassion and humanity, he is not, in E. M. Forster's formula, a "round character"; he is, rather, a "flat" one. The distinction is not one of quality but of construction. The distinction results from how an author intends to use her characters. "The test of a round character," Forster wrote in *Aspects of the Novel* (78), "is whether it is capable of surprising in a convincing way. If it never surprises, it is flat." Adhering to this definition, nearly all the characters in *To Kill a Mockingbird* are flat. Again, that is no deprecation. Most of the characters in the great novels of Charles Dickens are flat. The reader expects certain sorts of behavior from them and they do not disappoint but play their parts convincingly and satisfyingly. The characters in *To Kill a Mockingbird* are predictable; they live according to a particular given sensibility. The pleasure for the reader is to watch those sensibilities play out. We are not surprised when Atticus acts characteristically. We are glad of it. Predictable means dependable. The reader experiences the pleasure of having expectations met. It is the literary experience of wish fulfillment.

Tom is a stereotype. He is a good black man in a white racist society. Were he something other than an innocent victim, *To Kill a Mockingbird* would not be *To Kill a Mockingbird* but a far more complex book telling a far more ambiguous and difficult story. Tom's options, as a representative good black man in a white racist society are, at best, limited. He is the sacrificial offering that defines the culture which offers it and that allows the good whites to show their goodness. Others are defined by their response to Tom Robinson and to his lot. That includes the readers of the book, for it is noteworthy that Lee has constructed the novel in such a way that readers do not have definite authorial knowledge of Tom Robinson's innocence or guilt. The story is told from Scout's point of view, colored by it, and is constituted only by the things she has seen or heard. The only testimony against Tom comes from Bob and Mayella Ewell. It is presented as highly suspect. The only proof of his innocence is circumstantial. There are contextual circumstances. Solid, good, loyal, wise, and trustworthy Calpurnia vouches for him. So does his church congregation. So does Link Deas, Tom's white employer, who risks the judge's wrath when he springs up, out of order, "from the audience and announced: 'I just want the whole lot of you to know one thing right now. That boy's worked for me eight years an' I ain't never had a speck o' trouble outa him. Not a speck.'" The very circumstances of the case, Tom's crippled hand, Bob Ewell's left-handedness, Ewell's neglect to call a doctor, suggest that Tom was framed. So do the environmental circumstances of Southern racism, including the hidden guilty sexual attraction that conventionally characterizes the oppressing class's relationship to the oppressed. And there is the overriding circumstance that Scout's narrative voice is ingratiating and authoritative. She is a credible narrator because she has shown herself to be an honest and fair-minded person in the course of her account of Maycomb County so far. The reader can take her portrayal of Bob Ewell and his daughter at the trial as honest and credible because of the relationship she has forged with the reader, because of her portrayal of Atticus, and because the Ewells behave according to the reader's expectations of how such types do behave.

Atticus is rock solid, reliable and true. The incidents leading up to the trial have shown him so. Scout presents Mayella with a dimensionality that brings forward the reader's humane understanding that the girl is a victim, terrified of her father and humiliated by her circumstances. She is more sinned against than sinning, even as she frames her accusation against Tom Robinson. It is done in resentment at her own awful portion in life and in terror of her brutal, tyrannical, incestuous, unrelentingly proud and cruel father, a man in every way the opposite of Atticus. Mayella's shame, the forbidden attraction she harbored for Tom Robinson, and the belligerent behavior she shows in the court as she testifies, which suggests through her denial of shame a confession of it, further contribute to a sympathetic portrayal of her. In desperate need of help she is beyond help. And when her father is killed later, there is no reaction scene depicting her response. Ironically, like Tom Robinson, she and her father are props in the story of other people's experience. Within the context of the Southern racial and class system, Mayella is a girl ground down by abuse; she can have little self-regard. In that context, it is understandable that she is sexually attracted to a man from another, equally despised and more oppressed underclass. Outside the cultural context, simply within the context of basic humanity, she is denied the right to admit a natural biological imperative that causes her to find a strong, upright, good-looking, kind man like Tom Robinson desirable. In court, Bob Ewell comes across as the little bully the reader expects him to be. His subsequent behavior confirms the accuracy of Scout's account and the reader's impression of him. He is a quintessential Southern redneck. Even Atticus calls him trash. He is essential to the plot, but as an allegorical figure representing the madness of the spirit of segregation, not as a person to be understood.

The final chapters of *To Kill a Mockingbird* return to the mystery of Boo Radley and to the problem of his identity, the mystery that had haunted the children's imagination for the first third of the book. By linking the plot to make Boo Radley appear and reveal himself with the story of Bob Ewell's attempt to avenge himself upon Atticus, Lee merges the secular and the religious meaning of the word "mystery."

The mystery of Boo Radley suggests the revelation of a secret spiritual affinity that can join the souls of people together. He emerges like the god from the machine in Greek tragedy to save Atticus's children. The spiritual bond they have forged earlier with him by their fascination with him has made him their guardian angel.

5.

Like Boo Radley, Atticus has a complicated relationship with his community, but unlike Boo, he has made a sort of secret pact with himself to live within that community, as a member of that community. His creed is to show real regard and respect for people with whom he is in fundamental disagreement, even those who condemn his differences, especially regarding black people. The philosophy he has developed under these circumstances involves withdrawing into himself while not becoming anti-social. He holds as an article of faith that people who perform evil acts are not inherently evil but only removed from something essentially humane that is recoverable. His recurrent advice is to put oneself inside the skin of one's adversary. Talking about the Ku Klux Klan, Atticus tells the children how they once "paraded by Mr. Sam Levy's house . . . but Sam just stood on his porch and told 'em things had come to a pretty pass, he'd sold 'em the very sheets on their backs. Sam made 'em so ashamed of themselves they went away." Although a construction hardly true to life, Atticus's credo is validated in the novel when Scout singles out Mr. Cunningham in a mob come to the Maycomb jail to lynch Tom before the trial, brings out his humanity, and causes the mob to disperse. "That proves," Atticus says afterward, "that a gang . . . *can* be stopped simply because they're still human."

But the final episode, to say nothing of the real world, contradicts Atticus's optimism about the human character. When Bob Ewell spits in Atticus's face, Atticus simply walks away. He turns the other cheek and later tells the children that by taking Ewell's spit, he [Atticus] has spared Mayella a beating from a fuming father. He assures the children that Ewell will now calm down, that he has gotten his wrath out of his system. Atticus is wrong.

Despite Atticus's discipline, irredeemable evil, *To Kill a Mockingbird* asserts, does exist as an independent force. According to Atticus, it is beyond the pale of humanity. He calls Hitler a maniac. And of Bob Ewell, after he has tried to kill Jem and Scout, Atticus says, "He was out of his mind." In response, Heck Tate, the sheriff says, "Don't like to contradict you, Mr. Finch—wasn't crazy, mean as hell . . . there's just some kind of men you have to shoot before you can say hidy to 'em. Even then, they ain't worth the bullet it takes to shoot 'em." This is a cynical creed, perhaps, but some of the events of the story justify it. That people can become this mean gives purpose to the didacticism of *To Kill a Mockingbird*. Lee is trying to teach the reader to be human through a story of pain that is like a refiner's fire, as Jem becomes sensitive to suffering and will not even allow Scout to crush a roly-poly because he has seen how Tom's wife, Helen Robinson, "fell down in the dirt . . . like you'd step on an ant." Atticus's last words, therefore, as he tucks Scout into bed, "Most people are [real nice], Scout, when you finally see them," is less a statement of fact about others and more an ameliorating injunction to the self about how one must regard others, despite the flaws of mankind. That is his wisdom and the model perspective the book seeks to cultivate in its readers. That is also the faith and the emotional strength of its presence: perhaps reading this story can help make the wish actual.

Notes

1. "Bildungsroman" refers to a type of novel that traces the moral and spiritual growth of the heroine or hero as she or he encounters and comes to terms with her or his society.

2. "Wisdom literature" originally referred to certain books of Scripture, like *Job*, concerned with instructing readers how to live a virtuous life. In the form of manuals called "Mirrors," Renaissance writers composed books of wisdom literature instructing princes and others how to act and govern properly.

Works Cited

Forster, E. M. *Aspects of the Novel.* San Diego, Calif.: Harcourt Brace Jovanovich, A Harvest Book, 1927.

Lee, Harper. *To Kill a Mockingbird.* New York: J. B. Lippincott Company, 1960.

To Kill a Mockingbird as an
Introduction to Faulkner_____

Matthew J. Bolton

A reader who plans on tackling William Faulkner's novels might first want to reread Harper Lee's classic *To Kill a Mockingbird*, for its depiction of family life and race relations in the American south can serve as an introduction to the setting and themes that are central to Faulkner's body of work. Lee's novel was published in 1960, two years before Faulkner's death and a generation after he had published his most important novels (he would publish only one more, the light-hearted and picaresque *The Reivers*). While Lee's novel is rooted in her own childhood in Alabama, it is also in dialogue with Faulkner's vision of life in the deep south. This sort of implicit comparison may be inevitable when an author writes about a milieu that a predecessor has so thoroughly and successfully mined. Lee's childhood memories are her own, and the town in which she grew up would have been much the same whether or not Faulkner had ever picked up his pen. Yet once those memories of childhood in a small town are rendered objective in the form of a novel, they enter into the sphere of the literary and will be measured against other representations of similar experiences. Faulkner's depiction of life in the American south is powerful enough that it draws *To Kill a Mockingbird* into its orbit. This is particularly true for a modern reader who is not from the south, and who therefore knows the mores of that place and time through literature rather than through first-hand experience. Readers of Faulkner who revisit *To Kill a Mockingbird* may find themselves trying to locate Harper Lee's town of Maycomb on Faulkner's map of Yoknapatawpha county. None of this is to suggest that *To Kill a Mockingbird* is derivative. Rather, the book stakes its own claim, and in several important ways challenges Faulkner's depiction of life in the American south. It is a testament to the novel's lasting power that it can address settings and themes that were central to Faulkner's novels without being subsumed by those novels.

Yet to talk of one writer following another in orderly progression may be to place too much weight on the historical and the chronological. Readers themselves often encounter works in a very different order from the one in which they were written; after all, few toddlers choose as a bedtime story *Gilgamesh*, the *Iliad*, or *Beowulf*! Historically, Lee may have written after Faulkner, but in the reading history of most modern Americans, *To Kill a Mockingbird* comes before *The Sound and the Fury* and *As I Lay Dying*. Because of its long-established place on middle school required reading lists, *To Kill a Mockingbird* is often one of the first "serious" novels that an adolescent encounters. A teacher, professor, or lay reader may want to take advantage of the novel's canonical status (both in the school and in the intellectual development of many readers) by treating it as an initial foray into the territory that Faulkner will explore more fully. Lee's novel can serve as a guide that allows one to access the more densely constructed work of Faulkner. Connecting the two authors may help the reader who finds Faulkner's Latinate prose and fragmented narration a challenge. A great novel in its own right, *To Kill a Mockingbird* can also be a key to understanding several of Faulkner's great novels, particularly *The Sound and the Fury*.

To Kill a Mockingbird deftly intertwines two narratives: the story of Scout and Jem's fascination with the reclusive Boo Radley and the story of their father Atticus's defense of Tom Robinson, an African American accused of raping a white woman. Whereas the children, aided by their summer visitor Dill, are active participants in their campaign to draw Boo Radley out of his house, they are essentially witnesses to Atticus's legal battle and to the ire that he draws on himself from the town and the county. But a witness need not be passive, and the trial of Tom Robinson calls on Scout and Jem to actively reconsider their relationship to the society in which they have grown up. Jem, older than his sister by four years, is able more fully to articulate an understanding of Maycomb's divisions and hierarchies. He says:

You know something, Scout? I've got it all figured out, now. I've thought about it a lot lately and I've got it figured out. There's four kinds of folks in the world. There's the ordinary kind like us and the neighbors, there's the kind like the Cunninghams out in the woods, the kind like the Ewells down at the dump, and the Negroes. . . . [O]ur kind of folks don't like the Cunninghams, the Cunninghams don't like the Ewells, and the Ewells hate and despise the colored folks. (226)

Scout can't bring herself to accept Jem's cynical interpretation of life in Maycomb; she holds on, for now, to the hope that the divisions her brother describes are illusory, averring, "Naw, Jem, I think there's just one kind of folks. Folks" (227). But Jem's observation is an accurate one and can serve as a touchstone for exploring similar divisions in the society on which Faulkner's novels center. One might start by comparing the Finch family to the Compson family, the protagonists of *The Sound and the Fury*, and from there draw connections between Jem's "four kinds of folks" and the inhabitants of Faulkner's county.

Jem Finch takes as his standard for comparison his own family and their fellow townspeople, characterizing them as "the ordinary kind [of folks] like us and the neighbors." Social roles and relations between neighbors are clearly defined in a prototypical small southern town. Men have jobs connected with the town rather than with farms, working in business, trade, and local government, or in one of a handful of white-collar professions: a minister, lawyer, or doctor. Women keep houses and tend gardens, raise families, and play an active role in their churches. One's religious denomination plays an important part in defining who one is and with whom one associates. Yet all of this addresses only present-day circumstances. Coloring and defining these social relations is the legacy of family history. The social status of an individual or a family is rooted as much in the past as it is in the present. Status therefore cannot be measured empirically; one's education, profession, place of residence, and economic means do not tell the whole story. Above and beyond all of these factors is the tremendous value given to an old name. The Finches possess such an old name, one still borne by the ancestral seat of Finch's Landing. As such, they have a certain position and influence in town, despite their modest means. Scout and Jem's haughty Aunt Alexandra is quick to remind them of their distinguished lineage. Yet Scout sees the disconnect between her family's past and present, complaining to Jem, "all we've got's background and not a dime to our names" (226). In short, the Finches are landless gentry: they have retained some of their importance in the eyes of their neighbors but have lost possession of the property on which that importance was initially based. The old family of a southern town has a paradoxical relationship to the agrarian society that produced their initial wealth and prominence: they are caught between country and town, importance and irrelevance, past and present.

The Sound and the Fury, Faulkner's first great novel, concerns a family that, like the Finches, has "background and not a dime to [their] names." The Compsons are descended from greatness. One of their ancestors held the deed to a full square mile of land that would become the town of Jefferson, Mississippi. His son would become governor of the state, while his grandson would serve as a confederate general during the Civil War. Yet the present-day patriarch of the family, Jason III—known in *The Sound and the Fury* as Mr. Compson—never lives up to the legacy of his father and grandfather. His diminished state is encoded in his very title: "III" stands for the third, of course, for Mr. Compson is the third man to bear the given name Jason, but on a modern typewriter it could also read as "Ill," or "ill" with a capital "I." Mr. Compson is suffering from the modern condition. Like Atticus, Jason is a lawyer, a father, and a townsman. He and his family live on the last remnant of the Compson square mile, a house bordered by the pasture that his son Benjy loves. The Compsons have sold off their land parcel by parcel, and Mr. Compson will sell the final parcel, the pasture, to send his son Quentin to college. The Compsons flourished in an antebellum agrarian society, but in a modern economy they must trade in the land that defined their greatness for cash. Like Atticus Finch, Mr.

Compson has heritage but little inheritance. Mr. Compson's sons will destroy what little remains of the family legacy: Quentin will kill himself before he can come into his inheritance, Jason will divide the old house up into rooms for rent, and Benjy, the manchild, will eventually burn it to the ground. The Compson family reaches its peak with the Civil War general, but that larger-than-life ancestor seems to bequeath his descendants little but destruction.

Atticus Finch and Mr. Compson may find themselves in comparable economic and familial situations, but their attitudes toward those situations are quite different. Atticus possesses a nobility of spirit that may in fact be greater than that of his ancestors. He is quiet, droll, and unassuming, but beneath this modest surface lie great reserves of courage and conviction. One of the earliest indications of this hidden strength may be found in the scene where Atticus uses the sheriff's gun to dispatch a rabid dog. Most men would take pride in their once-vaunted skills as a marksman; Atticus, on the other hand, has deliberately refrained from mentioning his ability to his children. Knowing how to shoot a gun is part of his past, but it will not, if he can avoid it, be part of his children's future. Atticus has a quiet but unshakable conviction regarding his own identity, one rooted as much in a guardedly optimistic vision of what could be as it is in a realistic understanding of what has been.

If Atticus Finch is, behind his droll and an unflappable facade, a man filled with hope, Mr. Compson is a man filled with despair. He shares Atticus's wry sense of humor and his erudition, but in Compson these qualities are bent toward a cynical and fatalistic end. Such fatalism is inextricably bound up with his alcoholism; it is impossible to say whether he drinks because he is unhappy or is unhappy because he drinks. Much of Compson's despair centers on the problem of time. When he gives his son Quentin his pocket watch, a family heirloom, he says, "I bequeath to you the reliquary of all hope and desire." Quentin recalls other of his father's injunctions, such as ". . . was the saddest word of all there is nothing else in the world its not despair until time its not even time until it was . . ." (178). Quentin's unpunctuated prose reflects the speed of thought; these are words embedded in his memory, words that he can recall instantly rather than in the slow measure of speech and time. Punctuated and reconstituted, they might look like this: "Was: the saddest word of all. There is nothing else in the world. It's not despair, until time. It's not even time, until it was." Mr. Compson fills his intelligent and hypersensitive son with this sort of fatalism, and ultimately it will prove fatal to the boy. Whereas Atticus can see a better future and fosters in his children hope and conviction, Jason Compson is obsessed with the past and with the ceaseless passage of time. On the morning that he kills himself, Quentin deliberately breaks off the hands of the watch his father has given him. "Clocks slay time," Mr. Compson once warned Quentin, but the boy has lighted on a different way to remove himself from the despair of being in time. Slaying himself is the ultimate form of slaying the clock.

Yet it is the Compson children, like the Finch children, who are the main protagonists of their novel. If Mr. Compson has wandered into a twilight state of despair over the past and the passing of time, his children stand as a symbol of how time has diminished the Compsons' claim to greatness. Quentin, unable to cope with his desire for his sister Caddy and with the revelation that she has gotten pregnant without being married, will kill himself. Caddy, in disgrace once her husband realizes the baby she carries is not his own, will exile herself from Jefferson. Jason IV, who has always identified more with his mother's family than his father's, is at once a petty failure of a man and a thoroughgoing villain. But it is Benjy who stands as the clearest symbol of the Compsons' fall from greatness. A manchild, Benjy not only cannot speak but also cannot comprehend the passing of time. He is the "idiot" to which the novel's title refers; Shakespeare's Macbeth says of life: "It is a tale told by an idiot / Full of sound and fury, signifying nothing." Whereas Mr. Compson and Quentin have a paralyzing awareness of history, Benjy has no capacity for making distinctions between past and present. His consciousness shuttles between the perception of what is happening around him and his memories of what has happened before. Benjy's tragedy lies in his inability to accept the changes that time has wrought. He cannot accept that his sister Caddy is gone or that his pasture has been sold, because in a very real sense they are still with him. In his inability to comprehend the nature of time, Benjy is at once a refutation of his family's history and its embodiment.

Reading *To Kill a Mockingbird* in light of *The Sound and the Fury*, one might characterize Harper Lee's project as a normalizing of Faulkner's vision of the southern family. The Compsons are the stuff of Greek tragedy or the Gothic novel, a family doomed by a collective fatal flaw and by a raft of secrets and lies. Like the descendants of Cadmus, Agamemnon, or Oedipus, the Compson children are a refutation of their ancestor's crimes. To recast the family plot in terms of the Gothic, they are like the two generations that inhabit Wuthering Heights: Quentin and Caddy are as doomed as the quasi-siblings Heathcliff and Catherine. Scout, Jem, and their friend Dill, on the other hand, are free of history and fate in a way Faulkner's characters are not; they are, to use Jem's characterization, "ordinary." The relationship between the siblings in each novel is one clear marker of Lee's movement away from the Gothic. Quentin and Caddy's relationship is haunted by the specter of incest. The issue is not so much that Quentin literally desires his sister, as that a southern code of propriety has caused him to fixate on Caddy's loss of virginity and to imagine that it would have been better had he himself, rather than the rakish Dalton Ames, slept with his sister. Yet what Quentin really wants is to return Caddy and himself to the pre-sexual childhood state of innocence in which they happily shared a bed. If they commit incest, Quentin reasons, they can be doomed to hell forever, where the two of them could exist outside of time and society. He imagines:

> If it could just be a hell beyond that: the clean flame the two of us more than dead. Then you will have only me then only me then the two of us amid the pointing and the horror beyond the clean flame. (116)

Like the lovers Paolo and Francesca in Dante's *Inferno*, Quentin and Caddy would spend eternity at each other's side, doomed but undivided. Quentin goes so far as to make a false confession to his father. He later recalls the scene: "I have committed incest I said Father it was I it was not Dalton Ames" (79). Mr. Compson sees the confession for what it is: a fabrication rooted in Quentin's sense that he has lost his sister forever. He tells his son, "you wanted to sublimate a piece of natural human folly into a horror and then exorcise it with truth . . . you cannot bear to think that someday it will no longer hurt you like this" (177). It may be the realization that the pain he felt for his sister is diminishing, that drives Quentin to kill himself.

The brother-and-sister relationship in *To Kill a Mockingbird* is, of course, of an entirely different and more "ordinary" kind. It is marked not only by closeness and love and occasional squabbles, as Scout and Jem spend their summers playing together in and around the family's house, but also by a growing and healthy separation. In fact, the arc of their relationship is one in which Jem, four years older than Scout, gradually withdraws into the deeper waters of adolescence. The novel's two stories inform and interpenetrate each other, in that the Tom Robinson trial serves to mark the differences in maturity between the older brother and younger sister. Jem emerges from the experience with a keen awareness of the injustice inherent in the society in which he has grown up. Scout is not yet able to accept the damning conclusions that Jem has come to regarding Maycomb; their debate over the kinds of folks that make up their town is emblematic of the divide between the innocence of childhood and the experience of adolescence. Jem, by novel's end, has done what Quentin Compson cannot: he has passed from innocence to experience without allowing that loss of innocence to consume him. In so doing, he has also begun to pass beyond the circle of his immediate family, trading games in the backyard with Scout and Dill for games with the football team down at his high school. There are other compelling parallels between Jem and Quentin. Both indenture themselves for a time to a Civil War widow: Jem must read to the elderly Mrs. Dubose, while Quentin, in the later novel *Absalom, Absalom!*, listens to the story of Rosa Sutpen and then drives her out to revisit her family's estate. These relationships with the last of a generation are encounters with history itself, a grappling with the legacy of the Civil War and with an outmoded code of behavior and expectations. Jem survives his confrontation, just as he later shakes off the injuries he received in the attack by Bob Ewell, but Quentin cannot. The weight of history crushes Quentin. In this respect, *To Kill a Mockingbird* is a coming of age story, whereas *The Sound and the Fury* is a story about the end of an age.

Scout argues with Jem's bleak assessment of their town, but she will eventually come into a broader and more nuanced understanding of what the Robinson trial and all of the events surrounding it reveal about the virtues and inequities of southern life. Indeed, the novel itself, narrated by an older Scout reflecting on her childhood, is an expression of this understanding. Scout is still a child, albeit one who has made forays into the adult world, both in the domestic sphere of her Aunt Alexandra and in the worldly sphere of the courthouse in which her father argues Tom Robinson's case. Yet the reader has a clear sense of what kind of adult Scout will be, for it is this older version of her that tells the story. We do not know the particulars of her life—what she does for a living, whether she has a family of her own, where she has chosen to live—but we know her sensibilities. She has emerged from her tumultuous childhood and from the vicarious trauma of the Robinson trial as someone who can see the world in which she grew up steadily and whole. Scout's narratorial voice is therefore another way in which Lee breaks from the Gothic family plot that is central to *The Sound and the Fury*. In Faulkner's novel, each of the Compson brothers narrates his own chapter. Caddy, however, does not serve as a narrator, and the effect is to make her elusive, a presence invoked through absence. She is a fugitive from Jefferson in more ways than one, for her physical removal from the town is reinforced by her narratorial removal from her own story. Whereas each of her brothers takes a turn being the subjective "I" of the novel's narrator, Caddy remains an object. In speaking for herself, Scout gives voice to a girl's and woman's first-person perspective on southern culture—a perspective that is quite deliberately silenced in *The Sound and the Fury.*

Harper Lee's depiction of Boo Radley may represent another mode in which *To Kill a Mockingbird* normalizes Faulkner's Southern Gothic family. The trope of the manchild who cannot leave the house in which he grew up is central both to *The Sound and the Fury* and to *Absalom, Absalom!* In each novel, a prominent antebellum family ends its hereditary line in the form of a speechless last man who haunts the family seat. Benjy, grandson of General Compson, and James Bond III (another "ill" descendent), grandson of Colonel Sutpen, are the refutations of their ancestors' claims to greatness. If the generation that fought the war was somehow larger than life, their descendants are concomitantly diminished: Benjy and Bond lead lives that are as narrow and circumscribed as their grandfathers' were epic and grand. There is a central tension, therefore, animating the character of Benjy and informing his role in the novel. On the one hand, he represents pure, unadulterated love; his dedication to Caddy and his attachment to the pasture mark him as the most noble of the Compsons. More than any confederate officer, Benjy is filled with love for his family and his land. Yet at the same time, he serves as a symbol of the Compson family's fall from greatness. His mental retardation is, if not a judgment, an ironic comment on the fate of the antebellum Southern gentry's place in a modern world.

In *To Kill a Mockingbird*, the Faulknerian manchild is displaced onto another family. Boo is not himself a Finch, and his inability to live in the adult world is therefore not a direct comment on the legacy of the antebellum gentry. Like Benjy, Boo is a grown man who has remained a child; his refusal to leave his childhood home and his habit of leaving chewing gum and other artifacts of childhood for the Finch children to find speak to his state of arrested development. It is not surprising that the children are fascinated by and terrified of their unseen neighbor. By the novel's conclusion, however, Boo has emerged both from his house and from the gothic persona that Scout, Jem, and Dill have created for him. Even before Boo makes his appearance, Jem comes to realize that Boo's decision to retreat from the world is just that: an act of freewill, rather than the acting out of a family curse or a hereditary doom. Jem explains his realization to Scout: "I think I'm beginning to understand why Boo Radley's stayed shut up in the house all this time . . . it's because he *wants* to stay inside" (227). Boo shares in Jem's cynical assessment of Maycomb, and he has chosen to remove himself from an inherently unjust society. It is his affection for the Finch children, and the act of bravery that stems from that affection, that causes him to re-engage his neighbors. In walking Boo home at the novel's conclusion, Scout establishes a normative relationship with her neighbor, one that moves him forever out of the realm of the gothic and into that of the domestic and the ordinary. Boo is reintegrated into the life of the town in a way Benjy can never be.

One final parallel between the Finch and Compson families lies in the central role that an African-American housekeeper plays in each. Calpurnia in *To Kill a Mockingbird* and Dilsey in *The Sound and the Fury* write large the contradictions inherent to southern race relations. Both women are descendants of slaves whom the Finch and Compson families owned, and as such their personal histories are bound up with the legacies of each family. They are, on the one hand, members of the families they serve, acting as surrogate mothers to the white children in their charge and presiding in the kitchen, the seat of family life. Yet at the same time, their race marks them off as being entirely "other." The white families maintain such an intimate relationship with their black servants by being careful not to cross certain racial lines. Calpurnia and Dilsey likewise negotiate their roles as insiders and outsiders. They act a double part, living their private lives among fellow African Americans and their professional ones in the homes of the white families for whom they work. This switching between a black world and a white one is reflected in Calpurnia's pattern-switching between the standard

English of the Finches and the colloquial speech patterns of the town's African-American community. Scout marvels at Calpurnia's ability to alternate between the two dialects, an ability she can only witness by seeing Calpurnia interact with other African-American people. Scout reflects, "The idea that she had a separate existence outside our household was a novel one, to say nothing of her having command of two languages" (125). In both novels, the African-American housekeepers break a deeply engrained taboo by taking the children of their employers to their churches. Just as whites and blacks live separately in the Jim Crow south, so too do they worship separately. Calpurnia and Dilsey's fellow parishioners challenge them for bringing their charges—Jem and Scout, in the former's case, and Benjy in the latter's—into one of the few places that should be off-limits to whites. The trip to the African-American church is a crossing of the color line, a blurring of the boundary between the African American's role as a household servant and as a member of a separate, independent culture. For Scout, this trip is a revelation, and her subsequent interest in visiting Calpurnia at her home indicates how deeply concerned she has become with the doubleness and segregation that southern culture imposed on African Americans.

The white-aproned African-American servant in the kitchen reassured some white southerners that race relations remained fixed and stable; although slavery was long gone, the white population still held power while the African-American population was still thoroughly domesticated. Indeed, so powerful a symbol was the apron that in Faulkner's short story "A Rose for Emily," mayor Colonel Sartoris issues "the edict that no Negro woman should appear on the streets without an apron" (*Portable Faulkner*, 393). But if the sight of a black woman in a white family's kitchen assuaged whites' fears of their former slaves, another figure raised those fears: the long-standing stereotype of the black man as a violent and lusty predator. This figure is a powerful one, in that he crosses the most hard-and-fast of color lines by seducing or raping a white woman. So strong was the fear of miscegenation that a black man who had been accused of the crime often did not live long enough to stand trial. This is the cultural context in which Tom Robinson, an innocent man, stands accused of raping a white woman. The accusation taps directly into the deepest-seated Jim Crow notions of racial purity and of chivalry—a pathological shared anxiety about African-American male sexuality—and ultimately neither the jury nor the lynch mob is really concerned with whether Tom actually committed the crime of which he is accused. The issue is not so much one of getting at the truth, but of deciding which side of the color line to come down on. As Mayella tells the jury: "That nigger yonder took advantage of me an' if you fine fancy gentlemen don't wanta do nothin' about it then you're all yellow stinking cowards" (188). The jury does not need to believe Mayella's allegation (and in point of fact, it almost surely does not) to believe themselves justified in convicting Tom. In finding Tom guilty, the jury would not be passing judgment on a single man but rather maintaining the balance of power in southern race relations, in which a white woman's word must be taken over that of a black man's.

To understand the dynamics of the Robinson trial is therefore to understand the other three "kinds of folks" that Jem identifies as making up Maycomb society, "the kind like the Cunninghams out in the woods, the kind like the Ewells down at the dump, and the Negroes." Jem's parsing of Maycomb culture also lights a reader's way through many of the novels and stories that Faulkner wrote after *The Sound and the Fury*. *As I Lay Dying*, his subsequent novel, leaves the town and the descendants of the great families in order to focus instead on a family very much like the Ewells. The Bundren family, who live in shocking poverty and ignorance far from town, are worlds away from the Compsons. Their disastrous journey to town to bury their dead matriarch might be read as a comic inversion of the Compson family's tragedy. Readers of *To Kill a Mockingbird* will see something of Bob and Mayella Ewell in Faulkner's Anse and Dewey Dell Bundren. Juxtaposed against the ignoble Bundrens are Faulkner's own answer to Mr.

Cunningham: poor country folk who possess a quiet dignity and goodness. The Bundrens' neighbor Vernon Tull is one such character, as are the convict protagonist of *Old Man* and the hardworking and virtuous Byron Bunch in *Light in August*. *Go Down, Moses* likewise centers on people who live close to the land and hence to what Faulkner would later call "the verities of the human heart." A man like Atticus, who has spent much of his life reflecting on the character of his neighbors, can see both the virtues and the faults of these simple people. Mr. Cunningham is capable both of leading a lynch mob and of being the last holdout arguing for Tom Robinson's innocence. The mutually respectful if strained relationship between Atticus and Mr. Cunningham may echo the friendship in Faulkner's Snopes trilogy (*The Hamlet*, *The Town*, and *The Mansion*) between the Harvard and Oxford-educated town lawyer Gavin Stevens and the self-educated, itinerant sewing machine salesman V. K. Ratliff. Faulkner's work is shot through with a tension between town and country, book-smarts and earth-wisdom.

But it is *Light in August*, Faulkner's novel of miscegenation and mob violence, that may have the most direct bearing on the trial subplot of *To Kill a Mockingbird*. Joe Christmas, a man who cannot be sure whether he is white or black, is the logical extreme of the Jim Crow south's obsession with race. At the novel's conclusion, Reverend Hightower, who has tried but failed to defend Joe from a vengeful mob, falls into a dreamlike state in which he has a vision:

> In the lambent suspension of August into which night is about to fully come, it seems to engender and surround itself with a faint glow like a halo. The halo is full of faces. The faces are not shaped with suffering, not shaped with anything: not horror, pain, not even reproach. They are peaceful, as though they have escaped into an apotheosis; his own is among them. In fact, they all look a little alike, composite of all the faces which he has ever seen. But he can distinguish them one from another. (491)

Hightower's vision of faces that are at once composite and distinguishable challenges the notion that people can be divided into irreconcilable camps. Jem may be right to see in Maycomb divisions to which he was once blind, yet it would be a mistake for him to consider this social order as fixed and eternal. Nor would he be right to adopt his sister's overly reductive answer: "I think there's just one kind of folks. Folks." In the wake of the Robinson trial, Jem and Scout alike have taken up, with the steady dogmatism of youth, positions that are too static and black and white. Reverend Hightower's vision is a more nuanced one, for the minister sees people as both alike and different, united and divided, wholly individual and wholly of a single community. The wisdom to recognize these contradictions and ambiguities—to accept that the positions Jem and Scout have taken endlessly blur into each other—is born out of experience. It is a mature vision that Atticus Finch shares in and that, by novel's end, he has taught his children to share in.

Works Cited

Faulkner, William. *The Sound and the Fury*. 1929. New York: Random House, Vintage International, 1990.

_____. *Light in August*. 1932. New York: Random House, Vintage International, 1985.

_____. *The Portable Faulkner*, edited by Malcolm Cowley. New York: Viking Portable Library Series, 1977.

Lee, Harper. *To Kill a Mockingbird*. New York: Warner Books, 1960.

CRITICAL
READINGS

The Rise and Fall of Atticus Finch_____

Christopher Metress

In 1991, the Library of Congress and the Book-of-the-Month Club commissioned a "Survey of Lifetime Reading Habits" and discovered that *To Kill a Mockingbird* was second only to the Bible among books "most often cited as making a difference" in people's lives. A staple of high-school reading lists for more than four decades, and the source for one of the nation's most beloved films, Harper Lee's novel is bound to be on most short lists of contemporary American classics. While controversy has long surrounded the work (it remains to this day one of the books most frequently banned from high-school libraries), many readers would concur with the recent assessment of Lee's novel in *500 Great Books by Women: "To Kill a Mockingbird* only gets better with rereading; each time the streets of Maycomb become more real and alive, each time Scout is more insightful, Atticus more heroic, and Boo Radley more tragically human."

Despite these recent confirmations, however, all is not well in Maycomb. Beginning in the early 1990s, quick upon the heels of the Library of Congress survey, a new generation of critics began to reread Lee's classic. *To Kill a Mockingbird*, it appears, is not getting better with age, and each time these new readers revisit the streets of Maycomb, those streets look less insightful and less heroic. Hardest hit by these revisionary readings is the novel's purported hero, Atticus Finch. For forty years the source of continuous accolades, Atticus has now fallen on hard times. And as goes Atticus, so goes the novel. As a result, within the short span of a decade a new critical dissensus has emerged, one which suggests that *To Kill a Mockingbird* tells two stories—or, to borrow a phrase from the novel itself—speaks two languages. That second language tells a darker tale, one that warns us that our adulation of Atticus Finch and our praise for *To Kill a Mockingbird* have less to do with the merits of the hero and the liberal vision of the novel than they have to do with our own blind spots and prejudices. *To Kill a*

Mockingbird is not, as earlier readers claimed, a persuasive plea for racial justice, nor is its hero a model of moral courage. Instead, novel and hero are, at best, morally ambiguous or, at worst, morally reprehensible. Nowadays, many readers of the novel are like as not to emphasize Finch's complicity with, rather than his challenges to, the segregationist politics of his hometown, and, as a result, Lee's novel is beginning to lose its iconic status. Never in all its years has the song of the mockingbird sounded so unsweet.

It would be naive, of course, to suggest that before the 1990s there was no negative criticism of the work. Although *To Kill a Mockingbird* won the 1961 Pulitzer Prize, sold 500,000 copies in one year, and was immediately translated into ten languages—all this before going on to sell more than 30,000,000 copies worldwide, making it the third best-selling American novel of the twentieth century—there were scattered denunciations of Lee's classic. The most famous was by fellow Southerner Flannery O'Connor, who, in a letter to Alabama writer Caroline Ivey, called the novel "a child's book." "When I was fifteen," O'Connor claimed, "I would have loved it. Take out the rape and you've got something like *Miss Minerva and William Green Hill*[.] I think for a child's book it does all right. It's interesting that all the folks that are buying it don't know they're reading a child's book. Somebody ought to say what it is."

For the most part, however, those buying the novel in 1960 and since would have agreed more with James Carville than Flannery O'Connor. In the introduction to *We're Right, They're Wrong: A Handbook for Spirited Progressives*, Carville recalls that in the wake of *Brown v. Board of Education* he still "took segregation for granted and wished the blacks just didn't push so damn hard to change it." But then he read *To Kill a Mockingbird* "and that novel changed everything."

I got it from a lady who drove around in the overheated bookmobile in my parish—another government program, I might add. I had asked the lady for something on football, but she handed me *To Kill a Mockingbird* instead. I couldn't put it down. I stuck it inside another book and read it under my desk during school. When I got to the last page, I closed it and said, "They're right and we're wrong." The issue was literally black and white, and we were absolutely, positively on the wrong side.

From that moment on, Carville decided to devote his life to combating racial and legal injustice. Similar testimonies run up to the present moment. As one contemporary lawyer recently confessed, "I had lots of heroes growing up. Some were men, some were women; some were real and some were imaginary people in books I read. Only one remains very much alive for me. He is a character in Harper Lee's *To Kill a Mockingbird.* . . . Atticus Finch made me believe in lawyer heroes." Such testimonies have led Joseph Crespino to argue that "In the twentieth century, *To Kill a Mockingbird* is probably the most widely read book dealing with race in America, and its protagonist, Atticus Finch, the most enduring fictional image of racial heroism."

But in 1992, that all began to change. In the February 24th issue of *Legal Times*, Hofstra University Law Professor and contributing editor Monroe Freedman devoted an entire column to Lee's novel. In a provocatively entitled piece called "Atticus Finch, ESQ, R.I.P." Freedman rejected the notion that Finch was a model for lawyers. "If we don't do something fast," Freedman enjoined his readers—perhaps a few decades too late—"lawyers are going to start taking [Finch] seriously as someone to emulate. And that would be a bad mistake." Freedman's points are many, but his argument essentially boils down to this: "Atticus Finch does, indeed, act heroically in his representation of Robinson. But he does so from an elitist sense of noblesse oblige. Except under compulsion of a court appointment, Finch never attempts to change the racism and sexism that permeate life in Macomb [sic], Ala. On the contrary, he lives his own life as the passive participant in that pervasive injustice. And that is not my idea of a role model for young lawyers." "Let me put it this way," Freedman continues, "I would have more respect for Atticus Finch if he had never been compelled by the court to represent Robinson, but if, instead, he had undertaken voluntarily to establish the right of the black citizens of Macomb [sic] to sit freely in their county courthouse [and not segregated in the balcony]. *That* Atticus Finch would, indeed, have been a model for young lawyers to emulate."

And just how was this first witness for the prosecution against Atticus Finch received by the legal community? Total outrage, it appears. Finch was defended in the pages of *Legal Times* by none other than the president of the American Bar Association, who wrote, "Sixty years after Judge Taylor appointed Atticus Finch to defend a poor, black man in *To Kill a Mockingbird*, these two fictional heroes still inspire us. Contrary to what Professor Freedman asserts, Finch rose above racism and injustice to defend the principle that all men and women deserve their day in court represented by competent legal counsel, regardless of their ability to pay." Another contributor to the *Times* was much less considered in his response. "In my book," wrote Southern attorney R. Mason Barge, "any lawyer who takes on the establishment *pro bono publico* is a hero. I hope Mr. Freedman would agree, and if so, I'll make a deal with him. We'll worry about racism down here, and you just go on living in the good old days, when New York was marginally less racist than Alabama and its habitants could arrogate moral superiority to themselves. And when you get around to cleaning up those sewers you call cities, give me a call, and we can talk about what a bad guy Atticus Finch was."

Three months after his column appeared, Freedman informed his readers of the following:

> During the past two years, this column has dealt with cases and causes involving unethical lawyers, dishonest judges, criminal conflicts of interest in the White House, and widespread maladministration of justice in our criminal courts. But never has there been such a fulsome response as to the column making the rather modest suggestion that a particular fictional character is not an appropriate model for lawyers.

The mythological deification of Atticus Finch was illustrated by Atticans who wrote to equate my rejection of Finch, literally, with attacking God, Moses, Jesus, Gandhi, and Mother Teresa.

Now, if Freedman's revisionist dissent were the only controversial rereading of *To Kill a Mockingbird*, there'd be little reason to fear for Atticus Finch or Harper Lee's novel. But that is simply not the case. A second trial of Finch occurred not in the pages of another legal magazine, but in Tuscaloosa, Alabama, at a 1994 Symposium sponsored by the University of Alabama School of Law. Alabama Law Professor Timothy Hoff opened the symposium in terms that echoed the critical consensus that had marked the novel's first thirty years: "The continued popularity of *Mockingbird*," Hoff urged, "must be ascribed to its evocation of the lawyer as hero. . . . There is hope in the fact that readers and movie watchers are [still] drawn to such goodness." However, while some presenters did want to argue for the novel's "goodness," others at the symposium urged dissent. Freedman resurrected his position of 1992 and extended its reach, telling the Tuscaloosa audience that "[t]hroughout his relatively comfortable and pleasant life in Maycomb, Atticus Finch knows about the grinding, ever-present humiliation and degradation of the black people of Maycomb; he tolerates it; and sometimes he even trivializes and condones it." "Here is a man," Freedman concludes, "who does not voluntarily use his legal training and skills—not once, ever—to make the slightest change in the pervasive social injustice of his own town. . . . [As a state legislator] Could he not introduce one bill to mitigate the evils of segregation? Could he not work with Judge Taylor in an effort to desegregate the courthouse? Could he not take, voluntarily, a single appeal in a death penalty case? And could he not represent a Tom Robinson just once without a court order to do so?"

Strong words, but this time Freedman did not find himself alone. Teresa Godwin Phelps, a Professor of Law at Notre Dame, opened her remarks by noting the following: "For nearly a decade I have assigned

To Kill a Mockingbird to my Law and Literature class and for the most part class discussions have followed along typical lines. We are chagrined at the intractable racism of Maycomb; we admire Atticus and discuss whether his lie to save Boo Radley from public scrutiny is justified. We come away from *To Kill a Mockingbird* feeling good about being lawyers and law students." However, she now confessed, she could no longer teach the book this way. For Phelps, the most troubling aspect of the novel is voiced by Jem late in the book. "There are four kinds of folks in the world," Jem tells Scout. "There's the ordinary kind like us and the neighbors, there's the kind like the Cunninghams out in the woods, the kind like the Ewells down at the dump, and the Negroes." According to Phelps, "*To Kill a Mockingbird* is a valiant attempt to erase some of the barriers that exist between 'kinds of folks'; however, the books fails to recognize or acknowledge the barriers it leaves erect. While the novel depicts change in one facet of law and society, it reinforces the status quo in other troubling aspects." While granting that Lee's treatment of folks like the Cunninghams represents a "true liberal vision," Phelps argues against the "Far less liberal and far more disturbing vision . . . put forth of the Ewells" by both Lee and Atticus. "The book teaches us to desire to be like Atticus," Phelps concludes, "courageous in the face of our community's prejudices. But it also teaches us to fear and deplore the Ewells and Lula. . . . We readers, like the citizens of Maycomb, see what we want to see and are blind to much else. We, like Atticus, are implicated in the town's delusions as long as we read *To Kill a Mockingbird* with uncritical acceptance."

A year later, the dissent against Atticus moved from the lawyers to the literary critics. In a 1995 anthology entitled *The South as an American Problem*—a collection of essays written mainly by professors from Vanderbilt—Eric J. Sundquist, who is certainly one of the most influential critics of contemporary American literature, argued that, "For all its admirable moral earnestness and its inventory of the historical forces making up the white liberal consciousness of the late 1950s . . . [*To Kill a Mockingbird*] might well have been entitled

'Driving Miss Scout.'" Calling the novel "something of an historical relic," Sundquist argues that the work is "an icon whose emotive sway remains strangely powerful because it also remains unexamined." Sundquist's own examination takes twenty-nine pages as he reads the novel through the lens of the Scottsboro trials, *Brown vs. the Board of Education*, the lynching of Emmett Till, the rise of massive resistance, and the accomplishments of contemporary African-American literature. Here is one example, worth quoting at length, of where all this leads Sundquist:

> Atticus's moral courage forms a critical part of the novel's deceptive surface. Whether to shield his children from the pain of racism or to shield Lee's Southern readers from a confrontation with their own recalcitrance [on the race problem], Atticus, for all his devotion to the truth, sometimes lies. He employs indirection in order to teach his children about Maycomb's racial hysteria and the true meaning of courage, but he himself engages in evasion when he contends, for instance, that the Ku Klux Klan is a thing of the past ("way back about nineteen-twenty"), a burlesque show of cowards easily humiliated by the Jewish storeowner they attempt to intimidate in their sheeted costumes purchased from the merchant himself. Such moments are not distinct from the book's construction of analogies for moral courage in the face of communal racism . . . but rather part of it. Indirection and displacement govern both novel's moral pedagogy and, in the end, its moral stalemate.

According to Sundquist, the novel also has a "peculiar political morality" embodied in Atticus's warning to Scout that "This time we aren't fighting the Yankees, we're fighting our friends. But remember this, no matter how bitter this gets, they're still our friends and this is still our home." Such words, for Sundquist, are an "expression of near paralysis, which at once identifies the race crisis as only a *Southern* problem," which by 1960 it no longer was. "Just as the South closed ranks against the nation at the outset of desegregation," Sundquist concludes, "*To Kill a Mockingbird* carefully narrows the terms on which changed race relations are going to be brought about in the South" in the 1960s. Ultimately, "Atticus Finch's integrity"—and thus the integrity of the novel itself—"is circumscribed by his admonition that moral action must respect the prejudices of 'our friends' and ultimately abide by local ethics"—a stance that, because it argues against the need for federal intervention in the South, would have all but assured that racial justice would have never come to the black citizens of Maycomb. Thus, instead of Atticus being a hero who stands in opposition to his community, Sundquist reads him as an apologist whose moral vision embodies a subtle form of massive resistance to outside agitation.

In the few short years since Freedman, Phelps and Sundquist first began to cross-examine Lee's lawyer hero, Atticus Finch has been called repeatedly before the bar of judgment. One more example will suffice. In a mammoth essay comparing Atticus Finch to Gavin Stevens, the lawyer hero of Faulkner's *Intruder in the Dust*, Rob Atkinson, accuses Finch and Lee of "lawyerly paternalism" and hopes that *Intruder in the Dust* will replace *To Kill a Mockingbird* as America's most inspirational story of progressive legal ethics. Writing in the December 1999 issue of the *Duke Law Journal*, Atkinson argues that "the greater appeal of *To Kill a Mockingbird* may tell us something less than wholly laudable about ourselves," for Lee's novel expresses a "liberal-democratic vision" which suggests that lawyers are always "above" their clients because their clients are always beholden to them for uplifting. This is the "paternalistic" message of *To Kill a Mockingbird*, a message that can also be seen as supporting a larger assumption in the novel: that racial progress is in the hands of good, enlightened white people who know what is best for underprivileged, and thus always beholden, blacks. Under this approach, Atticus's legendary defense of Tom Robinson is radically reinterpreted. "When pressed to explain his motives for taking the case," Atkinson writes, "Atticus's focus is distinctly on himself, not his client. He makes clear several times that it is his own sense of personal rectitude and his need to be seen as virtuous by others that compel him to take Tom's case . . . Atticus [may allude] to 'a number of reasons,' but he elaborates only one: 'The main one is, if I didn't, I couldn't hold up my head in town, I couldn't represent this county in the legislature, I couldn't even tell you or Jem not to do something again.' Each explanatory clause begins with 'I'," Atkinson concludes. "Atticus does not mention Tom Robinson at all." So much for Atticus as an enduring fictional image of racial heroism.

Just a few years ago, the Alabama Bar Association placed a stone outside of the Monroeville County Courthouse and upon that stone a plaque commemorating the ideals of Atticus Finch. We should not, however, mistake that long overdue gesture as representing critical consensus about this man. No longer is the response to Lee's hero as clear-cut as when James Carville first read the work forty years ago. Ours is an age of pluralism and dissensus, and as Atticus Finch moves into a new century, some tough lawyers, and some even tougher literary critics, are beginning to build a strong case against him. The great defense lawyer is now himself on trial, and while the outcome of the proceedings are not a foregone conclusion, things are not looking good. Yes, Atticus still has his many defenders, among them most recently fellow Alabamians Claudia Durst Johnson and Wayne Flynt, but with each passing year these voices of praise meet with louder and more numerous denunciations. Although it is impossible to predict what perspective on the novel future generations will hold, when this new trial is over and Atticus Finch must once again leave the courthouse, it is just possible that, on that day, no one will rise to stand.

From *Chattahoochee Review* 24, no. 1 (Fall, 2003), pp. 95-102. Copyright © 2003 by Christopher Metress. Reprinted by permission of Christopher Metress.

Lawyers, Ethics, and *To Kill a Mockingbird*_____

Tim Dare

I

Lawyers are widely thought to be callous, self-serving, devious, and indifferent to justice, truth, and the public good. The law profession could do with a hero, and some think Atticus Finch of Harper Lee's *To Kill a Mockingbird* fits the bill.[1] Claudia Carver, for instance, urging lawyers to adopt Atticus as a role model, writes: "I had lots of heroes when growing up. . . . Only one remains very much 'alive' for me. . . . Atticus made me believe in lawyer heroes."[2] Not everyone endorses Atticus's nomination. Most influentially, Monroe Freedman argues that Atticus is hardly admirable since, as a state legislator and community leader in a segregated society, he lives "his own life as the passive participant in that pervasive injustice."[3]

Although there is plainly disagreement between Freedman and his opponents, there is also an important point of consensus. Both sides to the debate accept that Atticus's suitability as a role model is settled by his character. Freedman argues that Atticus should not be a role model because he is not the admirable figure he is made out to be: appointed counsel to an unpopular defendant, Atticus admits that he had hoped "to get through life without a case of this kind" (p. 98). He excuses the leader of a lynch mob as "basically a good man" who "just has his blind spots along with the rest of us" (p. 173). He sees that "one of these days we're going to pay the bill" for racism, but hopes that payment, and so justice for blacks, will not come during his children's life times (pp. 243-44).[4] On the other hand, a leading Atticus supporter, Thomas Shaffer, argues that Atticus shows us precisely that what matters in professional ethics is character rather than moral principle:

> One thing you could say about Atticus is that he had character. . . . We
> say that a good person has character, but we do not mean to say only that he
> believes in discernible moral principles and, under those principles, makes

good decisions. We mean also to say something about who he is and to relate who he is to his good decisions. When discussion proceeds in this way,
principles need not even be explicit. We can say, "How would Atticus see
this situation?" or "What would Atticus do" rather than, "What principles
apply?"[5]

So understood, the debate about Atticus connects with the recent
resurrection of virtue ethics and with concomitant suggestions that a
virtue or character-based ethics might provide a particularly promising
approach to professional ethics in general and to legal ethics in particular.

In the following essay, I argue that this character-based appeal to
Atticus is misplaced. Although Atticus can teach us important lessons,
they are not about the priority of virtue or character. Neither side to the
debate has Atticus quite right. Sorting out what it is about him that
makes him an appropriate or inappropriate role model for lawyers will
both enrich our appreciation of a fine novel and further our understanding of what it is to be an ethical lawyer. More generally, my analysis
will suggest that virtue ethics has little to offer toward an understanding of the moral responsibility of lawyers.

II

In brief, *To Kill a Mockingbird* is the story of the trial of a black man,
Tom Robinson, for the rape of a white woman, Mayella Ewell, in racist
Alabama in the 1930s. Appointed to defend Robinson, Atticus Finch
takes the task seriously, drawing upon himself and his children the
slurs and taunts of neighbors. At trial he proves that Robinson could
not have raped Mayella, showing that her attacker was left-handed
with two good arms, whereas Robinson had lost the use of his left arm
in a cotton-gin accident. Robinson is convicted nonetheless. The verdict does not surprise Atticus. Racism, "Maycomb's usual disease"
(p. 98), has made it a foregone conclusion. Indeed, shortly afterward,

Tom is killed, shot while climbing a prison fence in full view of guards. Tom's death completes one story in *Mockingbird:* an innocent black man has been falsely accused, wrongfully convicted, and killed.

"Tom's story" occurs in the middle parts of the novel, flanked by another focussing on the Finch's mysterious neighbor, Arthur 'Boo' Radley. Boo has been a recluse inside his family's house for close to twenty-five years, unseen for ten years since stabbing his father with a pair of scissors. The children regard him as a bogeyman, and play what seem to them dangerous games of brinkmanship with him. The reader knows that the children are mistaken about Boo. He is a gentle person: he leaves gifts for the children; he wraps a blanket around Scout as she watches a fire in the cold; he attempts to mend the trousers Jem has torn and abandoned in flight from a raid on the Radley property.

Tom and Boo's stories come together at the end of the novel. Mayella's father, Bob Ewell, attacks the Finch children. They are rescued by Boo, who kills Ewell. In an important moment for my account of the novel, Atticus goes along with the Sheriff's recommendation not to charge Boo over Ewell's death. Instead, Atticus and the Sheriff adopt the fiction that Ewell fell on his knife.

Atticus's daughter Scout narrates *Mockingbird*, and the novel is also the story of her moral development. Her innocence is a crucial aspect of the narration, highlighting the senseless racism and class divisions that rend Maycomb. Scout's innocence wanes during the course of the novel, but it gives way to informed goodness rather than prejudice, a transformation most evident in her attitude to Boo. At the beginning of the story, she regards him as an outsider and misfit, legitimately tormented and feared. The novel closes with her taking his hand to lead him home and seeing that things look the same from the Radley porch as they do from her own.

Much of the credit for Scout's moral development is owed to Atticus. He is a loving, patient, and understanding father who guides his children to virtue while respecting them as individuals capable of judgment and decision. He teaches them compassion and tolerance, frequently advising Scout to "step into the shoes" of others such as the Ewells and Boo Radley. Atticus treats everybody with respect, regardless of class or color. He is courageous, both in zealously pursuing Tom's defense while knowing that it will not succeed and in arming himself only with a newspaper though anticipating a confrontation with a lynch mob. In sum, Atticus's is a voice of decency, wisdom, and reason, courageously speaking out against bigotry, ignorance, and prejudice.

III

There are three moments in *Mockingbird* of particular significance for lawyers and legal ethics. The first is Atticus's summation to Tom's jury. One often hears, he remarks, that all men are created equal. On some construals, the assertion is simply ridiculous: people are not born equally smart or equally wealthy. Nevertheless, says Atticus:

> . . . there is one way in this country in which all men are created equal—there is one human institution that makes a pauper the equal of a Rockefeller, the stupid man the equal of an Einstein and the ignorant man the equal of any college president. That institution, gentlemen, is a court. . . . Our courts have their faults, as does any human institution, but in this country our courts are the great levellers, and in our courts all men are created equal. (p. 227)

This is as plain a statement of the role of courts as one could hope for. Whatever inequities people suffer outside the court, within it, they are to be treated as equals.

The second moment occurs after Tom's death. Mr. Underwood, the editor of the local newspaper, has published a courageous editorial condemning the death as sinful and senseless, likening it to the "slaughter of songbirds" (p. 265). Initially, Scout is puzzled by the editorial: how could Tom's death be sinful when he had been granted due process and vigorously defended in an open court? But then, she continues, "Mr. Underwood's meaning became clear: Atticus had used every tool available to free men to save Tom Robinson, but in the secret courts of men's hearts Atticus had no case. Tom was a dead man the minute Mayella Ewell opened her mouth and screamed" (p. 266). Again, the meaning of the passage seems clear: Tom was convicted because he had been tried not in a court of law but "in the secret courts of men's hearts." These courts were governed not by presumptions of equality and innocence, but by prejudice and bigotry. Atticus's plea to the jury had been ignored and Tom had been convicted and killed as a result.

In his summation, Atticus makes clear his commitment to the ideal of the rule of law, understood precisely as rule by public standards rather than by the private wishes and inclinations of individuals. Scout's explication of Mr. Underwood's editorial further emphasizes that commitment. An innocent man has died because a jury chose to try him by their own standards rather than by those of the public system of law. Thus far, the message of *Mockingbird* is one in favor of the rule of law. Lawyers should honor and protect the public judgments of courts in preference to and from the private judgments of individuals.

The third great moment occurs after Boo Radley rescues Atticus's children from Bob Ewell. Initially, all that is clear is that the children have been attacked and that their attacker lies dead. Atticus thinks that Jem has killed Ewell, wresting a knife away during the attack. He takes it for granted that Jem will go before a court, though he will be acquitted since "it was clear cut self-defense" (p. 300). Sheriff Tate interrupts, telling Atticus that Jem did not stab Ewell, that he fell on his own knife. Atticus assumes Tate is trying to hush up what has happened to protect Jem, and refuses to go along with the subterfuge. But soon Atticus realizes that it is Boo, not Jem, who the Sheriff is trying to protect. It would, Tate maintains, be a sin to bring Boo "and his shy ways" before a court. Atticus sits, looking at the floor for a long time before finally raising his head and saying to Scout, "Mr. Ewell fell on his knife. Can you possibly understand?" Scout's response demonstrates that she understands perfectly well: there has been a decision to accept a fiction. "Yes sir," she says, "I understand. . . . Mr. Tate was right. . . . Well, it'd be sort of like shootin' a mockingbird, wouldn't it?" (p. 304).

These three episodes pose an obvious challenge. The first two deliver a clear message in favor of the rule of law, put quite specifically as a warning about the danger of deciding upon guilt or innocence in the "secret courts of men's hearts." But this seems to be exactly what Atticus countenances in the final episode. Atticus and the Sheriff have decided that Boo should be spared a trial. They have tried him in the secret courts of their hearts and declared him innocent, and Scout endorses their decision: to try Boo would be like shooting a mockingbird. What was a wicked thing in Tom's case is a good thing in Boo's case.

IV

The ethical contradiction has not gone unnoticed, and some commentators have been mildly critical. For the most part, however, both Atticus's summation and his decision to spare Boo have been applauded. Indeed, the apparent inconsistency between the two episodes is taken to show Atticus's praiseworthy character and his laudable attitude toward the law. Claudia Johnson writes at length of Atticus's respect for law, before commenting that "despite [this] . . . he believes that reason must prevail when law violates reason. . . . In the case of Boo Radley's killing of Bob Ewell, law is proven inadequate, because on occasion reason dictates that laws and boundaries must be overridden for justice to be done."[6] And, although he thinks Atticus made a mistake over Ewell's death, Shaffer does not think the mistake diminishes Atticus as a hero, but that it shows us precisely "how a good man makes a doubtful choice" and demonstrates "that more is involved than whether the choice is sound in principle."[7] These commentators take the importance of *Mockingbird* to lie in its demonstration of the centrality of character in professional ethics. In effect, they render

Atticus's conduct consistent by subsuming it under the notion of "judgment." His conduct may well be inconsistent when viewed from the perspective of this or that general principle or rule of right conduct, but such a method just shows the inadequacy of principle or rule-governed approaches to ethical conduct.[8]

Assessments of Atticus that elevate judgment over principle reflect wider developments in contemporary ethics and moral philosophy, which have, strikingly, rediscovered Aristotle. At the heart of this renaissance is the idea that moral deliberation and justification cannot proceed deductively through the application of general principles to particular cases. Aristotle supposes that the phenomena with which ethical inquiry is concerned are marked by mutability, indeterminacy, and particularity such that they can never be subsumed under general principles of right action unproblematically. His view of the limitations of general principles of right action led him to stress the importance of "practical judgment" (*phronesis*), a practical reasoning skill which is neither a matter of simply applying general principles to particular cases nor of mere intuition. Both general principles and the particularities of a case play a role in *phronesis* which thus emphasizes judgment and brings the character of the practical reasoner to center stage. We cannot look to general principles to settle what is the right thing to do, hence we must look to the character—or virtues—of those doing the judging.[9]

Atticus supporters present him as the *phronimos*, an expert practical reasoner sensitive both to general principles and the particularities of cases. Atticus is one who knows what to do not by applying general principles, but by being the sort of person he is, by having the sort of character he has. Atticus recognizes that confining himself to general principles, such as those he defended at Tom's trial, would be a recipe for obtuseness.

V

I am not convinced that Atticus is an appropriate ethical role model for lawyers. He fails not, as Monroe Freedman would have it, because his character makes him unsuited to the role, but because the character approach itself is unable to provide an appropriate grounding for the ethical obligations of lawyers and similar professionals. That is Atticus's lesson for us. My starting point is a reiteration of the challenge posed by the three episodes set out above. Atticus's defenders, we have seen, respond to that challenge by subsuming Atticus's conduct under the notion of "judgment." His conduct may well be inconsistent when viewed from the perspective of this or that general principle or rule of right conduct, but this just shows the inadequacy of principle or rule-governed approaches to ethical conduct. I think there are textual difficulties with this reading, but will not dwell on them here. Instead, I will offer what I think is a more natural reading of Atticus's conduct.

We seek an interpretation of Atticus's conduct that renders it, if not consistent, at least coherent. We have such a reading if we regard Atticus as a tragic figure. *Mockingbird* has at least some elements of tragedy: an innocent man (Tom) falls victim to evil despite the best efforts of the novel's hero. Atticus's story too is tragic. Regarding the rule of law as tremendously important, he presents his arguments in its favor to the jury with passion and all of his professional ability, recognizing that the life of an innocent man rests upon his success. But he fails, and Tom dies. When a decision over Boo is required, Atticus is struck by the similarities between the cases. Both Tom and Boo are mockingbirds: innocents who it would be sinful to harm. Both Tom and Boo are 'outsiders'; Tom because he is black and Boo because he is a handicapped recluse, isolated from the dominant community. Each must rely upon the dominant community to ignore the fact that they are outsiders. In Tom's case, the community does not do so. When Boo kills Bob Ewell, Atticus, cast as protector of both men, must decide whether he will allow another outsider to face the same threat. Confronted with the possibility of another tragedy, Atticus's faith in the rule of law, and perhaps his courage as well, fail him. He cannot bear the possibility that he will be party to the death of another mockingbird.

In the end, Atticus abandons the principles that determined his self-understanding, secured his unique and valuable position in Maycomb, and received his passionate defense. That is the stuff of tragedy: a principled man has come to doubt the adequacy of principles by which he understands himself and abandons those principles. Whether or not it is wicked to try people in the secret courts of men's hearts now depends upon *which* men's hearts. Hence we need not strain for a reading which makes Atticus's conduct consistent: it is not consistent. Atticus is not throughout the *phronimos*, an eye firmly on substantive principles of justice and fairness, but a more human figure. Tragically though understandably, he is not prepared to risk a vulnerable person effectively in his care, having so recently seen how his legal system mistreated another similarly placed outsider.

The point of interpreting Atticus as a tragic figure is not to brand him as less than admirable and *therefore* as an unsuitable role model. Instead, this interpretation contrasts with that which portrays him as the *phronimos* and provides an alternative to the assumption shared by both sides of the debate that his significance for legal ethics is to be settled by reference to his character. Cast as a tragic figure, Atticus yields a very different message than that which he conveys as a wise figure. We are not meant to *admire* what he does but to be struck by the gravity of his loss. Viewed as a tragic figure, his message is one about the value of the principles he has abandoned, not one about the desirability of regarding them as disposable, trivial, or burdensome.

VI

A tenacious Atticus supporter might claim that even if Atticus did abandon the principles he defended in Tom's case, the decision to do so was a wise one, and does not show Atticus to have acted other than as the *phronimos*. However, there are reasons to reject this assessment. Some of these reasons are specific to Boo's case: they undercut the claim that Atticus's decision in Boo's case was a wise one. I begin with these Boo-specific issues.

Perhaps the most striking Boo-specific feature in this context is the fate from which Atticus and Sheriff Tate are attempting to save Boo. In portraying Atticus as a tragic figure, I suggested that he could not bear the thought of being party to the death of another mockingbird. The talk is warranted from Atticus's point of view. It explains why Scout speaks so effectively when she likens putting Boo on trial to "shootin' a mockingbird." However, it is rhetorical. No one seems to think Boo will really suffer Tom's fate. They take it for granted that he will be acquitted. The worst Sheriff Tate can imagine for Boo is that he will be besieged by grateful Maycomb ladies bearing angel food cakes (p. 304)! Plainly, this is not a trivial matter for Boo and his shy ways. Surely, however, it cannot be sufficient to warrant rejection of what on any reading of the novel is a fundamental principle of justice.

There are other factors that cast doubt on the wisdom of Atticus's decision. There is no consideration of how the decision will seem to other members of the community. No middle grounds are canvassed—there is no discussion of the possibility of putting Boo on trial and forbidding the Maycomb ladies from bombarding him with angel food cakes. Further, by the time of the episodes recounted in *Mockingbird*, Boo has been held in his family home for some twenty-five years. Might not Boo have been better served by giving him his day in court, bringing him out of the shadowy world he had occupied for so long? Surely one need not be terribly hard-hearted to think that the local community had an interest in knowing that someone with Boo's history had been about with a honed kitchen knife with which he had dispatched Bob Ewell, no matter how much Ewell deserved his fate or how clearly Boo had merely been trying to prevent a crime.

This is to suggest that Atticus makes a mistake in Boo's case, putting aside too easily fundamental principles in the face of insufficiently countervailing considerations. It is not hard to see why he does so. I have suggested that Atticus's deliberations about Boo are dominated by his experience in Tom's case and, in particular, by the perception that Boo, like Tom, is a vulnerable outsider. But Boo is a very different sort of outsider than Tom, and the difference is both plain and important. We see it illustrated starkly in the Sheriff's responses to Boo and Tom. After a somewhat perfunctory investigation of each episode, he immediately arrests Tom, with no apparent qualms about the reliability of the Ewells' accusation. Yet he decides on the spot to adopt a fiction to spare Boo a trial, evidencing sensitivity to Boo quite absent from his dealings with Tom. The Sheriff's apparent change of heart shows clearly that Boo, at least compared to Bob Ewell, is a privileged outsider, and Atticus seems not to have noticed this or to have given it too little weight. The second obvious explanation for Atticus's lapse is the involvement of his own children in Boo's case. His gratitude to the man who saved his children is surely understandable, and one can see why he would be loathe to insist that his children's rescuer be put through the ordeal of a trial and displays of public gratitude. But the involvement of his children should have led Atticus to be especially careful about trying Boo in the secret court of his own heart.

Hence, we might wonder whether Atticus gets it right in Boo's case. We have seen that Shaffer also describes Atticus's decision to spare Boo as a mistake, albeit one that reminds us of the importance of character. But I think that Sheriff Tate has it right when he says, "Mr. Finch I hate to fight you when you're like this. You've been under a strain tonight no man should ever have to go through. Why you ain't in bed from it I don't know. But I do know that for once you haven't been able to put two and two together. . . ." (p. 303).

This reading of Atticus's decision in Boo's case supports the interpretation of him as a tragic figure. He makes a poor decision in Boo's case because his focus on the common themes in the cases prevents him from paying sufficient detail to the particularities of Boo's situation. It is difficult to believe the details would not have moved a wise-

Atticus, but we would expect a tragic-Atticus to respond just as Atticus Finch does respond. This account also reveals the flaws of the character approach. If even Atticus cannot avoid the sort of understandable cognitive dissonance that seems to mark his deliberations in Boo's case, we should favor an alternative approach that places less emphasis upon the particular judgments of individuals. A rule or principle-based approach, though not eliminating the need for judgment, is such an alternative.

There is another point to be drawn from this discussion. Behind much of it has been the idea that the decision to spare Boo a trial may have been reasonable had there been a genuine risk that Boo would have suffered Tom's fate. I have suggested that the facts of Boo's case simply do not support that conclusion. But suppose for a moment that a Maycomb jury would have unjustly convicted him of wrongdoing in the death of Bob Ewell. The supposition renders *Mockingbird* the story of a legal system in crisis. We may think, indeed, that Tom's fate alone is enough to show that this is just what *Mockingbird* is. But what would its lesson be if this were correct? Not that identified by Atticus's defenders. Rather, assuming that *Mockingbird* is the story of a system in crisis, its lesson is that lawyers should not admire and emulate Atticus's alleged attitude to rules and principles. For on the reading of the novel which portrays it as the story of a legal system in crisis, it is precisely the jury's *disregard* for these constraints which generates the crisis. Here, once again, Atticus's lesson for us would be about the importance of rules and principles, not about their triviality.

VII

I remarked that there were two sorts of reasons to doubt that Atticus's decision in Boo's case was a wise one, some specific to Boo's case and others of more general import. I turn to the reasons of the second sort. As well as bearing again upon the question of Atticus's wisdom in Boo's case, these are reasons to think that we should reject the character approach to legal ethics itself.

I begin with an account of the nature and function of law. One of Atticus's most important moral lessons to his children is that of tolerance and appreciation of difference. Here Atticus gestures at what has been described as the problem of political liberalism: "How is it possible that there may exist over time a stable and just community of free and equal citizens profoundly divided by reasonable religious, philosophical and moral doctrine?"[10] A central part of the liberal response to this question has been the establishment of procedures and institutions that aspire to an ideal of neutrality between reasonable views represented in the communities to which they apply. The members of pluralist communities will often be able to agree on the structure of neutral institutions and practices even when they cannot agree on the right outcome of a policy question as a substantive matter. Of course, these institutions and practices cannot guarantee outcomes which will suit all the reasonable views: often there will be no such universally acceptable outcomes. The hope of liberalism, however, is that even those whose substantive preferences do not win the day on this or that occasion will have cause to accept the decisions of these institutions as fair and just. At the very least, they must have reason to believe that their views have been taken seriously and that the decision procedures have not simply turned the individual preferences of some members of the community into public policy.

Precisely these sorts of general political concerns lie behind the requirement that individuals are to be tried by public standards in public courts rather than by private or secret tribunals. Why object to trials in the secret courts of men's hearts? Not only because we are worried about whether or not we have the *right* men's hearts, but also because a crucial part of the role of law in pluralist communities is to allow individuals to see the mechanisms by which public decisions are made and to see that those mechanisms have indeed been used. Liberal community so understood is undercut by those who insist upon appeal to their own substantive views of the good rather than to public procedures.

Atticus has it right in his summation to the jury. A commitment to tolerance and equality leads to decision procedures that render trial within the secret courts of men's hearts illegitimate. Atticus's decision to spare Boo a public trial is a mistake not just because it fails to take account of the particular facts of Boo's case, but because it undercuts the role of law in securing community between people who hold a range of diverse and reasonable views. This view about the role of law in pluralist societies has consequences for the ethical obligations of lawyers. They act improperly when they substitute their own judgments for those of the procedures, acceptance of which makes pluralist community possible. An appreciation of the role of law should lead us away from rather than toward a character-based approach to legal ethics. The issue is not whether we have the right men's hearts, but whether any individual's heart will do.

This discussion provides a response to a recent and important contribution to the legal ethics debate. Anthony Kronman has argued that the legal profession is in the grips of "a spiritual crisis that strikes at the heart of [the lawyer's] professional pride" and threatens the very soul of the profession itself.[11] The crisis has resulted from the demise of a two-hundred-year-old professional ideal—that of the lawyer-statesman—which envisioned the outstanding lawyer as the *phronimos:* not a mere technician but a person of practical wisdom possessed of a range of honorable and more or less peculiarly legal character traits. Without this ideal, lawyers have come to regard law as an essentially technical discipline, requiring no particular character or virtue on the part of its leading practitioners, judges, and teachers.

As the lawyer-statesman epithet suggests, Kronman takes lawyers to have a significant leadership role. In the political sphere, the lawyer-statesman seeks a certain kind of political integrity, namely one that obtains despite the existence of significant and ineradicable conflict. The lawyer-statesman directs us to a condition of political wholeness in which "the members of a community are joined by bonds of sympathy, despite the differences of opinion that set them apart on questions concerning the ends, and hence the identity, of their community."[12]

The discussion of the role of law and lawyers given above provides a better account of these matters. There are a couple of points. First, the 'procedural' story is directed precisely at securing political community in the face of ongoing substantive dispute. The neutral institutions of political liberalism aim to give us ways of going on as a community which assure even those whose personal preferences have failed to carry the day that neither they nor their views have been ignored. Law is an essential part of the effort to secure stable and just political community between the advocates of diverse views of the good. Second, the procedural approach provides a response to Kronman's spiritual crisis as well: on the procedural account the various law jobs are extraordinarily important in pluralist communities and hence are ones in which lawyers can and should take pride. One might think, indeed, that some such story would be a source of considerably more comfort to lawyers than Kronman's—it tells them, after all, that what most of them are doing most of the time has moral and political value.

VIII

There are also reasons to be wary of character-based approaches to legal ethics that focus not upon the political or social significance of law in general, but upon the nature of lawyer-client relationships. We can relate these concerns to *Mockingbird* by noting a difference between Atticus's position and that of most contemporary lawyers. *Mockingbird* is importantly the story of an intimate community. A good deal of the book is concerned to place Atticus and his family within Maycomb, to show how he and his forebears came to the town, to show that the neighbors and the community know him well. Consequently, Atticus's professional relationships have much in common with relationships between family members or friends. In these latter relationships our intimate knowledge of the individual allows us to make assessments of the character of the person to whom we are vulnerable— of their motivations, their priorities and so forth—which explain our willingness to place ourselves in their hands. However, we do not have this sort of detailed knowledge of the character of our professionals. Hence we cannot rely upon their character as we rely upon the character of friends. The result is that the character aspect of the virtues approach makes it inappropriate for professional and legal ethics. Clients just do not have access to information about the character of their professionals that would make it reasonable to place themselves in positions of vulnerability in reliance upon character-based considerations.[13]

Given this analysis of professional-client relations, it is important not only that professionals are ethical, but that clients and potential clients have some way of knowing the ethical stance of practitioners even though they do not know them or their moral views personally. The adoption and promulgation of a distinct professional morality makes the ethics of the profession public in a way that the personal ethics of its members cannot be. Clients get the benefit of this public ethics, however, only if it is indeed given priority over personal ethical views in members' dealings with the public. Given this, to know what values at least should govern the professional's conduct, the client need only know what values the professional role requires the professional to adopt and that the professional is a role-occupant. In a different world, perhaps one characterized by the positive communal aspects of life in Maycomb, we may not need these guides to the ethical views of our professionals. However, Maycomb, both thankfully and sadly, is not our world.

IX

In sum, Atticus does have an important lesson for professional and legal ethics, but not one about the importance of character over rules and principles. On the contrary, Atticus allows us to see the importance of the principles of law he defends so eloquently in Tom's case and abandons so tragically in Boo's case. In doing so, he shows why we cannot found an adequate professional ethic on the character of practitioners. Character approaches make it less rather than more likely that professionals will fulfill the ethical obligations appropriate to their roles. Atticus's lesson is not that lawyers should throw over rule- and principle-based models of professional ethical obligation, but that they should be brought to appreciate the significance of the social roles they serve, and to understand and take pride in fulfilling the duties which flow from those roles.

From *Philosophy and Literature* 25, no. 1 (2001), pp. 127-141. Copyright © 2001 by The Johns Hopkins University Press. Reprinted by permission of The Johns Hopkins University Press.

Notes

1. Harper Lee, *To Kill a Mockingbird* (London: Heinemann, 1960). Subsequent references appear in parentheses in the text.
2. Claudia A. Carver, "Lawyers as Heroes: The Compassionate Activism of a Fictional Attorney is a Model We Can Emulate," *Los Angeles Lawyer* (July-August, 1988).
3. Monroe Freedman, "Atticus Finch, Esq., R.I.P.," *Legal Times*, 24 February 1992.
4. Monroe Freedman, "Atticus Finch—Right and Wrong," *Alabama Law Review* 45 (1994): 473-82. This volume contains a symposium on *To Kill a Mockingbird* and legal ethics.
5. Thomas L. Shaffer, *Faith and the Professions* (Provo, Utah: Brigham Young University Press, 1987), p. 5.
6. Claudia Johnson, "Without Tradition and Within Reason: Judge Horton and Atticus Finch in Court," *Alabama Law Review* 45 (1994): 483-510, 499. See also Timothy Hall, "Moral Character, the Practice of Law and Legal Education," *Mississippi Law Review* (1990): 511-25.
7. Thomas L. Shaffer, "The Moral Theology of Atticus Finch," *University of Pittsburgh Law Review* 41 (1981): 181-224, 196.
8. For other applications of virtue ethics to the legal profession, see Anthony Kronman, *The Lost Lawyer* (Cambridge, MA: Belknap Press, 1993), discussed below, and Gerald Postema, "Moral Responsibility in Professional Ethics," *New York University Law Review* 55 (1980): 63-89.
9. See, for instance, John McDowell writing that "one knows what to do (if one does) not by applying universal principles but by being a certain sort of person: one who sees situations in a certain way." "Virtue and Reason," *The Monist* 62 (1979): 331-

50, 347, reprinted in *Virtue Ethics*, eds. Roger Crisp and Michael Slote (Oxford: Oxford University Press, 1993), pp. 141-62. Crisp and Slote's collection contains many of the important contributions to the virtue ethics revival.

10. John Rawls, *Political Liberalism* (New York: Columbia University Press, 1993), p. xxv.

11. Kronman, p. 2.

12. Kronman, p. 93. It is no coincidence that Kronman appeals to historical examples of the lawyer-statesman, just as the Atticus supporters appeal to a fictional figure. Both characterize the *phronimos* ostensively, since they are suspicious of doing so by appeal to 'principles' of deliberation or good character. The use of such principles would undercut the character approach's rejection of principles.

13. This analysis may capture the compelling aspects of the idea that the professional is the client's "special purpose friend." See Charles Fried, "The Lawyer as Friend: The Moral Foundations of the Lawyer-Client Relation," *Yale Law Journal* 85 (1976): 1060-89.

Growing Up Good in Maycomb _____

Thomas L. Shaffer

"I am the sum total of those who preceded me," Elie Wiesel wrote recently, "and so are you. Am I responsible for what all of them have done before I came into this world? No. But I am responsible for what I am doing with the memory of what they have done."[1]

Jean Louise Finch (Scout), her brother Jeremy, their summer friend Dill, who comes to them from Meridian, Mississippi, and their school friends from the town and the farms around Maycomb grew up in memory and learned, or failed to learn, and accepted, or refused to accept, responsibility for what they did with the memory and in the name that memory gives to a place.[2]

These children in Maycomb learned the virtues before they learned that what they had learned were virtues.[3] The virtues they learned were virtues formed in the memory and in the name that the memory gives to a place. They grew up good in Maycomb. Their childhood story, told in large part as a story about their father Atticus, is about growing up in virtue. The epigraph Harper Lee chose for the novel is from Charles Lamb: "Lawyers, I suppose, were children once."[4] And the dedication of the novel is to Miss Lee's father, a Monroeville lawyer[5] ("to Mr. Lee"), and to her sister, who became a lawyer[6] ("and Alice"), and it is framed as if it were copied from a warranty deed in Atticus Finch's law office ("in consideration of Love & Affection").[7]

Growing Up a Lady

A slightly quaint example of growing up good in Maycomb is Scout's learning to be a Southern Lady,[8] told most directly in the chapter that describes the meeting of a group of Maycomb's Methodist ladies in the Finch home.[9] It is one of the few occasions on which Scout wears a dress rather than bib overalls, which is significant as well as symbolic: Throughout the story, Atticus's and Calpurnia's failure to put Scout in dresses is evidence of their failure to train her to be a lady.[10]

Scout's Aunt Alexandra, temporarily taking charge of the home in order to correct the failure and to provide what a single-parent male and a black woman could not be expected to provide, is hostess for the meeting of the missionary circle of the Maycomb Alabama Methodist Episcopal Church South. She recruits Scout and Calpurnia to help her entertain the members, who gather there to discuss the wretched condition of the children of polygamous and polytheistic Africa. Scout goes about her duties with reluctance: "Ladies in bunches always filled me with vague apprehension and a firm desire to be elsewhere . . . a feeling . . . Aunt Alexandra called 'being spoiled.'"[11]

As if to confirm Scout's misgiving, the young girl has hardly sat down to sip her lemonade when Miss Stephanie Crawford from across the street asks her if she wants to grow up to be a lawyer like her father. "Not me, just a lady," Scout answers,[12] and Miss Stephanie says that if Scout wants to be a lady she will have to wear dresses more often.[13] Miss Maudie Atkinson, from a different house across the street, secretly intervenes to teach Scout a lesson—or to confirm her in it—on the importance of meeting slight insults with quiet dignity: "Miss Maudie's hand closed tightly on mine, and I said nothing. Its warmth was enough."[14]

This becomes a lesson in judgment as much as a lesson in behavior, as, a few minutes later, Mrs. Merriweather begins idly to berate her absent black servant and Miss Maudie stops the conversation with a caustic comment.[15] The secret hand-squeeze was a lesson in quiet dignity, but the lesson in judgment is that silence is not always the virtuous response; sometimes a lady stands up against evil, in this case the customary racism that Atticus, elsewhere in the story, refers to as "Maycomb's usual disease."[16]

How is a lady-in-training to know when judgment—what the moral philosophers call prudence[17]—requires speaking out, and when judgment requires quiet dignity? The way ladies tell the difference, as Scout sees it at the meeting, rests on, or at least is confirmed by, an understanding about allies. The fact that morally influential others are present and supportive makes it possible to confront ordinary evil. All through this story, collaborators in the good[18] describe the distinction between ordinary evil and casual insult. In Tom Robinson's case[19] and Atticus's confrontative, uncivil defense of Tom Robinson, this looking around for allies becomes clear when Atticus learns that Braxton Bragg Underwood, publisher of the *Maycomb Tribune*, was standing by to defend him from the mob that had come to the jail at night to lynch Atticus's client.[20] At another point in the story, Atticus senses that the judge in the Robinson case is an ally because he seems sympathetic with the unpopular tactic Atticus has chosen for his client's defense. The judge seems to have appointed Atticus to defend Tom Robinson because he hoped for and expected just such an unpopular choice of legal theory for the courtroom.[21]

Scout, however, who learns about truth and courage from her father and from Mr. Underwood and Judge Taylor, has to learn to practice prudence as a lady among ladies. Scout learns that, among ladies, there is a sisterhood of sympathy and principle that does not operate in dramatic encounters such as the ones Atticus has with the mob in front of the jail, or with the racist prosecutor in the courtroom, or the mad dog in the street. Among ladies, the presence of collaborators in virtue is as quiet as Miss Maudie's hand-squeeze.

Collaboration occurs when Miss Maudie stops Mrs. Merriweather's ruminations on Southern black people with a caustic remark (which also operates as a defense of the unusual racial politics of the Finch house). After the remark, Scout notices a silent and unexpected alliance between Miss Maudie and Aunt Alexandra. The alliance is unexpected because the two women are not friends; they have seemed to Scout to be operating at cross purposes as Miss Maudie insists on being mildly unconventional and, worse, on supporting whatever Atticus does, in his house or out of it. By contrast, Aunt Alexandra is as uncomfortable with what Atticus is doing for Tom Robinson as most white people in Maycomb are, and is persuaded that Atticus and

Calpurnia are raising Scout to be unladylike. Despite what Scout has already seen to be cold courtesy between Miss Maudie and Aunt Alexandra, what Scout sees after Miss Maudie silences Mrs. Merriweather is a compact to protect the Finch house (and Atticus too). From this compact arises a bit of unexpected sisterhood that teaches Scout about the way Southern ladies get together when they have to without surrendering the independence[22] that keeps them apart:

[Aunt Alexandra] gave Miss Maudie a look of pure gratitude, and I wondered at the world of women. Miss Maudie and Aunt Alexandra had never been especially close, and here was Aunty silently thanking her for something. For what, I knew not. . . . There was no doubt about it, I must soon enter this world, where on its surface fragrant ladies rocked slowly, fanned gently, and drank cool water.[23]

And then the crisis of Tom Robinson's persecution and the gentle drinking of cool water meet. Atticus comes in the house, away from his office at an unusual time of day. He does not interrupt the meeting, except that his presence has already interrupted it. He asks Aunt Alexandra and Miss Maudie to speak with him in the kitchen; he tells them that Tom Robinson has been killed by his jailers and he asks Calpurnia to go with him to the Robinsons' home because he needs her to help him tell the new widow what has happened.

No one tells the other ladies at the meeting what has happened. No doubt that is because Atticus, his sister, and his neighbor know (and Scout learns) that decency requires that the widow learn first. And so the meeting, the fans, the rocking, and the cool water, go on as if nothing has happened—except that Scout and Aunt Alexandra have to take over Calpurnia's duties as well as their own. Scout then describes her duties: "I carefully picked up the tray and watched myself walk to Mrs. Merriweather. With my best company manners, I asked her if she would have some. After all, if Aunty could be a lady at a time like this, so could I."[24]

Scout's learning to be a Southern lady—learning the way the virtues are practiced in a subtle, demanding vocation—is essential to the story because she is becoming a woman in a place, in a family, in a neighborhood, that teaches children how to take responsibility for a memory and a name.[25] By the time Aunt Alexandra comes from Finch's Landing to take charge of Scout's education in manners Scout is ten years old and in the third grade. Most of her formation in virtue has already taken place,[26] and most of it appears to have been, as Alexandra fears, masculine education—not because women are absent but because Scout's only living parent is a man, a man of moral power and influence. Scout has to put together the training in virtue she appears to have from her father with the demands and expectations put on a Southern woman in the 1930s.[27]

The point I get from the meeting of the missionary circle is that the available notions of role are not adequate to describe Scout's moral formation. Scout cannot step from being her father's child into being a Southern lady and then back again, as she goes, say, from the tree house in the backyard to Sunday School. She has to be, as her father is, the same person in town and at home. The fact that she wears bib overalls under her dress when Aunt Alexandra drafts her into service at the missionary-circle meeting shows how she has begun to figure out how to wear ladies' clothing and at the same time accept and practice what she learned when she wore overalls. The women of Maycomb help Scout do this, as they have helped her understand the virtues she appears to learn from her father. Consider three of them, and then consider the ideal of Southern white womanhood:

Calpurnia, Scout and Jem's surrogate mother, is the person in the story who is, no doubt, Atticus Finch's best friend (although he would, in a small town in Alabama in 1935, not have put it that way). Calpurnia is a demanding teacher. She is the mistress of what feminist scholars, looking at our culture's moral past, call "the woman's sphere."[28] She is the one who teaches these white children, as Aristotle said,[29] the moral virtues and good habits, long before they choose to behave well—long before their virtues are virtues. Much of what the women in Scout's life think the children learned from their father they in fact learned from Calpurnia. Atticus exemplified and confirmed intellectual content, and added the right names—classical names, such as truth, courage, justice—to what they already knew and had begun, because of Calpurnia, both to practice and to choose to practice.

Calpurnia demands, nourishes, and comforts. "By watching her," Scout says, "I began to think there was some skill involved in being a girl."[30] When Scout criticizes Walter Cunningham for putting syrup all over his lunch (in Maycomb it's called dinner), after Jem induces Walter to come home from school to eat with the Finches, Calpurnia is an avenging angel on behalf of Walter and of Southern manners: "Yo' folks might be better'n the Cunninghams but it don't count for nothin' the way you're disgracin' 'em—if you can't act fit to eat at the table you can just set here and eat in the kitchen!"[31] But when Scout is in pain over the hypocrisy and drudgery of public education, Calpurnia is a comforter; she makes crackling bread and gives it to Scout, as a surprise, after school. She also tells Scout she missed her: "The house got so lonesome 'long about two o'clock I had to turn on the radio."[32] And Scout concedes some softening: "Calpurnia's tyranny, unfairness, and meddling in my business had faded to gentle grumblings of general disapproval. On my part, I went to much trouble, sometimes, not to provoke her."[33]

When Aunt Alexandra comes to Maycomb to see to Scout's refinement, the first thing she wants to do is send Calpurnia away. Atticus bears most of Alexandra's reforms with patience; when, for example, she tells Scout that Scout has to be a sunbeam in her father's life, he tells Scout (on the side) that the Finch family already has enough sunbeams.[34] But he is openly stubborn when it comes to his friend Calpurnia. He identifies her as a kinswoman: "She's a faithful member of this family and you'll simply have to accept things the way they are."[35] He disapproves of Alexandra's well-bred practice of not saying anything controversial within Calpurnia's hearing: "Anything fit to say at the table's fit to say in front of Calpurnia. She knows what she means to this family."[36]

Neither of these white children will ever have to live under the oppression Calpurnia lives under, although both of them will be called upon to take responsibility for what they do with the memory of old-style American racism sooner than their father—or anybody else in Maycomb—might have supposed they would. But one of the things they do have to learn—just have to—is that half the people in their town are cruelly oppressed, and it is Calpurnia's undertaking, as much as that of Atticus and Miss Maudie, to teach them about it. The fact that the children do not know, until they are preteens, that Calpurnia has a home and a family of her own justifies as much as anything in the story a nod to the irony of American history.[37] Jem and Scout find out about both Calpurnia's family and the community of Maycomb's black Christians when they go with Calpurnia to Sunday services at First Purchase African Methodist Episcopal Church. There they also find out that the black church is the one place in Maycomb that is not racist.

The children notice that Calpurnia speaks differently among black people than she does in the Finch home (and they sharpen the contrast as they remember that "Atticus said Calpurnia had more education than most colored folks"[38]) and, being children, they mention this to her. She says it is a matter of not putting on airs. It's not that she approves of the lack of education among most of her black neighbors, nor that she thinks black illiteracy is inevitable; she has, after all, taught her own son to read from a copy of *Blackstone's Commentaries* that she borrowed from Atticus. What the Finch children are asked to learn is that a person can work for moral gain in the community without being offensive about it: "[F]olks don't like to have somebody around knowin' more than they do. . . . [W]hen they don't want to learn there's nothing you can do but keep your mouth shut or talk their language."[39]

Mrs. Dubose, the suffering old white bigot who lives up the street from the Finches, was left out of the movie version of the story. My guess is that the omission was not due to the economics of film making alone, but demonstrates that the movie was a 1960s civil rights story, rather than the affectionate story of an Alabama town in 1935, and that the American civil-rights agenda when Horton Foote wrote the screenplay could not find a way to come to terms with Mrs. Dubose—with the fact that Atticus Finch could endure an old woman's ruthless and racist attack on him and his client and at the same time hold her out to his children as the bravest person he ever knew, a teacher of the virtue of courage.[40]

Mrs. Dubose was, Scout said, by unanimous neighborhood opinion, "the meanest old woman who ever lived."[41] She so taunted Jem that he stormed into her yard and beheaded her camellias. His training as a Southern gentleman required him to apologize, make his peace with her, and spend two weeks reading to her from *Ivanhoe*.[42] And then, when Atticus needed a way to teach his children what courage was, he dipped (a bit improperly[43]) into his professional knowledge of her affairs and told them, after Mrs. Dubose's death, that the reading of *Ivanhoe* was to help her overcome morphine addiction, cold turkey, before she died. Her determination to die free of the addiction which had come upon her as beneficent professional medical therapy, on the assumption that morphine addiction is all right for old, sick people,[44] was the lesson Atticus needed to overcome an impression he had created, in the mad-dog incident, that courage is a *man* with a *gun* in his hand. The movie leaves in the man and the gun and omits the brave old woman.[45] The memory was just different.

Miss Maudie Atkinson teaches the children independence (I again avoid the word autonomy) and friendship. She is a devoted gardener—so much so that her ability to continue to grow flowers is a genuine consolation for her after her house burns down. But certain elements in the white Christian church in Maycomb (the Foot Washing Baptists) disapprove of her garden; it is, in their theology, a worldly indulgence. Miss Maudie is also a faithful and understanding companion for the children, as well as a source of firm support for their father in his struggle with the town in the Robinson case. It is Miss Maudie who explains the novel's title, when she tells Scout and Jem what Atticus means when he says it is a sin to kill a mockingbird.[46] And it is Miss Maudie who defends the Finch home from the racism of Mrs. Merriweather's attack on black people. Scout says of Miss Maudie: "She had never told on us, had never played cat-and-mouse with us, she was not at all interested in our private lives. She was our friend. How so reasonable a creature could live in peril of everlasting torment was incomprehensible."[47] Not only does Scout find out that an adult can be as much a friend as her summer companion Dill; she also learns that growing up as a Southern Christian woman includes locating and understanding theological distinctions.

Southern White Womanhood. The ethos of Maycomb that clouds men's minds so badly that they will lynch an innocent black man is understood or, rather, rationalized, as the defense of Southern White Womanhood.[48] Arthur Radley, the strange recluse who lives hidden away next door to the Finch house, and who, at the end of the story, saves the children's lives, was locked away because of an offense to Southern White Womanhood. When he was a boy he was a member of an unruly group of juveniles accused of, among other offenses, "using abusive and profane language in the presence and hearing of a female."[49] The probate judge released Arthur (Boo) to his father, and his father locked him away.

When Atticus rushes home in the middle of the day, and interrupts the meeting of the missionary circle, after he learns that Tom Robinson has been killed, and asks Alexandra, Maudie, and Calpurnia to speak to him in the kitchen, he becomes so overwrought that he almost storms out of the room—but then checks himself, does not slam the door, and comes back briefly to make a lame joke. "I know what he was trying to do," Scout says, "but Atticus was only a man. It takes a woman to do that kind of work."[50]

The defense of Southern White Womanhood is an attitude nourished and promulgated by Aunt Alexandra, who, Scout says, "had river-boat, boarding-school manners; let any moral come along and she would uphold it; she was born in the objective case."[51] Hers is, though, an ethos that carries disadvantages to women—disadvantages that will be challenged, after the story ends, long before anybody in Maycomb would have predicted. What a lady-in-training, learning the memory and the name of Maycomb, does with the disadvantages is to notice them and store them away for later exercises of the discerning judgment that she is also, and at the same time, learning. For example, when the children go to church with Calpurnia, Rev. Sykes's sermon is on drinking, gambling, "and strange women. . . . Again, as I had often met it in my own church, I was confronted with the Impurity of Women doctrine that seemed to preoccupy all clergymen."[52]

The last scene in the novel provides a reminder of where Scout has been in her formation as a Southern Lady, as well as showing a bit of what lies ahead for her.[53] Her life and Jem's have been saved by their reclusive neighbor Boo Radley, who has come out of his house to save, be seen by, and be introduced to the children.[54] It is late at night; the children have been through a harrowing experience; Jem lies asleep in the Finch house, Aunt Alexandra by his side.[55] The doctor has come and gone. It is time for Boo Radley to go home, and he is afraid. He asks for an escort.[56] Scout is the only available escort, and she has learned enough about courage to be willing to take on the job; but a Southern Lady knows—as Mrs. Dubose did, from the reading of *Ivanhoe*—about proper appearance in the exercise of courage: "'Mr. Arthur, bend your arm down here, like that. That's right, sir.' I slipped my hand into the crook of his arm."[57] That way, if Miss Stephanie Crawford was looking out her window, "she would see Arthur Radley escorting me down the sidewalk, as any gentleman would do."[58]

There are other virtues to be learned in growing up good in Maycomb. They are not so evidently a matter of a young girl, already trained in the virtues by her surrogate mother and already under the influence of an upright Southern Gentleman, finding out what it means to be a lady. These virtues can, perhaps, be talked about without being quite as lamely gender specific as I have been in reflecting on Maycomb's memory, and what good women learn to do with its memory and in its name. Part of this broader consideration of virtue involves respect for religion and for ordinary morals. Part is conscious reflection on what it means to be rooted in a community, and part is focused formation on the virtues of discrimination and respect.

Religion and Ordinary Morals

The most frequent moral lesson Atticus Finch announced to his children, and practiced for them by example, was a curious and respectful wonder at the mystery of each of the other people they met as they grew up in Maycomb. "You never really understand a person until you consider things from his point of view," he said, "until you climb into his skin and walk around in it."[59] That moral lesson is, I think, a matter of *faith*. It is related to but not the same thing as his *religion*.[60]

Walter Cunningham's father (also Walter), a stubborn, proud farmer—one of "a set breed of men," as Atticus put it[61]—and a client of Atticus's, is an example. It was Mr. Cunningham who brought the produce of his farm to the back door of the Finch house, in payment of a fee Atticus charged him for docking the entail on the Cunningham farm property.[62] It was also Mr. Cunningham who joined the mob (Faulkner's Mississippi lawyer Gavin Stevens called it "the Face"[63]) that came at night to the jail in Maycomb—came to lynch Tom Robinson—and were confronted first by Atticus, guarding his client, and then by the children.[64] Scout saw Mr. Cunningham in the mob and called him by name.[65] She asked him about his son,[66] the children's erstwhile luncheon guest.[67] "How's your entailment gettin' along?"[68] she asked him. Scout chooses this topic because "Atticus had said it was the polite thing to talk to people about what they were interested in, not about what you were interested in."[69] "I'll tell him [Walter, Jr.] you said hey, little lady," Mr. Cunningham finally said, and then he led the mob away and the crisis passed.[70]

Later, Atticus told the children that

> Mr. Cunningham's basically a good man, . . . [h]e just has his blind spots
> along with the rest of us. . . . [Y]ou'll understand folks a little better when
> you're older. A mob's always made up of people, no matter what. Mr.
> Cunningham was part of a mob . . . but he was still a man. Every mob in ev-
> ery little Southern town is always made up of people you know. . . .[71]

In the screenplay, Atticus had told Scout earlier not to call him to the
door when Mr. Cunningham brought nuts and vegetables from his
farm. "I think it embarrasses him to be thanked. . . . He is paying me . . .
the only way he can . . . he has no money. . . . The Cunninghams are
country folks, farmers, and the crash hit them the hardest."[72]

The theology that explains such a faith is a theology that sees that
the world is redeemed. In specifically Christian terms, it sees the Word
spoken of in the opening verses of St. John's Gospel as working in nature, in society, and in each person—sees the action of the Word in the
world as not limited by the creeds and principles with which religion
seeks to explain Who God is and what God is doing in the world. And
so every other person is not only interesting, not only fits in, but is also
inexplicable: "The Word generates faith rather than religion,"[73] as
Milner S. Ball puts it. "Our faith is our faith, but as it is the faithfulness
of God, it cannot be restricted by formulas or definitions or anything
applied from without, as though in some way unauthorized by the
Word."[74] He quotes Karl Barth: "True Christians can only remember
that the first might also be the last, so that at the very best they can only
believe that they believe."[75]

As Scout's character is formed in such a faith, she develops respect
even for the racist prosecutor, Mr. Gilmer, who abuses Tom Robinson
during the trial—abuses him by mocking him for saying he felt sorry
for a poor and ignorant white woman, Mayella Ewell, the prosecuting
witness against him, on a capital charge of rape.[76] When Mayella is on
the witness stand, Atticus addresses her as "Miss Mayella" and calls

her "ma'am," until Mayella complains that Atticus is mocking her, just as Mr. Gilmer mocks Tom Robinson. Judge Taylor has to intervene: "Mr. Finch is always courteous to everybody . . . he's trying to be polite. That's just his way."[77] As a matter of faith, though, Atticus's habit and his lesson are more than courtesy. When he tells Scout, after she asks him about his being accused of being a "nigger lover," that he tries to love everybody, he means it.[78] It is a matter of faith, rather than a matter of religion.

The habit and the lesson operate up close as well as outside the house. No doubt the up-close part of this faithful regard for the redeemed other person comes first in a child's moral development; it is something that is learned first at home and among the people at home.[79] It becomes a virtue in this story when Scout realizes that she is herself treated as redeemed: "I found myself wondering . . . what I would do if Atticus did not feel the necessity of my presence, help and advice. Why, he couldn't get along a day without me. Even Calpurnia couldn't get along unless I was there. They needed me."[80] And then she sees it as something to *do*, to apply, as the practice of getting into the other person's skin. Thus, Scout bites her lip and refuses to fight Cecil Jacobs, after Cecil insults her father, because Atticus asked her not to fight and she feels she has to do something for Atticus: "Atticus so rarely asked Jem and me to do something for him, I could take being called a coward for him. I felt extremely noble for having remembered, and remained noble for three weeks."[81] When the children go to church as Calpurnia's "company," each of them takes the customary Sunday dime for the collection plate, but they then have to accept Calpurnia's saying that putting money in the plate would show disrespect for the church and for their status as her "company": "Jem's face showed brief indecision . . . but his innate courtesy won and he shifted his dime to his pocket."[82]

When she finally, at the end of the story, meets Boo Radley, Scout tells Atticus that she finds Boo "real nice," and Atticus says, "Most people are, Scout, when you finally see them."[83] But not all people are "real nice" after one sees them—which means, if I have the ethical theory right, that one will never see them. Mayella Ewell, who falsely testifies against Tom Robinson, is an example of the first half of this distinction, and people who are "trash" are an example of the second. For example, Mayella is redeemed in a world in which the Word is at work: Scout, learning how to practice faith, sees Mayella Ewell lie in court to condemn Tom Robinson but comes to some compassion for her, as Atticus does in his jury speech. Scout remembers that the Ewells live next to the Maycomb town dump and salvage trash from the dump. Mayella, the eldest and caretaker of several motherless children, has salvaged makeshift pots from the trash and used them to put beauty in her miserable home. Scout remembers a picture in her mind as Mayella falsely testifies: There "against the fence, in a line were six chipped-enamel slop jars holding brilliant red geraniums, cared for as tenderly as if they belonged to Miss Maudie Atkinson."[84] What Mayella does to Tom Robinson is, so far as the law is concerned, unforgivable. And neither Atticus nor his children can ignore what she does. But Mayella is also redeemed; it is a matter of faith. The geraniums are a reminder of unseen grace.

The Finch children are also raised to be religious; they are moored, religiously, in the low-church, old-South Protestantism that their ancestor brought to that part of Alabama when he fled English restrictions on the Methodist movement. Church is, Scout says, "Maycomb's principal recreation," and anybody who does not go to church is, she says, unforgiven, even though the town supposes that they worship at home.[85] When Atticus is gone to the capital to serve in the legislature, and therefore not at home to take the children to church services, they go to the black Methodist church with Calpurnia.

Atticus's faith includes his religion, though they are not the same thing. "Faith," Karl Barth said, "is neither religion nor irreligion, neither sacred nor profane; it is always both together."[86] Faith includes so much more than religion, but as Milner S. Ball points out, religion cannot be discarded by a faithful believer.[87] Barth says religion "must be borne as a yoke which cannot be removed."[88] To destroy temples "is not better than to remove them."[89] Membership in the church, which was important to people in Maycomb, is, seen from the standpoint of faith, not something to be envied.[90] As Ball notes, Barth said that a true Christian can only "remember that the first might also be the last."[91] And so, Scout says, Atticus sits by himself in church; he goes there to pray, in and as part of the church. He tells Scout that he took on the painful burden of Tom Robinson's defense because it was important to him to go to church and to pray there, and he could not pray in church and at the same time refuse to help Tom Robinson.[92]

Ordinary morals. Maycomb has an ethic and a web of moral rules and customs, not all of them traceable to its conventional religion, and a few of them inconsistent with any thoughtful exercise of Christianity.[93] Scout explains some of these: "Finders were keepers unless title was proven. . . . [H]elping ourselves to someone's scuppernongs was part of our ethical culture, but money was different."[94] Southern children learn from the crib to call elders "sir" and "ma'am," and not to point at people. Ritual neighborliness is characteristic of small Southern towns. "Neighbors bring food with death and flowers with sickness and little things in between."[95] Even Boo Radley's brother and his jailer,[96] a man capable of firing his shotgun at children in his garden,[97] comes out of his house when neighborliness requires him to come out.[98] People in Maycomb do not vote for Republicans; they maintain a caste system that puts "the older citizens" at the top, followed by "the present generation of people who had lived side by side for years," all of their manners toward one another refined by time.[99] There are those at the top of the system who are still young enough to accept the burden of leadership. Atticus goes to the legislature and there takes on the least glamorous tasks,[100] while Aunt Alexandra fits into the social hierarchy of the town "like a hand into a glove."[101] Southerners of that time and place sometimes named their children after Confederate generals, although it was a practice, Atticus said, that tended to make "slow steady drinkers."[102] Atticus gives his children air rifles for Christmas, but he does it with distaste. Scout says, "[M]y father . . . hated guns and had never been to any wars."[103] Atticus tells his brother Jack that Jack will have to show them how to use the rifles: "That's your job. . . . I merely bowed to the inevitable."[104] Still, Atticus says, "it's a sin to kill a mockingbird"—the one time, Scout says, that Atticus described anything as sinful.[105]

Ordinary morals are, in the way the Finch children grow up, subordinate to the direction and the witness indicated by faith, including the part of their faith that is religious. That is the importance of Atticus's insistence on truth in the Robinson trial (even at the expense of his client's life and almost of his children's) and of the courage that, he insists, is better illustrated by a bigoted old woman overcoming morphine than by his being the best rifle shot in Finch's Landing. The biblical word for such a moral stance is "prophet"—one who reminds a community of what its deepest commitments are and of what it might cost to bear witness to those commitments.[106]

The critical prophetic events in the story are, of course, the trial of Tom Robinson and the death of Bob Ewell, at the end of the story, when Atticus Finch, uncommonly devoted to the truth, goes along with Sheriff Tate's public lie to protect the reclusive Boo Radley. The Sheriff says to the town that Ewell fell on his own knife, as he tried to kill Scout and Jem; in fact, as the Sheriff and the Finches know, he was killed by Boo Radley.[107] But sometimes the narrative events are more mundane: use of the commonest of all epithets in that time and place, the word "nigger," is perhaps an example. Atticus tells his children that use of the word by white people is "common," and he tells them that Hitler is a maniac (this in 1935).[108] But, in the closer-to-home case, he feels that he has to say more, lest the children fail to understand white people who are "common." Atticus explains that white people who use the word "nigger" have been corrupted; the word, he says, has "slipped into usage with some people like ourselves, when they want a common, ugly term to label somebody."[109]

Atticus says that the corrupters in this case were people who are "trash," meaning what my grandmother from Kentucky called "poor white trash," and meaning as well to invoke the harshest and most judgmental word Atticus—or, I suppose, any Southern gentleman—used. The Ewells, for example, are trash (Mayella excepted). Atticus tells the children that the "Ewells had been the disgrace of Maycomb for three generations. . . . They were people but they lived like animals."[110] He uses the word again to condemn white merchants who cheat black people; that practice, he says, is "ten times worse than cheatin' a white man . . . the worst thing you can do."[111] He seems to distinguish the merchant who preys on black people from the jurors who condemned an innocent man in the Robinson case; the jurors have lost their good sense—temporarily. The merchant is trash: "As you grow older, you'll see white men cheat black men every day of your life but let me tell you something and don't you forget it—whenever a white man does that to a black man, no matter who he is, how rich he is, or how fine a family he comes from, that white man is trash."[112]

The judgment Atticus hands down to his children regarding people who are trash seems to contradict the ethic he otherwise announces to them, namely, the ethic of climbing into the other person's skin. Maybe that is because the story needs a villain and Bob Ewell, who is trash, is it; maybe, too, there is a limit to the extent to which a good mentor can follow his own principles.[113] We are all subject, more than we might like to think, to the deviance systems our communities maintain for us. In any event, there are distinctions. Dolphus Raymond, the strange river dweller who comes to town at the time of the Robinson trial and comforts the children after they hear Mr. Gilmer abuse Tom Robinson in court, is ruled outside of decent society because he has married a black woman. However, the children, who talk to him and learn that he pretends to be drunk in public so that people will have a comfortable reason to condemn him, know he is not trash.[114] Dolphus might even cause the children to reflect on the category.

Community. After the trial and the Finches' return home, Atticus notices and explains to Scout that Jem has been deeply hurt by what he saw in the courthouse and that it will take time for his wounds to heal. Atticus becomes unusually voluble:

> They're ugly, but those are the facts of life. . . . [P]eople have a way of carrying their resentments right into a jury box. . . . Don't fool yourselves—it's all adding up and one of these days we're going to pay the bill for it. I hope it's not in you children's time.[115]

He does not seem to consider the possibility that he could leave Maycomb to pay its bills without him or that his children might leave before the bills have to be paid. He does not claim immunity from the debt. He recalls a point he made to Scout before the trial, after he told her they would not win the case: "We're fighting our friends," he said. "But remember this, no matter how bitter things get, they're still our friends and this is still our home."[116] And, to Alexandra, referring to what Maycomb is doing to Tom Robinson, he says, "This is their home, sister. . . . We've made it this way for them [the children], they might as well learn to cope with it."[117]

When Scout wonders, to Dill, why Boo Radley has never left the home in which his family keeps him prisoner, Dill, who knows a bit more than Scout about being rootless, says, "Maybe he doesn't have anywhere to run off to."[118] These Southern people regard their community as organic and inevitable—as fate. It is an attitude described by a Southern gentleman I know as a matter of "staying put."[119] Staying put is characteristic of stories about the South, as it is characteristic of stories of the Hebrew prophets. In one case Jeremiah stays in the city and goes into the dungeon; Socrates refused to flee Athens and suffered capital punishment instead. In the other, the Southerner stays put and accepts complicity in his community's evil. Complicity simply because, try as he might, no person can see clearly everything his community does to perpetuate its injustices. Staying put, even in complicity, reflects what Isaiah said when he accepted his commission from God:

Then said I "Woe *is* me! For I am undone; because I *am* a man of unclean lips, and I dwell in the midst of a people of unclean lips. . . . Also I heard the voice of the Lord, saying, "Whom shall I send, and who will go for us?" Then said I, "Here *am* I; send me." And he said, "Go. . . ."[120]

Class, Discrimination, and Respect. The moral culture in which the Finch children are formed is not an egalitarian culture. When Atticus, in his jury speech, reminds the jury that, in court, all people are equal,[121] he means to draw a contrast between the ethos they find in the law (an irony, surely, as he must have realized even as he said it) and the ethos they find outside the courtroom. Maycomb's is a class-based social order; children there are made to understand that what Miss Maudie calls "people of background" should control the society, and, if they cannot or do not control it, the society is worse for the absence of control.[122] The highest tribute the town can pay a person, she says, is to trust him with the sort of mission Atticus undertook when he agreed to defend Tom Robinson, but only "the handful of people in this town with background" understand.[123] Aunt Alexandra, for all of Atticus's scoffing at her snobbery, impresses on the children the peculiar and superior status of the Finch family in and around Maycomb and the burdens of leadership that go with superiority. Atticus accepts what is important in her campaign when he says to her, "I just hope that Jem and Scout come to me for their answers instead of listening to the town."[124]

Class is buffered in Maycomb by the practice of what Shirley Letwin calls the virtue of discrimination,[125] and by the virtue of respect. Discrimination is the practiced ability to tell people from one another and to treat them in a way that is consistent with their differences.[126] It is what causes the Sheriff and Atticus to lie to protect Boo Radley's seclusion when neither of them would have lied to protect Jem, the gentleman in training.[127] Discrimination is what caused Atticus to rush into Miss Maudie's burning house and rescue her old heavy oak rocking chair, when the other men in the neighborhood were trying to rescue more valuable property—"sensible of him," Scout thought, "to save what she valued most."[128] It is what causes Atticus to tell the children not to bother the Radleys, when he seems not to worry about them bothering Miss Maudie or Miss Stephanie Crawford, or even Mrs. Dubose (although he also, when he first heard of Boo's confinement, "shook his head and said, 'Mm, mm, mm'").[129]

Respect is the virtue that accepts the differences discrimination helps a person notice and then treats each person with dignity.[130] It is, as the Finch children learned it, a theological virtue.[131] It follows from the faith that the world and each person in it has been redeemed, is, as the Finches' Methodist ancestors would have put it, a child of God. Respect practiced at home causes Atticus to listen carefully to each side when his children come to him to adjudicate one of their quarrels;[132] it causes Dr. Jack, their uncle, to tell them in advance what he is going to do when his treatment of them causes pain; it causes Atticus to tell Mrs. Dubose that she is as pretty as a picture,[133] and the tyrannical Mr. Radley to come out of his house and greet Alexandra, to "come up in the front yard and say he was glad to see her."[134]

Scout, who at that point in the story has never seen Boo Radley, imagines what might happen if he were to come out of his house and sit on the front porch: "'Hidy do, Mr. Arthur,'" she would say, "as if I had said it every afternoon of my life. 'Evening, Jean Louise,' he would say, as if he had said it every afternoon of my life, 'right pretty spell we're having, isn't it?' 'Yes sir, right pretty,' I would say, and go on."[135]

When Boo does come out, after the attack on the children and after he kills Bob Ewell, he joins the Sheriff and Atticus on the front porch of the Finch house. He does not have a chair. Scout gets one for him, but she puts it at a distance from the others, "in deep shadow. Boo would feel more comfortable in the dark."[136] She is practicing respect, as well as discrimination, as the children are when they turn their snowman into what Miss Maudie calls "an absolute morphodite," by putting an apron on him, because they at first made the snowman look too much like their neighbor Mr. Avery.[137] This sort of thing is often spoken of as Southern courtesy, and it is that; but in this story, which is a story about how children are taught the virtues, it is shown to be a practice that is necessary when a society preserves both its memory and a faith that says every person is redeemed.

Conclusion

Growing up good in Maycomb is as ordinary and as deep and profound as Patrick Henry's "Johannanine Haiku":

> The Word became Flesh
> and dwelt among us and said
> "Come and have breakfast"—
> which is not
> Exactly
> what we would have expected.[138]

Notes

1. Elie Wiesel, *Nostra Aetate: An Observer's Perspective*, 67 *Thought* 366, 368 (1992).

2. "[A] name means continuity with the past and people without a past are people without a name." Milan Kundera, *The Book of Laughter and Forgetting* 157 (Michael H. Heim trans., Alfred A. Knopf, Inc. 1981) (1978).

3. "[I]f Plato is correct . . . if our environment shapes our perceptions and judgments of goodness," Gilbert Meilaender argues, "one whose vision of the good is not properly shaped in childhood may never come to see." Gilbert C. Meilaender, *The Theory and Practice of Virtue* 54 (1984). Plato's program, as Meilaender describes it, begins in early childhood, to attachments he calls "erotic"—so that the child will "praise the fine things; and, taking pleasure in them . . . be reared on them and become a gentleman." *Id.* at 55 (quoting Socrates). This is done largely through stories, because "we must *learn* to delight in what is good" even before we learn that what we delight in is good. *Id.* (emphasis added). "If we want to teach morality . . . we must begin by teaching something else." *Id.* at 56. At the end, Plato's program leaves the reasoning adult

with a capacity for moral conversation and with what a traditional Catholic would call a settled conscience: If, at that time, moral argument seems fruitless—as it often must have seemed to Atticus Finch—it is not because what is good "is only a matter of opinion, but because our character and commitments help to determine what we see." *Id.* at 68. Some do not see. When Atticus recommends that his children imagine themselves to be inside the skin of Boo Radley's brother, or the new school teacher from North Alabama, or Mr. Cunningham, it is not because what is good is a matter of opinion, but so that the children will imagine the world as it appears to another person—not so that they will see the world, themselves, that way, but so that they will learn to love. *See infra* notes 40 and 46. Aristotle also discusses the origin of virtue:

> [N]one of the moral virtues is implanted in us by nature, for nothing which exists by nature can be changed by habit. . . . Furthermore, of all the qualities with which we are endowed by nature, we are provided with the capacity first, and display the activity afterward. . . . The virtues . . . we acquire by first having put them into action. . . . For the things which we have to learn before we can do them we learn by doing: men become builders by building houses, and harpists by playing the harp. Similarly, we become just by the practice of just actions, self-controlled by exercising self-control, and courageous by performing acts of courage. . . . For that reason, we must see to it that our activities are of a certain kind, since any variations in them will be reflected in our characteristics. Hence it is no small matter whether one habit or another is inculcated in us from early childhood; on the contrary, it makes a considerable difference, or, rather, all the difference.

Aristotle, *Nicomachean Ethics* 33-35 (Martin Ostwald trans., 1962). *See* Alasdair MacIntyre, *Whose Justice? Which Rationality?* 113-14, 195-96 (1988).

4. Charles Lamb, *Epigraph to* Harper Lee, *To Kill A Mockingbird* (Popular Library 1962) (1960).

5. Amasa Lee, of the Monroeville, Alabama, Bar. Charles Moritz ed., *Harper Lee, Current Biography Yearbook*, 1961, at 260. Judge Walter Jones's compilation of all lawyers licensed to practice in Alabama from 1818 until 1948 lists 19 lawyers named Lee. Walter B. Jones, *Alabama Lawyers, 1818-1918*, 9 Ala. Law. 123, 158 (1948).

6. Alice F. Lee, of the Monroeville, Alabama, Bar. Amasa Lee and his wife Frances Finch had three children; Nelle Harper, born in 1926, was the youngest. *Current Biography Yearbook, supra* note 5.

7. James McMillan wrote of Lee's work: "*To Kill a Mockingbird* is a superior book because it was written by a superior person." James B. McMillan, *Book Reviews*, 14 Ala. Rev. 233 (1961).

8. "[Southern] women were 'ladies'—gentle, refined, ethereal beings, passion and devotion wrapped in forms of ethereal mould, and surrounded by an impalpable effulgence which distinguished them from all others of the sex throughout the world." Merrill Maguire Skaggs, *The Folk of Southern Fiction* 5 (1972). I write "slightly quaint" because I am worried about being only a man—but there is evidence that the ideal here is not, after all, so quaint. *See, e.g.*, Bailey White, *Mama Makes Up Her Mind* (1993).

9. Harper Lee, *To Kill a Mockingbird*, ch. 24 (Popular Library 1962) (1960).

10. *See infra* notes 11 and 17 and accompanying text.

11. Lee, *supra* note 9, at 232; *see also* Christiane Bird, *Harper Lee*, in *Two American Women Writers: A Critical Reference Guide From Colonial Times to the Present* 540 (Lina Mainiero, ed., 1980) (speaking of the theme of the novel as a "gradual moral awakening."). If so, this attitude in Scout occurs a moment after sleep.

12. Lee, *supra* note 9, at 233.

13. Lee, *supra* note 9, at 233.

14. Lee, *supra* note 9, at 233.

15. Lee, *supra* note 9, at 234-36.

16. Lee, *supra* note 9, at 93.

17. Prudence is necessary to the exercise of the other virtues because we need prudence in order to exercise judgment and undertake action in particular situations; it is through judgment and action in particular situations that we acquire and strengthen the virtues. MacIntyre, *supra* note 3, at 196. Karen Lebacqz speaks of prudence, in particular reference to living virtuously as a professional, as a matter of moral discernment—"perceiving accurately what is required." Karen Lebacqz, *Professional Ethics: Power and Paradox* 105 (1985). Prudence is, William May says, "to be still, to be silent, to listen," and "readiness for the unexpected." William May, *The Virtues in a Professional Setting*, in *The Annual of the Society of Christian Ethics* 71, 83 (1984).

18. Aristotle describes friendship as collaboration in the good. *See* Thomas L. Shaffer, *The Legal Profession's Rule Against Vouching for Clients: Advocacy and "The Manner That Is the Man Himself,"* 7 *Notre Dame J.L. Ethics & Pub. Pol'y* 145, 169-75 (1993) (discussing the virtue of friendship). An example: Scout says that Atticus, in talking to Mrs. Dubose about her flowers, "gets her interested in something nice, so she forgets to be mean." Horton Foote, *The Screenplay of To Kill a Mockingbird* 17 (1964). It is important to notice what this casual and courteous effort to draw Mrs. Dubose's attention away from her bigotry is. The collaboration Aristotle associated with friendship is not just any sort of collaboration. Human beings are manifestly able to combine their talents in order to do evil as some of Mrs. Dubose's neighbors collaborated in her bigotry. As Santayana's Rev. Darnley, the vicar of Effley, put it:

> [T]o serve our neighbour and to love him is to serve and to love God. But that is only when you love and foster in your neighbour his participation in divine life, his approach to some sort of perfection. If you love him for his weakness, because he succumbs to you, or serve him in his folly, you are devoting yourself to the service of his vices; you are his worst enemy, as well as God's; and you hate his soul and destroy it.

George Santayana, *The Last Puritan* 253 (Charles Scribner's Sons 1936) (1935). *See infra* note 40.

19. With some misgiving I am preserving here the custom in Maycomb, at the time of the story, of not referring to black people with courtesy titles.

20. Lee, *supra* note 9, at 157.

21. The novel does not describe the moment in which Atticus accepted the appoint-

ment. The screenplay for the movie version does describe it, although the exchange, on the front porch of the Finch home, in the evening, Scout and Jem listening through the window, is prosaic: Judge: "I was thinking about appointing you to take the case. . . ." Atticus: "Yes Sir. (*Reflects thoughtfully.*) I'll take the case." Horton Foote, *To Kill a Mockingbird, Tender Mercies, and The Trip to Bountiful: Three Screenplays* 18 (1989).

22. I intentionally avoid the word autonomy. Independence, as I discern it from American cultures, is an aspect of what my daughter Mary and I have called the virtue of respect (in Italian, *rispetto*), which is the virtue that trains a child to hold on to her selfhood as she lives out the given anthropology of a life that first puts her in the family, then in the neighborhood, then in the town, etc. Thomas L. Shaffer & Mary M. Shaffer, *American Lawyers and Their Communities* chs. 6-7 (1991). Community in a person's life is, then, like concentric circles, or the ripples that form from a stone dropped into still water. Love begins and is always most intense in the closest circle, the communities in which one is fixed by biology and in which one is dependent. Pope argues that it is natural for us to love those closest to us, from which, he says, follow three things: (i) a preference for kin and friends; (ii) the presence of friendship in "egoistic and reciprocal relationships" (what Aristotle called "base friendship"); and (iii) the development of altruism (in the increasingly broader succession of communities in which the person finds herself) from these two sources (family and base friendships). Stephen J. Pope, *The Order of Love and Recent Catholic Ethics: A Constructive Proposal*, 52 *Theological Studies* 255, 287 (1991). An anthropology of self-rule (autonomy) says or assumes that values and habits have value because they are *chosen*; it seems to me a profoundly false account of the way people are. *See* Shaffer & Shaffer, *supra* at ch. 1.

23. Lee, *supra* note 9, at 236.

24. Lee, *supra* note 9, at 240.

25.

Education in the spiritual life means that children must see before them adults who don't go to pieces over a lost job or damaged property, who are not bitter over a death or illness, who don't envy the rich, or condemn as a coward one who doesn't take vengeance. Despite the pain and sorrow that such events bring, we are not to become unglued by them, as though we had no source of strength beyond ourselves. Children need models of virtue.

Margaret Lucy Dodds, *A Handy Pocket Guide to the Christian Life*, 97 *The Christian Century* 441, 443 (1980). *See* George A. Lindbeck, *The Nature of Doctrine: Religion and Theology in a Postliberal Age* 60-62 (1984) (speaking of a child's learning in this way—from models—as similar to the way we learn a language). *See also supra* note 3 (discussing how children learn morality).

26. June Tapp and Felice Levine provide evidence that this is the way moral education in fact takes place—that "strong affective attachment . . . is . . . more important . . . than punishment power," for example. June L. Tapp & Felice J. Levine, *Persuasion to Virtue*, 4 Law & Soc'y Rev. 565, 576 (1970). Persuasion is a more effective teacher than coercion. *Id.* at 580. Evident virtue persuades to virtue: "If authority figures . . . are to have positive impact, it will be largely through strong and manifest displays of 'good,'" particularly in the way the adult teacher and model treats children. *Id.* at 577.

This moral training is prior to and more powerful than training in rules. For example, children in the Tapp-Levine study were asked when it is moral to break a moral rule. One child said, "It depends on what's going on." *Id.* at 573. Another says, "If it's a matter of . . . something pretty important, then it's all right." *Id.* These children were being trained in the virtue of prudence. *See* May, *supra* note 17, at 83.

27. This is like a role, and in that way like much of what one reads in the modern literature of legal ethics, about lawyers having to take on roles. It is like that, but it is also a denial. See Thomas L. Shaffer, *Faith and the Professions* ch. 3 (1987).

28. *Id.* at 42-47; see Shaffer & Shaffer, *supra* note 22, at 58-65.

29. See Aristotle, *supra* note 3, at 33-35.

30. Lee, *supra* note 9, at 118.

31. Lee, *supra* note 9, at 29.

32. Lee, *supra* note 9, at 33.

33. Lee, *supra* note 9, at 38.

34. Lee, *supra* note 9, at 86.

35. Lee, *supra* note 9, at 139.

36. Lee, *supra* note 9, at 159.

37. Irony "depends upon an observer who is not so hostile to the victim of irony as to deny the element of virtue which must constitute a part of the ironic situation; nor yet so sympathetic as to discount the weakness, the vanity and pretension which constitute another element." Reinhold Niebuhr, *The Irony of American History* 153 (1962). Miss Lee describes with great skill irony as childish honesty and clear vision.

38. Lee, *supra* note 9, at 29.

39. Lee, *supra* note 9, at 128.

40. See Thomas L. Shaffer, *American Legal Ethics* 16-17 (1985) (discussing Mrs. Dubose and the filmmakers' treatment of the last scene in the novel).

41. Lee, *supra* note 9, at 39.

42. This aspect of the episode is, perhaps, an example of what Fred Erisman refers to as traditional Southern romanticism. Fred Erisman, *The Romantic Regionalism of Harper Lee*, 26 Ala. Rev. 122, 123 (1973). Another "Southern gentleman" example is in a family recollection of the behavior of William Faulkner. Faulkner's niece, Dean Faulkner Wells, remembered when her uncle (whom she called Pappy) took her to a tea given for fourth-grade girls and their escorts.

> Miss Jenkins [the lady pouring tea] said to me, "lemon or cream?" Not wanting to say the wrong thing, I finally replied, "both." She glanced at me, but went ahead and poured. Pappy was behind me in line. . . . When Miss Jenkins asked him which he preferred, he said, "both," as calmly as you please. Neither of them smiled. I felt an immense relief. Pappy sat down beside me and we stared at the mess in our delicate china cups and tried to drink some of it.

Susie James, *Homage to William Faulkner's Homestead, Wash. Post*, Aug. 13, 1980, at B-2.

43. It was a clear violation of the confidentiality rule stated in the Alabama Code of Ethics for Lawyers. Code of Ethics adopted by Alabama Bar Association, No. 21, 118

Alabama Reports xxiii (1899); compare *Model Rules of Professional Conduct* Rule 1.6 (1992).

44. This is like the Sheriff's (and Atticus's) view that being shut away was the moral thing to do for Boo Radley. See Lee, *supra* note 9, at 279.

45. A brave old woman is also important to the formation in truthfulness and courage of Gavin Stevens's nephew Chick, in Faulkner's similar story, *Intruder in the Dust*. William Faulkner, *Intruder in the Dust* (Vintage Books 1972) (1948). What good old women show in these stories is not only what is to be done, but the strength for doing it—both the intellectual content in the virtue of courage and the aspect of courage that keeps us from being so afraid that we are disabled. They thus complete the inadequate ethic that is formed by rules: "Both God and Miss Manners expect people to behave well in their daily life, but while Miss Manners is willing to supply them the rules for doing so, she does not presume to tell them where to get the strength." Judith Martin, *Miss Manners, Wash. Post*, Nov. 4, 1979, at G-17.

46. Lee, *supra* note 9, at 94.

47. Lee, *supra* note 9, at 49.

48. See William Faulkner, *Dry September*, in *Collected Stories of William Faulkner* 169-83 (1934).

49. Lee, *supra* note 9, at 14.

50. Lee, *supra* note 9, at 137.

51. Lee, *supra* note 9, at 131.

52. Lee, *supra* note 9, at 124.

53. Fred Erisman thinks that what lies ahead is indicated in the novel and that it is "a newer and more vital form of romanticism . . . reasonable, pragmatic, and native . . . truly regional in its vision." Erisman, *supra* note 42, at 123.

54. Lee, *supra* note 9, at 271-73.

55. Lee, *supra* note 9, at 280.

56. Lee, *supra* note 9, at 281.

57. Lee, *supra* note 9, at 280.

58. Lee, *supra* note 9, at 281.

59. Lee, *supra* note 9, at 34.

60. Cynthia Ozick treats this faith as the disciplined use of metaphor. Reflecting on the Lord's saying to Israel (through Moses), "You were strangers in Egypt," for example:

> [D]octors can imagine what it is to be their patients. Those who have no pain can imagine those who suffer. Those at the center can imagine what it is to be outside. The strong can imagine what it is to be weak. . . . We strangers can imagine the familiar hearts of strangers.

Cynthia Ozick, *The Moral Reality of Metaphor*, 272 *Harper's* 62, 68 (1986). Christian theology tends to relate a recognition of "the familiar hearts of strangers" to forgiveness. *Id.* Forgiveness through understanding others involves, and I follow here, a theology developed (from Karl Barth) by Milner S. Ball, in his important new book, *The Word and the Law*. Using the critical designation "Word" to identify the Christ, from the opening verses of St. John's Gospel, Ball says: The Word generates faith rather than religion. However, faith is not necessarily separable from religion. As Barth said:

> Faith is neither religion nor irreligion, neither sacred nor profane; it is always both together. Religion is not to be discarded. . . . Religion is the attempt to know God. God's self-revelation does not correspond to religion but contradicts it. Nevertheless, revelation can and does adopt religion. This is so not because religion is privileged or especially apt to revelation, but because religion belongs to the human condition. . . . In embracing humanity, the Word embraces religion.

Milner S. Ball, *The Word and the Law* 100 (1993) (quoting Karl Barth, *Epistle to the Romans* 128 (Edwyn Hoskyns trans., 6th ed. 1933)).
   61. Lee, *supra* note 9, at 26.
   62. Lee, *supra* note 9, at 25.
   63. Faulkner, *supra* note 45.
   64. Lee, *supra* note 9, at 153-55.
   65. Lee, *supra* note 9, at 155.
   66. Lee, *supra* note 9, at 156.
   67. Lee, *supra* note 9, at 27-28.
   68. Lee, *supra* note 9, at 155. In reference to her conversation with Mr. Cunningham, in front of the jail, Scout says, his "legal affairs were well known to me; Atticus had once described them at length." *Id. See supra* note 43 (discussing violation of the ethics code). Scout has absorbed much of Atticus's straight talk about law. She complains, for example, that "the only message Jem got from Atticus was insight into the art of cross-examination." Lee, *supra* note 9, at 55. Scout, too: "Never, never, never, on cross-examination ask a witness a question you don't already know the answer to, was a tenet I absorbed with my baby-food." Lee, *supra* note 9, at 179.
   69. Lee, *supra* note 9, at 156.
   70. Lee, *supra* note 9, at 156.
   71. Lee, *supra* note 9, at 159-60.
   72. In the screenplay, Foote describes the scene:

> (ATTICUS *holds the sack of nuts.* SCOUT *is on the steps behind him.* SCOUT *leans on Atticus' shoulders as they watch* MR. CUNNINGHAM *leave.*)
> Scout, I think maybe next time Mr. Cunningham comes, you better not call me.
> SCOUT: Well, I thought you'd want to thank him.
> ATTICUS: Oh, I do. I think it embarrasses him to be thanked.

Foote, *supra* note 21, at 6-7.
   73. Ball, *supra* note 60, at 100.
   74. Ball, *supra* note 60, at 101.
   75. Ball, *supra* note 60, at 101 (quoting Karl Barth, *Church Dogmatics*, I/2 at 485).
   76. Lee, *supra* note 9, at 198-201.
   77. Lee, *supra* note 9, at 184.

78. Lee, *supra* note 9, at 113. The love commandment, Victor Furnish says, is not given as impractical

> and therefore used to convict people of sin or to engender a sense of guilt. On the contrary, in every instance it is formulated as an eminently practicable commandment for readers who are presumed to understand themselves as members of a community called and empowered by God to be a new people. . . . In every case the commandment is conveyed as a specific rule for behavior or . . . the means by which all the other rules are to be interpreted.

Victor P. Furnish, *Love of Neighbor in the New Testament*, 10 *J. Religious Ethics* 327, 333 (1982). Jesus had that understanding as an educated and observant Jew.

79. *See supra* note 22. The model is primarily parental. *See* Arthur Dyck, *Loving Impartiality in Moral Cognition*, in *The Annual of the Soc'y of Christian Ethics* 55-72 (D. M. Yaeger ed., 1989).

80. Lee, *supra* note 9, at 145.

81. Lee, *supra* note 9, at 81.

82. Lee, *supra* note 9, at 122.

83. Lee, *supra* note 9, at 284.

84. Lee, *supra* note 9, at 173.

85. Lee, *supra* note 9, at 13.

86. Karl Barth, *Epistle to the Romans* 128 (Edwyn Hoskyns trans., 6th ed. 1933); *see supra* note 56 (discussing Milner Ball's theology developed from Karl Barth).

87. Ball, *supra* note 60, at 100.

88. Barth, *supra* note 86, at 258.

89. Barth, *supra* note 86, at 176.

90. Ball, *supra* note 60, at 101.

91. Ball, *supra* note 60, at 100.

92. "Faulkner is a profoundly religious writer; . . . [h]is characters come out of a Christian environment, and represent, whatever their shortcomings and whatever their theological heresies, Christian concerns; . . . they are finally to be understood only by reference to Christian premises." Cleanth Brooks, *The Hidden God* 22-23 (1963). I see this hidden God (partially) in *To Kill a Mockingbird* as well. But I mean, with reference to Atticus, in the church, to suggest as well a religion that is encompassed by faith. In a more faithful representation, the church Atticus belongs to would be more than a subculture of the Maycomb community. See Julian N. Hartt, *A Christian Critique of American Culture* (1967). The church, Barth says, is

> held together by the fact that it has the freedom, and no choice but to use this given freedom, to call God our Father. . . . As the community of the one Lord, it is not a monolith or collective in which the individual can be no more than a functioning organ, one among many moved and moving wheels in a mechanism. It is a people in which, as all these freed and free persons have a common Father, they are related, responsible, and united to one another.

Karl Barth, *The Christian Life* 82-83 (Geoffrey W. Bromiley trans., 1981). The church, so understood, and faithful in this way, would not, I think, have supported racism—support that is casually described in the story by the fact that the black and white Methodist churches are separate and that the white Methodist church is part of a denomination divided from its counterpart in the North.

Of course Barth's notion of the church has, throughout the history of Christianity, been more a theological proposition than a social reality. *See* Thomas L. Shaffer, *Erastian and Sectarian Arguments in Religiously Affiliated American Law Schools*, 45 *Stan. L. Rev.* 1859 (1993), and Shaffer, *supra* note 40, at ch. 8. What prophets like Atticus do in the formal worshipping community is to remind the *religiously* faithful both of their collective failure and of the fact that this *people* (who they are), this community, has within itself the guidance and the energy to overcome its failure. I have used and recommend three modern and powerful texts in teaching law students about these two theological arguments—which, as I say, Atticus might have made—Walter Brueggemann, *Interpretation and Obedience: From Faithful Reading to Faithful Living* (1991); Stanley Hauerwas & William H. Willimon, *Resident Aliens: Life in the Christian Colony* (1989); and John P. Reeder, Jr., *Visions of Community*, 16 *Religious Stud. Rev.* 28 (1990).

93. It is, nonetheless, an organic community. Cf. Thomas L. Shaffer, *The Legal Ethics of Radical Individualism*, 65 *Tex. L. Rev.* 963 (1987) (viewing the organic community as prior to individuality). Maycomb was, I think, a community in which moral discourse was possible. The community, as it forms its children, may mislead and shape badly. The answer is to provide enough space "for differing visions of what is good." Meilaender, *supra* note 3, at 69. I would say that moral discourse is possible where the community leaves enough space for prophets to speak and to be heard. See Shaffer, *supra* note 27. Neither Meilaender's argument nor my way of putting it means that all visions are true; we mean that it is possible, in such a community, to look, to see, and to talk to our neighbors about what we see—all of that within a coherent vision of the good:

> Successful moral education requires a community which does not hesitate to inculcate virtue in the young, which does not settle for the discordant opinions of alternative visions of the good. . . . For moral education requires that virtuous exemplars be presented the young, not that a thousand choices be given. At the same time . . . communities which do not permit the virtues they inculcate to be transcended by what is good . . . cut themselves off from the very source which inspired their efforts to shape character. Perhaps communities which seek seriously to inculcate virtue while also gathering regularly to confess their failures and recommit themselves to what is good are the best we can manage.

Meilaender, *supra* note 3, at 72.
94. Lee, *supra* note 9, at 39-40.
95. Lee, *supra* note 9, at 281.
96. Lee, *supra* note 9, at 17.
97. Lee, *supra* note 9, at 58.

98. When Miss Maudie's house burned down, Nathan Radley joined the rest of the neighborhood in helping put out the fire. Lee, *supra* note 9, at 76.

99. Lee, *supra* note 9, at 134.

100. The children puzzle over an editorial cartoon that shows Atticus, the legislator, "barefooted and in short pants, chained to a desk" and ignoring "frivolous-looking girls" who are yelling "yoo-hoo" at him. Jem says the point is that Atticus does "things that wouldn't get done if nobody did 'em. . . . [I]t's like reorganizing the tax systems of the counties and things." Lee, *supra* note 9, at 119. I think of Trollope's parliamentary gentleman, Plantagenet Palliser, who devoted himself to devising and attempting to sell (to a smug and uninterested Victorian society) a decimal system of coinage. Trollope, *The Prime Minister* (Oxford 1951) (1876).

101. Lee, *supra* note 9, at 134.

102. Lee, *supra* note 9, at 158.

103. Lee, *supra* note 9, at 105.

104. Lee, *supra* note 9, at 84.

105. Lee, *supra* note 9, at 94.

106. W. Sibley Towner includes the prophet's use of the rhetoric of secular life and the fact that the prophet's constituencies are the community of court, cult, and school. The prophet's message is one he finds in sacred tradition, particularly the tradition of covenant that one finds in Judaism and in Calvinist Christianity. The prophet compares that heritage with what the community is doing. The prophet in this biblical model is an insider (e.g., the prophet Nathan, in King David's court, II *Samuel* 12). W. Sibley Towner, *On Calling People "Prophets," in 1970*, 24 *Interpretation* 492 (1970). *See* Thomas L. Shaffer, *On Being A Christian and a Lawyer* ch. 10 (1981). Like saints, as James William McClendon argues, prophets have a faith which is against the church. But this faith is *in* the church and it sustains the church. James W. McClendon, Jr., *Biography as Theology* 204-15 (1974). A prophet, in Gaylord Noyce's phrase, is "always . . . chipping away at wrong. The wrong is in us and it is in the structures around us." Gaylord Noyce, *The Dilemmas of Christians in Business*, 98 *The Christian Century* 802, 803 (1981). A slightly more debatable notion is that the prophet is also *in complicity* with the wrong that his community is doing; that, I think, is an important aspect of the Southern gentleman-lawyer as prophet in stories such as Atticus's and Gavin Stevens's. *See* Shaffer & Shaffer, *supra* note 22, at ch. 4. John Reeder puts it as, "one stands on part of the raft while repairing another part. . . . The individual always works with an inherited social repertoire even when elements are discarded or radically reinterpreted." John Reeder, *Visions of Community*, 16 *Religious Stud. Rev.* 28, 29 (1990). It may be useful, on this point about complicity, to notice Karl Jaspers's and Calvin Schrag's distinction between community and conformity; they present those as *alternatives*—so that the person I am calling a prophet can either conform to what his community is doing or take the alternative course. This would be particularly important in biblical theology, where Israel is a priestly people chosen and rechosen, disciplined and redeemed, by the God of history—a people who need prophets to remind it of what it is. It would also be important to an adequate notion, for Christians, of what the church is.

107. Lee, *supra* note 9, at 276-78.

108. Lee, *supra* note 9, at 113.

109. Lee, *supra* note 9, at 113. Children are, by hearing and imitating such usage, trained in vice. Faulkner tells of a seven-year-old white boy, growing up with his black foster-brother: "Then one day the old curse of his fathers, the haughty ancestral pride based not on any value but on an accident of geography, stemmed not from courage and honor but from wrong and shame, descended to him." William Faulkner, *Go Down, Moses* 111 (Vintage Books 1973) (1942). See Kundera, *supra* note 2.

110. Lee, *supra* note 9, at 35.

111. Lee, *supra* note 9, at 204.

112. Lee, *supra* note 9, at 223. The mob that comes to lynch Tom Robinson includes such people, but it also includes Mr. Cunningham and other farmers and the sort of citizens who served on the jury. It is interesting that it does not involve the Ku Klux Klan: Jem suggests to Atticus that the Klan was involved, but Atticus says not. Jem says he had heard that the Klan in Maycomb got after some Catholics once. Atticus says he never heard of any Catholics in Maycomb. "You're confusing that with something else," he says. "Way back about nineteen-twenty there was a Klan, but it was a political organization more than anything. Besides, they couldn't find anybody to scare." Lee, *supra* note 9, at 149. He remembers that the Maycomb Klan did attempt to intimidate Mr. Sam Levy, but Mr. Levy, farmer and leader of a family that, Scout says, were among Maycomb's "Fine Folks," made them feel ashamed of themselves. Lee, *supra* note 9, at 149. Atticus is naive when he tells Jem, in reference to the broader community, "The Ku Klux Klan's gone. It'll never come back," but there is no evidence in the story that it came back to Maycomb. Lee, *supra* note 9, at 149.

113. It is easy to imagine that the trials and appeals in the Scottsboro case were in Miss Lee's mind when she told the story of Tom Robinson's trial. *See* Dan T. Carter, *Scottsboro: A Tragedy of the American South* (1969). It is interesting, though, that Atticus did not make an issue, as defense lawyers in some of the Scottsboro trials and appeals did, of the exclusion of black people (or, for that matter, of women) from juries, and did not insist, as those lawyers sometimes did, that courtesy titles be used when addressing black witnesses. *See supra* note 19.

114. Lee, *supra* note 9, at 163, 203-04.

115. Lee, *supra* note 9, at 223.

116. Lee, *supra* note 9, at 81.

117. Lee, *supra* note 9, at 215.

118. Lee, *supra* note 9, at 146.

119. Staying put is a principal theme in Faulkner's *Intruder in the Dust* and appears as a theme in his other work. William Faulkner, *Intruder in the Dust* (Vintage Books 1972) (1948). "A gentleman can live through anything," the grandfather in *The Reivers* says. "He faces anything. A gentleman accepts the responsibility of his actions and bears the burden of their consequences, even when he did not himself instigate them but only acquiesced to them, didn't say No though he knew he should." William Faulkner, *The Reivers* 302 (1962). "In accepting his fellow townspeople as necessarily flawed human beings," Carol R. Rigsby says of Gavin Stevens's nephew Chick, "he is no longer ashamed to count himself among them." Carol R. Rigsby, *Chick Mallison's Expectations and Intruder in the Dust*, 29 *Miss. Q.* 389 (1975-1976). Edmund Wilson might have said of Miss Lee's story what he said of Faulkner's stories, when he wrote:

> I do not sympathize with the line of criticism which deplores Faulkner's obstinate persistence in submerging himself in the mentality of the community where he was born, for his chivalry, which constitutes his morality, is a part of his Southern heritage, and it appears in Faulkner's work as a force more humane and more positive than almost anything one can find in the work of even those writers of our more mechanized society who have set out to defend human rights.

Edmund Wilson, *Books: William Faulkner's Reply to the Civil-Rights Program*, 24 *The New Yorker* 35 (Oct. 23, 1948). The bond that makes staying put possible is affection. As Walker Percy put it, "These Louisianians, for all their differences and contrariness, have an affection for one another. It is expressed by small signs and courtesies, even between strangers, as if they shared a secret." Walker Percy, *The Thanatos Syndrome* viii (1987).

120. *Isaiah* 6:5, 6:8-9 (King James).

121.

> [T]here is one way in this country in which all men are created equal—there is one human institution that makes a pauper the equal of a Rockefeller, the stupid man the equal of an Einstein, and the ignorant man the equal of any college president. That institution, gentlemen, is a court.

Lee, *supra* note 9, at 208.

122. Lee, *supra* note 9, at 239.

123. Lee, *supra* note 9, at 239.

124. Lee, *supra* note 9, at 93.

125. Shirley R. Letwin, *The Gentleman in Trollope: Individuality and Moral Conduct* 68 (1982). "His honesty leads him to speak differently to friends and to strangers, in private and in public. He will lie to a murderer in order to save his friend, though his honesty will keep him from pretending . . . that he has not lied." *Id.* at 72. "When faced with transgressors," she says, "the gentleman will consider whether he is faced with an eccentric, a ruffian, or a villain." *Id.* at 69. And he will act differently with each of them. *See* Shaffer, *supra* note 40, at 45 (discussing gentlemen's eccentricities).

126. See Letwin, *supra* note 125, at 68.

127. At first, Atticus thinks that Jem killed Bob Ewell and that the Sheriff's lie is meant to hide the fact.

128. Lee, *supra* note 9, at 74.

129. Lee, *supra* note 9, at 15.

130. See Letwin, *supra* note 125, at 68.

131. Finally, respect is love bestowed, and, as such, it is constituent of faith and of the discernment of God's action in the world. *See supra* note 18 and accompanying text. Respect is here a virtue that causes the virtuous person to go beyond perception, because love is *bestowed* on the other as well as *perceived* in him—or, rather, because it is bestowed it is perceived:

[L]ove outstrips valuation and respects the dignity of other persons rather than merely computing their utility. Given these facts, putting charity first is actually the surest means to the *avoidance* of cruelty. It furthermore limits the sort of ubiquitous irony that must eventually be self-defeating because it is insufficiently other-affirming.

Timothy P. Jackson, *The Disconsolation of Theology: Irony, Cruelty, and Putting Charity First*, 20 *J. Religious Ethics* 1, 29 (1992). The other person is then approached, as I think both Professor Ball and Karl Barth would put it, as redeemed. *See supra* note 92 and accompanying text. Stanley Hauerwas speaks of this as a method of perception, as a way of finding out what is going on in the world and what God is doing in it; he borrows Iris Murdoch's phrase, "just and loving gaze" and notices that convention (*cf.* Jackson's references to irony and the avoidance of cruelty) is as much an obstacle to such perception as neurosis is. Stanley Hauerwas, *Vision and Virtue* 30-45 (1974). The late Professor Warren Lehman, referring to the lawyer-client relationship as moral discourse in much the same spirit, said, "We are dealing with the most difficult problems of the interior and virtuous life. . . . We must speak . . . gently to the spirit." Warren Lehman, *The Pursuit of a Client's Interest*, 77 *Mich. L. Rev.* 1078, 1078 (1979).

132. *See* Lee, *supra* note 9, at 90.

133. Lee, *supra* note 9, at 104.

134. Lee, *supra* note 9, at 131.

135. Lee, *supra* note 9, at 245.

136. Lee, *supra* note 9, at 275.

137. Lee, *supra* note 9, at 72.

138. Patrick Henry, *Johannanine Haiku*, 38 *Theology Today* 479 (1982). "What is a home?" Walker Percy asked. "A home is a place, any place, any building, where one sinks into one's self and finds company waiting." Walker Percy, *The Second Coming* 242 (1980). I am grateful, as if I had been served breakfast at their hands (as I am, rather often), for the kind assistance of Mary M. Shaffer-Seytre and Nancy J. Shaffer.

Atticus Finch and the Mad Dog:
Harper Lee's *To Kill a Mockingbird*_____

Carolyn Jones

> One must think like a hero to behave
> like a merely decent human being.
>
> —May Sarton

In the spring of 1960, in the midst of the major events of the civil rights movement, J. B. Lippincott and Company published Harper Lee's *To Kill a Mockingbird*. A Pulitzer Prize winner which was made later into an Academy Award-winning film, the novel became and remains a bestseller. Yet, this novel which captured the imagination while it criticized the morality of American adults is classified as "young adult literature." This classification has caused the work to be ignored by the critical community and has undercut the power of the image of the modern hero that it presents. The dominant voice of *To Kill a Mockingbird* is not that of a child but that of a woman looking back at an event that tore at the fabric of childhood and of her community and that shaped her adulthood.

To Kill a Mockingbird is about three years (approximately 1933-1936) in the childhood of Jean Louise Finch, better known as Scout, and the coming of age of Scout and her brother Jem in the household of their father, Atticus Finch. It is also about two seemingly unrelated things—the trial of a black man, Tom Robinson, for rape and the attempts of Jem, Scout and their friend Dill to make Boo Radley come out of his house. Boo, a man who, for his lifetime, is confined to his house, first, by his father and, later, by his uncle for committing a minor offense as a teenager, becomes a catalyst for the imagination and a symbol by which the children come to understand, in their particular ways, Tom Robinson's trial. For Jem, the boy coming into manhood, the desire to see Boo is abandoned with Tom's conviction, and Jem moves into the adult world. For Scout, however, who is a child of about nine, Boo becomes the source of her imagination and the inspiration for her career as a writer. Thus, *To Kill a Mockingbird* shows the reader the importance of the imagination in the formation of the moral human being.

Yet, the children do not reach their understandings of Boo and Tom alone. The relationship of Boo Radley to Tom Robinson is mediated by Atticus Finch, the hero of the novel. Through the actions and thoughts of her father, Scout is able to make sense of Boo and Tom as she criticizes the morality of 1930s and 1960s America. Atticus's moral structure gives form to the imagination that Scout's meeting with Boo fires. Atticus is not the typical modern hero: he is neither angst-ridden nor decontextualized. He is a widower, a father, a lawyer and a neighbor—in short, an ordinary man living his life in a community. Yet, he stands as a supreme example of the moral life, and he communicates that morality to his children and, ultimately, to the community by his actions. Atticus's ordinary heroism embodies three components: the call for critical reflection on the self, the rule of compassion, and the law that it is a sin to kill a mockingbird. This heroism is illustrated in three key scenes in which he confronts mad dogs.

The first of these scenes introduces the theme of the mad dog and its importance to the novel. Jem and Scout have been bemoaning the fact that their father is the most uninteresting man in town; "Our father," Scout tells us, "didn't do anything" (94). When he gives Jem and Scout air rifles for Christmas, he also refuses to teach them to shoot. This winter, however, is one of amazing portents, foreshadowing the trial of Tom Robinson and the emergence of Boo Radley: it snows for the first time in years; the Finchs' neighbor, Miss Maudie's house burns down; and a mad dog named Tim Johnson appears in February on the main street of Maycomb.

Heck Tate, the sheriff, refuses to shoot the mad dog himself. Much to the children's amazement—they nearly fainted, Scout says—Tate turns the job over to Atticus.

In a fog, Jem and I watched our father take the gun and walk out into the middle of the street. He walked quickly, but I thought he moved like an underwater swimmer: time had slowed to a nauseating crawl.

Atticus pushed his glasses to his forehead; they slipped down, and he dropped them in the street. In the silence, I heard them crack. Atticus rubbed his eyes and chin; we saw him blink hard.

In front of the Radley gate, Tim Johnson had made up what was left of his mind. He had finally turned himself around, to pursue his original course up our street. He made two steps forward, then stopped and raised his head. We saw his body go rigid.

With movements so swift they seemed simultaneous, Atticus' hand yanked a ball-tipped lever as he brought the gun to his shoulder.

The rifle cracked. Tim Johnson leaped, flopped over and crumpled on the sidewalk in a brown-and-white heap. He didn't know what hit him. (100)

What Tim Johnson sees when he raises his head is Atticus Finch. Atticus allows himself to be the target of an irrational force and to absorb its violence as he acts to protect innocent people. This stance, his putting himself between the innocent and danger, characterizes the man. And this action, which occurs two more times in the novel, thematically binds the rite-of-passage of Jem and Scout to the rape trial of Tom Robinson and to the emergence of Boo Radley.

Mad dogs are easy; the courage to deal with a mad dog involves taking a concrete action: picking up a gun and shooting. Human beings are difficult; to respect their humanity, especially when they are wrong, makes concrete action difficult. In defending Tom Robinson, Atticus has to find a way both to respect the humanity of even his most belligerent opponents and to protect his innocent client. The alleged rape of Mayella Ewell presents the white citizens of Maycomb with something that "makes men lose their heads [so that] they couldn't be fair if they tried" (223). Like the dog infected with rabies, the citizens of Maycomb are infected with Maycomb's "usual disease," racism, which makes them just as irrational and just as dangerous as Tim Johnson. Atticus's neighbors and friends, therefore, are those "mad dogs" that he must confront. In an attempt to confront their irrational fears and to educate them that "Maycomb had . . . nothing to fear but fear itself" (10), Atticus must find a different kind of courage than that of picking up a gun, the kind of courage that one has when "you know you are licked before you begin but you begin anyway and you see it through no matter what" (116). This definition of courage provides the transition from facing the animal in the street to facing the citizens of Maycomb. Atticus, throughout the novel, then, repeats morally the stance that he takes physically in the city street.

That physical and moral stance embodies two philosophical components. The first is Atticus's "dangerous question," "Do you really think so?" and the second is Atticus's admonition to Scout to stand in another person's shoes before judging him or her. Fred Erisman, in "The Romantic Regionalism of Harper Lee," calls Atticus Finch an Emersonian hero who is able to cast a skeptical eye on the conventional ideas of goodness, to supplant those virtues that have lost their value, and to preserve those that work (135). Edwin Bruell, playing on Atticus's name, says Atticus is "no heroic type but [is like] any graceful, restrained, simple person like one from Attica" (660). Bruell sees Atticus as the Greek rational hero: "Know thyself. Nothing too much." Both are correct, as far as they take their arguments. Both account for Atticus's self-knowledge, but neither attempts to bind the "Know thyself" to Atticus's equally powerful assertion that we must know others as well. How can these be reconciled?

To ask the question "Do you really think so?" asks us to begin to understand ourselves by articulating the meaning of the actions and thoughts that, often, are reflections of the unspoken values of our communities. Alasdair MacIntyre, in *After Virtue*, reminds us that we inherit such values along with our bonds of family, city, tribe and nation. These relationships "constitute the given of my life, my moral starting point" (220). The moral inheritance of the whites of Maycomb includes set ways in which to see those different from themselves, particularly blacks. Their assumptions about blacks are, as Atticus says in his closing argument "that *all* Negroes lie, that *all* Negroes are basically immoral beings, that *all* Negro men are not to be trusted around our women" (207). Atticus, through his defense of Tom Robinson and by his very presence, brings into question these assumptions, forcing those ideas to become conscious and, perhaps, to be articulated. His question invites expression but is also threatening because of its disorienting effect. "Do you really think so?" forces us to confront our deepest beliefs, dreams and fears.

James Baldwin gives us an example of this kind of confrontation in an essay on Martin Luther King, in which he recalled the silence that he encountered on an integrated bus not long after the Montgomery boycott was settled:

> This silence made me think of nothing so much as the silence which follows a really serious lovers' quarrel: the whites, beneath their cold hostility, were mystified and deeply hurt. They had been betrayed by the Negroes, not merely because the Negroes had declined to remain in their "place," but because the Negroes had refused to be controlled by the town's image of them. And without this image, it seemed to me, the whites were abruptly and totally lost. The very foundations of their private and public worlds were being destroyed. (95)

This angry silence indicates that the white people resist and resent the change in the structure and story that has guided and undergirded their lives. Atticus's question potentially breaks through the kind of silence that Baldwin encountered on that Montgomery bus, forcing that silence to speak, perhaps creating a dialogue, between the self and the "other." Atticus, the man, becomes the catalyst for this dialogue in Maycomb.

Maycomb is, Scout tells us, "an old town . . . an old tired town" (9). It has been, as Erisman points out, "a part of southern Alabama from the time of the first settlements, and isolated and largely untouched by the Civil War, it was, like the South, turned inward upon itself by Reconstruction. Indeed its history parallels that of the South in so many ways that it emerges as a microcosm of the South" (123). Maycomb clings to its ideals, its traditions and its rigid caste system as ways of affirming its identity. People, especially blacks and poor whites, are, as Baldwin noted, expected to remain in their "places." The alleged rape of Mayella Ewell violates this order and throws the town and the individuals involved into confrontation with their community identity.

Atticus, in the second mad dog incident, confronts two very different sets of Maycomb's white citizenry, both with the same assumptions. The first group is "good" citizens—"merchants, in-town farmers" (148), even the town doctor—who come to warn Atticus that Tom Robinson is in danger. They ultimately confront Atticus about his defending a black man who has been accused of raping a white woman and tell Atticus that he has everything to lose. Atticus asks, "Do you really think so?" The men, angered, advance on Atticus: "There was a murmur among the group of men, made more ominous when Atticus moved back to the bottom front step and the men drew nearer to him" (148). The tension is broken when Jem, afraid for his father, yells to Atticus that the phone is ringing.

Not long after, Scout disperses the second group of Maycomb's citizens—this time, poor white citizens who smell of stale whiskey and the pigpen (154)—who come to the jail to lynch Tom Robinson. Scout watches her father push back his hat, fold his newspaper and confront the angry men. The men assume that Atticus is powerless because they have called away the sheriff, but Atticus's response is "Do you really think so?" Scout, hearing the question for the second time that evening, thinks this is "too good to miss" (154) and runs to see what is going to happen. Scout's presence and her personalization of the mob, her singling out Mr. Cunningham, the father of one of her school friends, disrupts the mob psychology, ending the danger. Only later does Scout realize the implications of what she has witnessed:

I was very tired, and was drifting into sleep when the memory of Atticus calmly folding his newspaper and pushing back his hat became Atticus standing in the middle of an empty waiting street, pushing up his glasses. The full meaning of the night's awful events hit me and I began crying. (158)

Atticus's question penetrates to the heart of the images and ideas that sustain the citizens of Maycomb as surely as the bullet penetrates the body of the mad dog. Faced with a challenge to their identity, both groups of men react; they lose their reason and become like a mad dog, attacking the man who calls their truth into question.

Why do the children have to save Atticus? Herein lies another dimension of the problem and potential danger of Atticus's question. Atticus's Apollonian virtues are based on the assumption that he is dealing with rational and reflective people. Scout indicates that when Atticus asks the question of her and Jem, he follows the question with a lesson or proof that forces the two of them to prove the validity of their ideas:

"Do you really think so?"
This was Atticus's dangerous question. "Do you really think you want to move there, Scout?" Bam, bam, bam, and the checkerboard was swept clean of my men. "Do you really think that, son? Then read this." Jem would struggle the rest of an evening through the speeches of Henry W. Grady. (148)

What reforming action can Atticus offer to these angry and emotional men confronted with a black man whom they think has gotten "above his place"? None. Tom Robinson is not part of their community in any vital and human way. They do not *see* Tom Robinson. He is not one of them; he exists either outside of the community or on its periphery. He is not their neighbor, either in the literal or in the religious sense. Atticus forces the men, if they cannot see Tom Robinson, to see Atticus

Finch. Their anger, however, nearly makes them forget that they *do* consider Atticus their neighbor. Only the intervention of the children restores their reason. Reflection, however, can take the men only as far as the experience of Atticus Finch; to see Tom Robinson, another kind of action is demanded. The first half of Atticus's ethic, the demand for reflection, therefore, is useless without the second half, the standing in another's shoes, the demand for compassion.

Civilization can be seen as "the agreement, slowly arrived at, to let the abyss alone," as Allen Tate says in *The Fathers* (185-86). Then, the Tom Robinsons of the world are defined as the abyss around which we create impenetrable boundaries. Or civilization can be a structure based on compassion—on the fact that, as Martin Luther King, Jr. said in *Strength to Love*, the "other" "is a part of me and I am a part of him. His agony diminishes me, and his salvation enlarges me" (35). Compassion has limits: it contains the realization that I can never know your experience as you experience it, but that I can, because of our "human fellow feeling" (11-12), as Joseph Conrad termed it, make an attempt to know what you feel and, thereby, bring you into the narrative of my experience. Hermeneutics creates the neighbor.

Atticus explains this to Scout as walking in another person's shoes:

> "First of all," he said, "if you can learn a simple trick, Scout, you'll get along a lot better with all kinds of folks. You never really understand a person until you consider things from his point of view . . . until you climb into his skin and walk around in it." (34)

Atticus asks Scout to "see with" others, to be compassionate. But compassion must be bound to the critical question "Do you really think so?" in order to respect the humanity of the neighbor. Critique without compassion threatens to become force; compassion without critique may dissolve into sentimentalism or emotionalism. Either stance alone turns the "I" into an "It," either an object to be controlled or a creature to be stereotyped or pitied. Both are required in order to see clearly, and though they may not lead to truth, they often lead, as Atticus tells Scout, to compromise (36). Reflection gives us humility, forces us to confront our own frailties and limitations; and compassion helps us love, lets us make, as Iris Murdoch says, "the connection of knowledge with love and of spiritual insight with apprehension of the unique" (209). Scout will exercise this ethic in the most essential way at the end of the novel.

In the third of the mad dog scenes, the trial of Tom Robinson becomes a symbol for the attempt to stand in another's shoes and see an event from that person's perspective while maintaining a critical capacity. Atticus says that serving on a jury "'forces a man to make up his mind and declare himself about something. Men don't like to do that'" (225). This case not only questions the jury, but it questions Atticus himself. When Scout learns that Atticus was appointed to the Robinson case, she asks why he cannot refuse it. He replies,

> For a number of reasons. The main one is, if I didn't I couldn't hold up my head in this town. I couldn't represent this county in the legislature. I couldn't even tell you and Jem not to do something again . . . Scout, simply by the nature of the work, every lawyer gets at least one case in his lifetime that affects him personally. This one's mine, I guess. (80)

He later tells his brother Jack, within Scout's hearing,

> "You know, I'd hoped to get through life without a case of this kind, but John Taylor pointed at me, and said, 'You're it.'"
> "Let this cup pass from you, eh?"
> "Right. But do you think I could face my children otherwise?" (93)

Atticus realizes that he is defeated before he begins but that he must begin if he is to uphold his values. The legal system offers at least a *chance* of success. In contrast to the lynch mob in the dark, the court represents the light of reason. Scout and Jem, in their innocence, believe that the

---

court is the structure in which Atticus can defeat the mad dog of irrationality and racism. Scout thinks, "With [Atticus's] infinite capacity for calming turbulent seas, he could make a rape case as dry as a sermon. . . . Our nightmare had gone with daylight, everything would come out all right" (171-72).

In the trial, Atticus attempts to make the jury and the town see the incident from the perspectives of both Mayella Ewell and of Tom Robinson and, thus, to understand that Mayella's accusation is a lie born from fear, emotional need, ignorance and poverty. From Mayella Atticus elicits the story of a lonely young woman imprisoned in poverty by her father's alcoholism (185). The Ewells, "white trash," are as alienated from Maycomb as Tom Robinson. Yet in the squalor of Ewell life, there is one disjunctive sight: Mayella's geraniums, as carefully tended as those of Miss Maudie Atkinson. These represent Mayella's desire to escape the life she lives, but that escape is denied her both by her own nature and by the rigid caste system of Maycomb. Scout compares her to the half-black and half-white children of Dolphus Raymond:

> She was as sad, I thought, as what Jem called a mixed child: white people wouldn't have anything to do with her because she lived among pigs; Negroes wouldn't have anything to do with her because she was white. . . . Tom Robinson was probably the only person who was ever decent to her. (194)

This decency is Tom Robinson's undoing. He is a black man who finds himself in the most dangerous of circumstances. He is accosted by a white woman, and whether he struggles with her or runs, he is guilty. What emerges before the astonished eyes of the court is that Tom Robinson could not have raped Mayella Ewell. The evidence, that she was beaten by someone left-handed, becomes moot when Tom Robinson faces the court and all see that "[h]is left arm was fully twelve inches shorter than his right and hung dead at his side. It ended in a small shriveled hand, and from as far away as the balcony I could see that it was no use to him" (188).

Mayella, when confronted with her obvious lie, falls back on her whiteness as her defense. Her father Bob had disrupted the court earlier when he testified that, through the window, "I seen that black nigger yonder ruttin' on my Mayella!" (175). His language illustrates the assumption that blacks are uncontrollable animals—mad dogs who must be exterminated. Mayella falls back on the same argument. The caste system of Maycomb names, categorizes and limits her, just as it names, categorizes and limits Tom Robinson. The boundary between them is an absolutely rigid one. Maycomb defines Tom Robinson as nonhuman; thus, Mayella only has to appeal to her whiteness—that which makes her "one of us"—to be right:

> Suddenly Mayella became articulate. "I got somethin' to say . . . an' then I ain't gonna say no more. That nigger yonder took advantage of me an' if you fine fancy gentlemen don't wanta do nothin' about it then you're all yellow stinkin' cowards, stinkin' cowards, the lot of you." (190)

Scout says that "Atticus had hit her hard in a way that was not clear to me" (191). His questions are the "Do you really think so?" They force her to face the truth of her self, but faced with that truth, she, angrily and stubbornly, falls back within the safety of the community ethos, leaving critique and compassion behind.

Tom Robinson's real crime is not the rape: it is that he shows himself to be more than the definition that Maycomb has created for him. Scout says that Tom is, in his way, as much a gentleman as her father (197). Indeed, Tom is convicted because he acts out Atticus's maxim and stands in another's shoes. When asked why he helped Mayella,

> Tom Robinson hesitated, searching for an answer.
> "Looked like she didn't have nobody to help her, like I says . . . I felt right sorry for her, she seemed to try more'n the rest of 'em—"

"You felt sorry for *her,* you felt *sorry* for her?" Mr. Gilmer seemed ready to rise to the ceiling.

The witness realized his mistake and shifted uncomfortably in the chair. But the damage was done. (199-200)

This is Tom Robinson's crime.

The real mad dog in Maycomb is the racism that denies the humanity of Tom Robinson. Atticus takes on that mad dog. When Atticus makes his summation to the jury, he literally bares himself to the jury's and the town's anger: he "unbuttoned his vest, unbuttoned his collar, loosened his tie, and took off his coat. He never loosened a scrap of his clothing until he undressed at bedtime, and to Jem and me, this was the equivalent of him standing before us stark naked" (205). Atticus tells the jury that what has happened between Mayella Ewell and Tom Robinson is a crime because it violates the rigid code and social structure of Maycomb. Mayella, willfully breaking this code by kissing a black man, now has to put the evidence of her crime out of her sight, for truly to see Tom Robinson is to have to confront and to redefine herself: "of necessity she must put him away from her—he must be removed from her presence, from this world. She must destroy the evidence of her offense" (206).

Atticus also appeals to the jury in the terms of his ethic. Arguing that the legal system is the place where community codes and caste systems must be left behind, he asks the jury to think rationally and critically, to ask themselves "Do you really think so?":

A court is only as sound as its jury, and a jury is only as sound as the men who make it up. I am confident that you gentlemen will review *without passion* the evidence you have heard. . . . In the name of God, do your duty. (208, emphasis added)

He also asks them to acknowledge Tom Robinson's humanity, to have for Tom the compassion that Tom had for Mayella Ewell. Atticus finishes his argument with a prayer: "In the name of God, believe him" (208).

This is not to be. As the town waits for the verdict, a sleepy Scout watches her father in the hot courtroom, and, in her thoughts, she binds the mad dog theme to Tom Robinson:

> But I must have been reasonably awake or I would not have received the impression that was creeping into me. It was not unlike one I had last winter, and I shivered, though the night was hot. The feeling grew until the atmosphere in the courtroom was exactly the same as a cold February morning, when the mockingbirds were still, and the carpenters had stopped hammering on Miss Maudie's new house, and every wood door in the neighborhood was shut as tight as the doors of the Radley Place. A deserted waiting, empty street, and the courtroom was packed with people. A steaming summer night was no different from a winter morning. Mr. Heck Tate, who had entered the courtroom and was talking to Atticus might have been wearing his high boots and lumber jacket. Atticus had stopped his tranquil journey and had put his foot onto the bottom rung of a chair; as he listened to what Mr. Tate was saying, he ran his hand slowly up and down his thigh. I expected Mr. Tate to say any minute, "Take him, Mr. Finch . . ." (213)

She continues, finding in the courtroom the images of Atticus's facing Tim Johnson, the mad dog, in the street:

> What happened after that had a dreamlike quality: in a dream I saw the jury return, moving like underwater swimmers, and Judge Taylor's voice came from far away and was tiny. I saw something only a lawyer's child could be expected to see, could be expected to watch for, and it was like watching Atticus walk into the street, raise a rifle to his shoulder and pull the trigger, but watching all the time knowing that the gun was empty. (213)

Though Tom Robinson is convicted, Atticus wins a small victory; the jury's deliberation lasts well into the night. Miss Maudie Atkinson confirms that Atticus's role is to face the mad dogs. He makes Maycomb question itself in a way no one else could, even though they, like Mayella, cannot bind love to power and act in creative justice.

> "We're the safest folks in the world," said Miss Maudie. "We're so rarely called on to be Christians, but when we are, we've got men like Atticus to go for us. . . . [As] I waited, I thought, Atticus Finch won't win, he can't win, but he's the only man in these parts who can keep a jury out so long in a case like that. And I thought to myself, well, we're making a step—it's just a baby step, but it's a step." (218-19)[1]

This baby step is not enough for Tom Robinson. He cannot trust that he can have justice, so he attempts to escape from prison and is shot dead in the attempt. This man who performed a loving act is treated like a rabid mad dog. The prison is a metaphor for Tom's position in the Maycomb of the 1930s. What is a baby step for the town is merely continuing oppression for Tom, the innocent man. Charles H. Long points out that, potentially, "passive power is still power. It is the power to be, to understand, to know even in the worst of historical circumstances, and it may often reveal a more clear insight into significant meaning of the human venture than the power possessed by the oppressor" (195). This Tom Robinson cannot believe, so he cannot wait. His is the silence of the oppressed person who has reached despair.

Jem, moving into adulthood, also feels Tom's despair. Tom Robinson's conviction and his death mark Jem's fall from innocence; as he tells Miss Maudie, his life until now has been "like bein' a caterpillar in a cocoon. . . . Like somethin' asleep wrapped up in a warm place" (218). Now, he must come to terms with what he has witnessed. Atticus tells Scout, who does not understand Jem's despair, that "Jem was trying hard to forget something, but what he was really doing was storing it away for a while. . . . When he was able to think about it, Jem would be himself again" (250). Yet Jem is marked forever by the experience. Scout begins the novel by describing Jem's arm:

When he was nearly thirteen, my brother Jem got his arm badly broken at the elbow. When it healed, and Jem's fears of never being able to play football were assuaged, he was seldom self-conscious about his injury. His left arm was somewhat shorter than his right; when he stood or walked, the back of his hand was at right angles to his body, his thumb parallel to his thigh. (7)

Jem's arm, broken in his and Scout's "longest journey together" (256), the night they survive Bob Ewell's vengeful attack, parallels Tom Robinson's withered arm, lost in a piece of machinery. Tom's lost arm and hand are ultimately crippling; they symbolize his inability to climb out of the prison of racism, his being crushed in its machinery. As Tom tries to escape, he is hindered by his loss: "They said if he'd had two good arms he'd have made it" (238). Jem is crippled and lives; but, the injury is the sign of the experience's "leaving its mark" on Jem's body and on his soul.

Similarly, Boo Radley makes his mark on Scout. *To Kill a Mockingbird* is divided into two parts: the first is the children's attempt to make Boo Radley come out of his house, and the second is the trial of Tom Robinson. At first, the two seem unrelated; however, one soon realizes that Boo Radley is a hermeneutical device for the children's coming to understand the adult world represented by the rape trial. Like Tom Robinson, Boo Radley, who commits a childhood offense and is imprisoned by his family as punishment, is one of the least powerful members of Maycomb society. Parallel to Tom's trial, from which the truth about the community's racism emerges, is the children's attempt to see Boo Radley and to make him emerge from hiding.

Tom Robinson's trial and death make Jem realize that the very limited kind of communication that Boo has with him and Scout—for example, his leaving them gum and soap dolls in the knothole of a tree—is the only connection with the outside world that Boo can claim. Jem decides that, in a world in which a Tom Robinson is falsely accused and convicted and, finally, dies, Boo Radley does not *want* to come out

(230). In Maycomb, there is no vital role for either Boo Radley or for Tom Robinson except as phantom and monster. For the disillusioned Jem, there is no longer a place for the childhood wonder that Boo represents. But in that mysterious role of ghost and phantom, Boo makes one powerful act as he emerges to save the children from Bob Ewell's attack.

Scout, too young to understand exactly what Tom Robinson's death means, does not lose her capacity for wonder. She sees Boo, and their meeting is Scout's rite of passage in the novel. Boo is the catalyst for the wonder that is the beginning of understanding. Scout and Jem's friend Dill sets in motion the children's investigation of the mystery of Boo Radley: "[H]e would wonder. 'Wonder what [Boo] does in there. . . . Wonder what he looks like'" (17). Scout, true to her name, enters this uncharted territory. She is willing to risk the exploration of the unknown, and her discovery is a profound one.

This risk almost causes her death. Bob Ewell, seeking revenge, attacks Jem and Scout as they walk home from a school play. Jem and Scout are saved by their mysterious phantom, Boo Radley, and Scout gets to see the man who has been the object of the children's speculations:

> His lips parted in a timid smile, and our neighbor's image blurred with my sudden tears.
> "Hey, Boo," I said.
> "Mr. Arthur, honey," said Atticus gently correcting me. (273)

This "gray ghost" that Scout desires to see appears and is given a name, and he gives Scout a gift beyond measure. As Scout walks Boo Radley home, she realizes that he, this "malevolent phantom" (13), is her neighbor:

> Neighbors bring food with death and flowers with sickness and little things in between. Boo was our neighbor. He gave us two soap dolls, a bro-

ken watch and chain, a pair of good-luck pennies, and our lives. But neighbors give in return. We never put back into the tree what we took out of it: we had given him nothing, and it made me sad. (281)

What follows is both another gift from Boo and a gift to Boo; it is a gift that she will share with her wounded, sad brother and with us, the readers. Scout stands in Boo's shoes and sees the world and the turbulent events of this time from his front porch:

> I had never seen the neighborhood from this angle.
> . . . Atticus was right. One time he said you never really know a man until you stand in his shoes and walk around in them. Just standing on the Radley porch was enough . . . (281)

Scout learns Atticus's ethic completely. Looking at her life from Boo's perspective, she is able to see herself and her experiences in a new way. This is the imaginative "Do you really think so?" and is the birth of Scout the writer and is the education of Scout the moral agent. She also makes an act of compassion—and this is her gift, as the neighbor, to Boo: she sees the world from his point of view and gains an understanding of him that no one else in Maycomb has ever had and, since he enters his house never to emerge again, ever will have. Scout looks into the face of the phantom and into Arthur Radley's human heart and realizes that her life and Boo's have been and are interrelated: that she is Boo's child (282) as well as Atticus's, nurtured and protected by both to this moment. Maycomb had been told recently that "there was nothing to fear except fear itself" (10), and Scout realizes the truth of this. She tells Atticus that "nothin's real scary except in books" (283) and that Boo was "real nice" (284). Atticus replies, "Most people are, Scout, when you finally see them" (284).

Atticus, then, casts his ethic in visual terms, and in the metaphor of vision, the function and the content of the novel merge. In the preface to "The Nigger of the 'Narcissus,'" Joseph Conrad links compassion

---

with vision and imagination with morality and makes clarity of vision the task of the artist. The artist, he says, creates community by appealing to the "human fellow feeling" that links us with all humankind:

> My task which I am trying to achieve is, by the power of the written word . . . to make you see. . . . If I succeed, you shall find there according to your deserts: encouragement, consolation, fear, charm . . . and, perhaps, also that glimpse of truth for which you have forgotten to ask. . . . And when it is accomplished—behold!—all the truth of life is there: a moment of vision, a sigh, a smile—and the return to eternal rest. (13-14)

The adult Scout telling us her story is the artist who grounds this call for vision in a character: her father.[2] She, in insisting with her father that seeing is a hermeneutical act, gives us true a meeting with the "other" and brings us, perhaps, to a moment of insight into our own lives, our own assumptions and our own frailties. The work of art becomes, potentially, a moral and ethical reference point, a pair of shoes in which we can stand.

The deepest symbol in the novel is Atticus Finch himself. Atticus, when he gives the children their air rifles, states the moral lesson of the novel. He tells them that it is a sin to kill a mockingbird; that is, it is wrong to do harm to something or to someone who only tries to help us or to give us pleasure. That rule, combined with critical reflection on the self and with compassion for others, keeps us from becoming mad dogs, from destroying each other and, finally, ourselves. Scout understands this lesson as she, along with Sheriff Heck Tate and her father, agree that Boo should not be charged for Bob Ewell's murder. When Atticus asks Scout if she understands this adult decision, she responds: "Well, it'd be sort of like shootin' a mockingbird, wouldn't it?" (279).

Atticus stands at the novel's heart and as its moral and ethical center: a man who knows himself and who, therefore, can love others. Scout presents her father to us as a gift and a guide. She shows us a man who gives up himself as he forces us to see and, thus, to know others by seeing through him, yet he is far from being a "gray ghost." Atticus emerges clearly, as a particular, ethical human being—as May Sarton's heroic, decent man—but also as an enduring symbol of the good. Toni Morrison calls such "timeless, benevolent, instructive, and protective" people "ancestors" because they so perfectly represent humanity that their wisdom transcends their physical being (343). For Scout, the child as well as the artist, and for us, because of her art, Atticus is ancestor, eternally present as comforter and critic, as structure and source:

> He turned out the light and went into Jem's room. He would be there all night, and he would be there when Jem waked up in the morning. (284)

From *The Southern Quarterly* 34, no. 4 (Summer, 1996), pp. 53-63. Copyright © 1996 by The University of Southern Mississippi. Reprinted by permission of The University of Southern Mississippi.

Notes

1. The black community recognizes this as well. Scout and Jem have sat, throughout the trial, in the balcony with the black spectators. As Atticus leaves the courtroom, a sleepy Scout tells us:

> Someone was punching me, but I was reluctant to take my eyes from the people below us, and from the image of Atticus's lonely walk down the aisle.
> "Miss Jean Louise?"
> I looked around. They were standing. All around us and in the balcony on the opposite wall, the Negroes were getting to their feet. Reverend Sykes's voice was as distant as Judge Taylor's.
> "Miss Jean Louise, stand up. Your father's passin'." (214)

The black community acknowledges that Atticus has made this attempt. They cannot acknowledge the judge or the justice that was meted out, but they honor the just man.

2. For a very interesting article about ethics, narrative, and character, see Christina Hoff Sommers, "Teaching the Virtues," *Public Interest* (Spring 1992) 3-13. Professor Hoff Sommers argues that teaching "situation ethics" or specialized ethics, as we have in the academy for some time, only leads to an ethical relativity among our students. She calls for grounding ethics in story and in character, in showing the importance of the virtue through exemplary characters.

Works Cited

Baldwin, James. "The Highroad to Destiny." *Martin Luther King, Jr.: A Profile*. Ed. C. Eric Lincoln. New York: Hill and Wang, 1970. 90-112.

Bruell, Edwin. "Keen Scalpel on Social Ills." *English Journal* 53 (Dec. 1964): 658-61.

Conrad, Joseph. Preface. "The Nigger of the 'Narcissus.'" *The Nigger of the 'Narcissus'/Typhoon and Other Stories*. New York: Penguin, 1963. 11-14.

Erisman, Fred. "The Romantic Regionalism of Harper Lee." *Alabama Review* (April 1973): 122-27.

King, Martin Luther, Jr. *Strength to Love*. Philadelphia: Fortress P, 1963.

Lee, Harper. *To Kill A Mockingbird*. New York: Popular Library, 1962.

Long, Charles H. *Significations: Signs, Symbols, and Images in the Interpretation of Religion*. Philadelphia: Fortress P, 1986.

MacIntyre, Alasdair. *After Virtue: A Study in Moral Theory*. Notre Dame: U of Notre Dame P, 1984.

Morrison, Toni. "Rootedness: The Ancestor as Foundation." *Black Women Writers, 1950-1980*. Ed. Mari Evans. New York: Doubleday, 1984. 340-45.

Murdoch, Iris. *Christian Ethics and Contemporary Philosophy*. Ed. Ian Ramsey. London: S. C. M. P, 1966.

Tate, Allen. *The Fathers and Other Fiction*. Baton Rouge: Louisiana State UP, 1977.

The Margins of Maycomb:
A Rereading of *To Kill a Mockingbird*_____

Teresa Godwin Phelps

To Kill a Mockingbird has been widely and justly praised as a great American novel: on one level, it is a tender family narrative; on another level, a poignant depiction of the slow and painful emergence of the New South from the ashes of its slaveholding past. The principal agent in the family and in this metamorphosis of the South is Atticus Finch, who is revered both as a model lawyer and an exemplary parent.[1] Atticus is held up by those in legal circles as the quintessential lawyer, the lawyer unafraid to confront his community with its own prejudices. So ubiquitous is reader reverence for him that we, like his daughter Scout, the book's narrator, call him by his first name: not "Finch" but "Atticus."

The merest suggestion that we might temper our admiration for Atticus results in thorough reprobation. Monroe Freedman's 1992 article proposing that Atticus was not a good role model for lawyers met with unprecedented response.[2] When Freedman wrote that Finch was complicitous in a racist society, made excuses for the Ku Klux Klan and for the leader of a lynch mob, and generally acted out of "an elitist sense of noblesse oblige"[3] rather than true compassion, he received more responses than he had even to other seemingly more controversial issues: "The mythological deification of Atticus Finch was illustrated by Atticans who wrote to equate my rejection of Finch, literally, with attacking God, Moses, Jesus, Gandhi, and Mother Teresa."[4]

Thematic discussions of *To Kill a Mockingbird* have likewise tended to adhere to a strict party line and to focus either on Atticus's exemplary character[5] (particularly as a lawyer) or on problematic race relations depicted in microcosm in Maycomb, Alabama. We read *To Kill a Mockingbird* as lawyers and legal academics for what Louise Rosenblatt would call an "efferent transaction"; that is, we are motivated to read it not for purely aesthetic reasons but rather for a lesson, for something to carry away.[6] What is it, then, that we carry away from *To Kill a Mockingbird*? Or, for those of us who teach this book year after year, what is it that we are hoping that our students will take away?

Some answers are clear. We do not read *To Kill a Mockingbird* for plot; in fact, it is curiously plotless and lacking in suspense. The outcome of Tom Robinson's rape trial is never in doubt; when Scout asks her father if they are going to win, that is, achieve Robinson's acquittal, Atticus's reply is brief and unambiguous: "No, honey."[7] Nor do we read *To Kill a Mockingbird* for other traditional plot-driven reasons: Will Scout marry Dill? Will Atticus marry Miss Maudie? Nor do we stay with the novel to find out why Jem's arm was broken; by page two hundred (or even earlier) we have forgotten Lee's introductory teaser about Jem's arm: "When he was nearly thirteen, my brother Jem got his arm badly broken at the elbow."[8] We stay with *To Kill a Mockingbird* for two reasons: we are engaged by Scout's voice and Atticus's character. Lee's carefully constructed beginning invites us not to stay glued to the book to see how it turns out but rather to learn more about Scout, Jem, and Atticus. Lee's opening gambit serves to introduce us to Atticus's conciliatory nature and to his ability to hold two competing ideas in his head at once: "We were far too old to settle an argument [about why Jem's arm got broken] with a fist-fight, so we consulted Atticus. Our father said we were both right."[9] The opening pages invite us to come to know this peacemaker Atticus and to be similarly instructed by him. We thus read (and teach) *To Kill a Mockingbird* to learn about character. A generation of young lawyers and law students has identified with Atticus and emulated his values.

Indeed there is much to admire about Atticus. He manages at once to be of and not of Maycomb; he has defined an individual self not in opposition to others, as have so many heroes of twentieth century fiction,[10] but as part of a community—a self *in relation* to others. Or as Tom Shaffer puts it: "It is important to understanding Atticus Finch to see that he was able to tell the truth about his community but still remain fond of his community. . . ."[11] The truth that Atticus "tells" is of what he calls "Maycomb's usual disease," the inbred racism that compels jurors to convict Tom Robinson even when they know that he could not be guilty.[12]

For nearly a decade I have assigned *To Kill a Mockingbird* to my Law and Literature class and for the most part class discussions have followed typical lines. We are chagrined at the intractable racism of Maycomb; we admire Atticus and discuss whether his lie to save Boo Radley from public scrutiny is justified. We come away from *To Kill a Mockingbird* feeling good about being lawyers and law students.

From time to time, however, students have raised awkward, disquieting questions that have punctured my complacency about my unqualified admiration for Atticus Finch and *To Kill a Mockingbird*. Trying to answer their questions has led me to a rereading of the book and to writing this article. I am now of the opinion that there is another disease in Maycomb that Atticus does not see: the disease of marginalization, of class distinctions that lead us to bifurcate our world into "us" and "them." *To Kill a Mockingbird* contains chilling depictions of members of what Richard Delgado calls "outgroups, groups whose marginality defines the boundaries of the mainstream, whose voice and perspective—whose consciousness—has been suppressed, devalued, and abnormalized."[13] Not only does Atticus fail to see them—so also do we.

Discussions of class distinctions are not absent from *To Kill a Mockingbird*.[14] Jem sums it up late in the book:

> You know something, Scout? I've got it all figured out, now. I've thought about it a lot lately and I've got it figured out. There's four kinds of folks in the world. There's the ordinary kind like us and the neighbors, there's the kind like the Cunninghams out in the woods, the kind like the Ewells down at the dump, and the Negroes.[15]

Although Scout protests—"Naw, Jem, I think there's just one kind of folks. Folks"[16]—it is Jem's vision that is lived out in the novel. Although Atticus's homely wisdom of not really knowing about someone until you've walked around in his shoes represents Lee's attempt to break down the impenetrable barriers that exist between the classes, the author (unknowingly, I would guess) leaves solidly in place certain discomforting barriers.

This article discusses Jem's "four kinds of folks" to analyze what the novel says about class distinctions and what it does not say but nonetheless reveals about marginalization. It describes Jem's four kinds of folks—the Finches, the Cunninghams, the Ewells, and the Negroes—and it also discusses each group's relationship to the other groups and to the legal system. *To Kill a Mockingbird* is a valiant attempt to erase some of the barriers that exist between "kinds of folks"; however, the book fails to recognize or acknowledge the barriers it leaves erect. While the novel depicts change in one facet of law and society, it reinforces the status quo in other troubling aspects. In rereading and to some extent criticizing the ethical message of *To Kill a Mockingbird*, I do not mean to suggest that we should not continue to read and teach it. As Wayne Booth points out, "ethical quarrels always take place against a backdrop of agreement."[17] We can quarrel over aspects of *To Kill a Mockingbird* only because we agree that it is worth the quarrel, and that it embodies ethical norms worthy of our consideration and respect.

"The Ordinary Kind Like Us and the Neighbors"

The "ordinary" folks depicted in *To Kill a Mockingbird* are the old aristocracy of Maycomb, represented at their best by Atticus and at their worst by Aunt Alexandra and her missionary ladies. *To Kill a Mockingbird* is essentially their story. Despite considerable differences among them as individuals, the ordinary folks comprise a single, unified community. Even Atticus, who is seen as a bit eccentric, remains one of them: "He Atticus liked Maycomb, he was Maycomb County born and bred; he knew his people, they knew him, and because of Simon Finch's industry, Atticus was related by blood or marriage to nearly every family in the town."[18] They are what is meant by Maycomb, and they can trace their ancestry to the beginnings of the town.

Lee is clearly most comfortable and most familiar with the "ordinary" folks, and she portrays numerous variations on this kind of people; its circumference is flexible enough to contain Mrs. Dubose, Boo Radley, Miss Maudie, Miss Stephanie, and many others. Their various and decided eccentricities are never judged; they are gossiped about but tolerated. Nothing, not even Atticus's spirited defense of Tom Robinson, can divide them. As Atticus explains to his children, "no matter how bitter things get, they're still our friends and this Maycomb is still our home."[19]

Lee resorts to heavy parody when describing the ladies of Aunt Alexandra's missionary circle, who are "fighting the good fight"[20] to bring western civilization and Christianity to the "sin and squalor"[21] of the Mrunas in far-off jungles while remaining blind to the lives of the "darkies" who live, if not in sin, at least in the squalor of poverty on the outskirts of Maycomb. Ironically, the missionary ladies are the ones in need of a good dose of Christian tolerance and compassion. Lee plays to readers' least flattering beliefs about Southerners, and the missionary circle scene highlights the differences between this type of Southerner and others, such as the Finches and Miss Maudie. When Mrs. Merriweather, "the most devout lady in Maycomb,"[22] obliquely criticizes Atticus as "good but misguided"[23] because his defense of Tom Robinson served to "stir 'em [the Negroes] up,"[24] Miss Maudie reacts: "When Miss Maudie was angry her brevity was icy. Something had made her deeply angry, and her gray eyes were as cold as her voice."[25] This scene throws into sharp relief the emerging new South, embodied in Miss Maudie and Atticus, against the old South, embodied in Mrs. Merriweather. Miss Maudie could not have gone so far as to defend Tom Robinson, but she understands why Atticus did. She represents the transition from intolerance and ignorance to an awakening awareness of the plight of the southern Black.

Atticus steps into the sanctimoniousness of the missionary circle in one of the most chilling juxtapositions in the book. He arrives pale and disturbed with the news that Tom Robinson is dead, shot in an escape attempt.[26] Mrs. Merriweather's abstracted "good works" and even Miss Maudie's passive sympathy likewise pale when compared to the harsh reality that these attitudes are not merely "ideas" or "disagreements"; the intolerance of the old South and the sympathetic impassivity of Miss Maudie cause violence.

Of this group, Atticus is obviously the most enlightened: he is the one, as Miss Maudie puts it, "who was born to do our unpleasant jobs for us. . . . We're so rarely called on to be Christians, but when we are, we've got men like Atticus to go for us."[27] Yet Atticus too is transitional; he rejects old values and speaks for new ones, but without confidence. He is willing to mouth Aunt Alexandra's "wisdom" to his children, albeit uneasily:

> Your aunt has asked me to try and impress upon you and Jean Louise that you are not from run-of-the-mill people, that you are the product of several generations' gentle breeding . . . and that you should try to live up to your name. . . . She wants to talk to you about the family and what it's meant to Maycomb County through the years, so you'll have some idea of who you are, so you might be moved to behave accordingly. . . .[28]

Aunt Alexandra has it all wrong, of course, and Lee means for us to see the irony. To "behave accordingly" would mean to behave like the missionary ladies and we, as readers, are far more drawn to the inappropriate behavior of Atticus and Scout, because they act from true human compassion, not from some sense of who they are. To "behave accordingly" means to know your place and to stay within your sphere, not mixing with the Cunninghams or Calpurnias, who belong to other spheres. Yet no matter how one behaves—as drunks, recluses, drug addicts, open-minded lawyers, or free-spirited little girls—one unconditionally belongs to this group as a birthright. To belong to this group is to move through life with advantage and privilege that is unquestioned, unacknowledged, and often unknown. Scout seems utterly unaware of her privileged status even as she narrates events such as the teacher calling on her on Scout's first day at school because the teacher knows Scout's name. Or to use Aunt Alexandra's words, the teacher knows who Scout *is*.

Most importantly, this group includes the caretakers of the law. Atticus, their representative both literally and figuratively, is both lawyer and lawmaker. The law orders their lives, guarantees their rights, and insures their supremacy. The law would not work for Tom Robinson at all if he did not have Atticus to speak for him; and when this group decides that the law does not apply to other folks, as it does not apply to the Ewells, their decision is final.

"The Cunninghams Out in the Woods"

The Cunninghams are the poor whites and they are physically separated from the Finches and the neighbors in that they live on the outskirts of Maycomb, in the woods. Lee first introduces this group when Scout goes to school: "the ragged, denim-shirted and floursack-skirted first grade, most of whom had chopped cotton and fed hogs from the time they were able to walk."[29] Their dress sets them apart from the teacher, who wears fingernail polish, high-heeled pumps, and a red-and-white striped dress, and from Scout, who fights throughout the book to be allowed to wear overalls instead of dresses. The overt differences in dress, moreover, mirror the more profound differences in intellect. Scout has read for as long as she can remember, and the teacher, Miss Caroline, reads classic children's literature to the class. The Old Sarum children, however, are "immune to imaginative literature."[30]

Representative of these children is Walter Cunningham, whom Lee describes in minute detail:

Walter Cunningham's face told everybody in the first grade he had hookworms. His absence of shoes told us how he got them. People caught hookworms going barefooted in barnyards and hog wallows. If Walter had owned any shoes he would have worn them the first day of school and then discarded them until midwinter. He did have on a clean shirt and neatly mended overalls.[31]

Beyond his characteristic appearance, Walter demonstrates equally characteristic Cunningham financial pride. Discovering that Walter has not brought his lunch to school, Miss Caroline tries to lend Walter a quarter to eat downtown. Scout attempts to explain his refusal to her succinctly: "Miss Caroline, he's a Cunningham."[32] But Miss Caroline, an outsider who does not know Maycomb's shorthand for class distinctions, does not understand and Scout must elaborate. Scout thinks:

I thought I had made things sufficiently clear. It was clear enough to the rest of us: Walter Cunningham was sitting there lying his head off. He didn't forget his lunch, he didn't have any. He had none today nor would he have any tomorrow or the next day. He had probably never seen three quarters together at the same time in his life.[33]

Out loud she says:

That's okay, ma'am, you'll get to know all the county folks after a while. The Cunninghams never took anything they can't pay back—no church baskets and no scrip stamps. They never took anything off of anybody, they get along on what they have. They don't have much, but they get along on it.[34]

The Cunninghams are poor but proud; they do not take charity but fend for themselves and when that is not possible, they find a way of paying. When Walter's father required Atticus's legal expertise because of his "entailment," he paid with sacks of hickory nuts and turnip greens and crates of smilax and holly.[35] And despite their lack of intellectual zeal, their children remain in school although "most of the first grade had failed it last year."[36] Although at this point the Cunninghams are outside of a possible future audience for *To Kill a Mockingbird* because they are "immune to imaginative literature,"[37] Lee suggests that with perseverance, they may become part of it.

Indeed, Scout's friendship with Walter Cunningham sows the seeds for the possibility of Walter's upward social mobility. Again we see Aunt Alexandra's attitudes contrasted with those of Atticus and Scout. Aunt Alexandra sees inviolable social lines: "[Y]ou can scrub Walter Cunningham till he shines, you can put him in shoes and a new suit, but he'll never be like Jem . . . [b]ecause—he—is—trash. . . ."[38] Jem, on the other hand, thinks nothing of solving Walter's missing lunch problem by inviting Walter home for lunch and despite Walter's initial hesitancy, "[b]y the time we reached our front steps Walter had forgotten he was a Cunningham."[39] More importantly, Walter shares the Finches' language if not their rules of etiquette. He converses comfortably with Atticus and seems oblivious to the fact that his pouring syrup all over his food brands him as different from his hosts.[40]

Although they live on the margins of Maycomb, the Cunninghams are becoming full-fledged participants in the legal community. They are members of the jury, and it is their relationship with the aristocracy that brings them from outside the law to within it. The scene at the jailhouse explicates this transition. Walter Cunningham arrives with members of a lynch mob, ready to take Tom Robinson and the law into their own hands. Neither the presence of Atticus nor the illegality of their proposed act serves to deter them. But Scout, in a scene central to the novel, talks to Mr. Cunningham as an equal:

"Don't you remember me, Mr. Cunningham? I'm Jean Louise Finch. You brought us some hickory nuts one time, remember?" I began to sense the futility one feels when unacknowledged by a chance acquaintance.

"I go to school with Walter," I began again. "He's your boy, ain't he? Ain't he, sir?"

Mr. Cunningham was moved to a faint nod. He did know me, after all.

"He's in my grade," I said, "and he does right well. He's a good boy," I added, "a real nice boy. We brought him home for dinner one time. Maybe he told you about me, I beat him up one time but he was real nice about it. Tell him hey for me, won't you?"[41]

Scout speaks from innocence, naivety and true friendship, and we see her as untainted by Aunt Alexandra's class consciousness and free of condescension. When Mr. Cunningham tells the mob to clear out, he responds to Scout's openness and warmth.[42] Scout erases the boundaries between the old aristocracy, the caretakers of the law, and the poor whites, the would-be lawbreakers. In so doing, she draws the Cunninghams into the circle of the law-abiding and they back down on their intentions to lynch Tom Robinson. The Cunninghams and the Finches still belong to separate spheres, but they are overlapping and increasingly concentric. They are separated only by table manners and education, both fairly easily remedied. The true liberal vision put forth by *To Kill a Mockingbird* is that of the rise of the Cunninghams.

"The Ewells Down at the Dump"

Far less liberal and far more disturbing is the vision put forth of the Ewells, who live on the margins of Maycomb, by the dump, past the Cunninghams but not as far out as the Negroes. Their place by the dump is highly symbolic in that they are truly the discards of society.

The reader is first introduced to the Ewells just after meeting the Cunninghams in Scout's first grade class. Burris Ewell, the boy with the cootie that frightens Miss Caroline, is immediately contrasted with Little Chuck Little, "a born gentleman,"[43] of the Old Sarum clan.

The boy [Burris Ewell] stood up. He was the filthiest human I had ever seen. His neck was dark gray, the backs of his hands were rusty, and his fingernails were black deep into the quick. He peered at Miss Caroline from a fist-sized clean space on his face. No one had noticed him. . . .[44]

This is a very strange passage. How can it be that no one notices this incredibly filthy human being? It is almost as though Burris is made visible only when his cootie crawls out of his hair. He alone is too insignificant to be seen.

Little Chuck Little takes the aghast Miss Caroline by the arm and offers her a drink of water.[45] Burris, on the other hand, has a severe reaction to her offer of a remedy for cooties:

"And Burris," said Miss Caroline, "please bathe yourself before you come back tomorrow."

The boy laughed rudely. "You ain't sendin' me home, missus. I was on the verge of leavin'—I done done my time for this year."

Miss Caroline looked puzzled. "What do you mean by that?"

The boy did not answer. He gave a short contemptuous snort.

One of the elderly members of the class answered her: "He's one of the Ewells, ma'am," and I wondered if this explanation would be as unsuccessful as my attempt. But Miss Caroline seemed willing to listen. "Whole school's full of 'em. They come the first day every year and then leave. The truant lady gets 'em here 'cause she threatens 'em with the sheriff, but she's give up tryin' to hold 'em. She reckons she's carried out the law just gettin' their names on the roll and runnin' 'em here the first day."[46]

Because Burris is "one of the Ewells," the legal system does not function in forcing him to attend school. This, however, is an odd kind of freedom for a first-grader who lives by the dump. This "freedom" from legal coercion ensures that Burris Ewell, unlike Walter Cunningham, will never move from the margins of Maycomb into the world of the Finches and their neighbors.

Burris, moreover, has a language and temperament to match his marginalization. When Miss Caroline asks him to sit down, she realizes that she has stepped over an invisible line: "The boy's condescension flashed to anger. 'You try and make me, missus.'"[47] And when Miss Caroline tells him to go home:

> The boy snorted and slouched leisurely to the door.
>
> Safely out of range, he turned and shouted: "Report and be damned to ye! Ain't no snot-nosed slut of a school-teacher ever born c'n make me do nothin'! You ain't makin' me go nowhere, missus. You just remember that, you ain't makin' me go nowhere!"
>
> He waited until he was sure she was crying, then he shuffled out of the building.[48]

Lee intends this scene to prepare the way for Bob Ewell and his attitude at the trial and afterwards. She reveals much more, however. The Ewells are separated from everyone else by the barriers of language and appearance. The other school children, Finches and Cunninghams alike, band together to support Miss Caroline against Burris's attack:

> Soon we were clustered around her desk, trying in our various ways to comfort her. He was a real mean one . . . below the belt . . . you ain't called on to teach folks like that . . . them ain't Maycomb's ways, Miss Caroline, not really. . . .[49]

Everything about the child Burris differs from the other children: his appearance—he is dirtier than the worst of them; his demeanor—he slouches and shuffles; his language—he swears and uses words as weapons; his hope for an education. The law, designed to protect just such children from their parents' neglect, utterly fails him.

Maycomb makes no effort to remedy any of it. Atticus explains and justifies the Ewells' exclusion from the legal system. When Scout complains that she is forced to go to school whereas Burris Ewell is not, that the truant lady is content to get Burris's name on the roll, Atticus launches into a lengthy description of the Ewells to rationalize maintaining them in an outsider status:

> "You can't do that, Scout," Atticus said. "Sometimes it's better to bend the law a little in special cases. In your case, the law remains rigid. So to school you must go."
>
> . . . .
>
> Atticus said that the Ewells had been the disgrace of Maycomb for three generations. None of them had done an honest day's work in his recollection. He said that some Christmas, when he was getting rid of the tree, he would take me with him and show me where and how they lived. They were people, but they lived like animals. . . . "There are ways of keeping them in school by force, but it's silly to force people like the Ewells into a new environment. . . ."
>
> . . . .
>
> "Let us leave it at this," said Atticus dryly. "You, Miss Scout Finch, are of the common folk. You must obey the law." He said that the Ewells were members of an exclusive society made up of Ewells. In certain circumstances the common folk judiciously allowed them certain privileges by the simple method of becoming blind to some of the Ewells' activities. They didn't have to go to school, for one thing. Another thing, Mr. Bob Ewell, Burris's father, was permitted to hunt and trap out of season.[50]

The common folk visit the Ewells only to deliver annual Christmas baskets, as the Ewells, unlike the Cunninghams, are not too proud for charity. Maycomb's way, in which Atticus is fully complicitous, is to keep the Ewells down by the dump with old Christmas trees and everything else they discard.

Yet if the law fails to protect Burris, it fails even more miserably in its protection of Mayella Ewell. Although it is clear that Mayella perjures herself and accuses Tom Robinson of a rape he did not commit, it is equally clear that Mayella is the victim of both violence and incest.

Tom Robinson may not have inflicted the bruises on Mayella, but someone did. As they do with Burris's truancy, the citizens of Maycomb (including the Finches) choose to look the other way. Among the extralegal "privileges" they afford Bob Ewell are the privileges of beating and raping his daughter.

During Atticus's cross-examination of Sheriff Tate, Ewell's abusive treatment of Mayella becomes explicit, as does Maycomb's knowing passivity:

"Did you call a doctor, Sheriff? Did anybody call a doctor?" asked Atticus.

"No sir," said Mr. Tate.

"Didn't call a doctor?"

"No sir," repeated Mr. Tate.

"Why not?" There was an edge to Atticus's voice.

"Well I can tell you why I didn't. It wasn't necessary, Mr. Finch. She was mighty banged up. Something sho' happened, it was obvious."[51]

The edge in Atticus's voice is due to the fact that there is no official report of Mayella's injuries. No one in Maycomb seems very concerned (nor does the book seem to acknowledge) that Mayella, who was "mighty banged up . . . beaten around the head,"[52] received no medical attention. Mayella's injuries become detached from her person and treated as impersonal evidence that can prove Tom Robinson's innocence.

Mayella's sad life is treated in a similar fashion. Atticus uses her narration about her home life to build his case that Mayella enticed Tom Robinson onto the property. Atticus's compassion for Mayella seems feigned and unconvincing and any concern for the Ewell children is completely absent:

Atticus was quietly building up before the jury a picture of the Ewells' home life. The jury learned the following things: their relief check was far from enough to feed the family, and there was strong suspicion that Papa drank it up anyway—he sometimes went off in the swamp for days and came home sick; the weather was seldom cold enough to require shoes, but when it was, you could make dandy ones from strips of old tires; the family hauled its water in buckets from a spring that ran out at one end of the dump—they kept the surrounding area clear of trash—and it was everybody for himself as far as keeping clean went: if you wanted to wash you hauled your own water; the younger children had perpetual colds and suffered from chronic ground-itch. . . .[53]

Importantly, Mayella does not have the opportunity to actually tell her own story. The story of her life is filtered through Atticus's cross-examination. Lee sets up the context for this passage in such a way that we are so focused on Atticus and Tom Robinson that we, like all of Maycomb, fail to hear just what is being said. This passage and others from the trial depict neglect and abuse so compelling that one wonders how one could have been blind to it.

When Tom Robinson testifies, Mayella's plight becomes even more transparent:

[I]t came to me [Scout] that Mayella Ewell must have been the loneliest person in the world. . . . [W]hite people wouldn't have anything to do with her because she lived among pigs; Negroes wouldn't have anything to do with her because she was white. . . . Maycomb gave them Christmas baskets, welfare money, and the back of its hand.[54]

Maycomb's disregard for the Ewells results not only in neglect, but also in abuse. Tom testifies that Mayella "says she never kissed a grown man before. . . . She says what her papa do to her don't count."[55] Yet it seems that the reader, like Maycomb, is not supposed to respond to this short, chilling line. *To Kill a Mockingbird* never again refers to the Ewell children and their living conditions. They have been used to develop the plot and explicate the conflict and then tossed back on the dump. Burris, at seven or eight years of age, and Mayella, at nineteen, have no hope for anything else. They, like Scout and Jem, must live up to their birthright. They will stay on the margins of Maycomb, outside the reach of its laws. As the trial scene also makes clear, they do not even share a language in which they might tell their own story. Mayella can read and write as well as her father (which I suspect is not well at all) and the rest of the children are denied the chance to become literate. Mayella and her father both have difficulty understanding what Atticus is saying at the trial and need interpretation. The reader's sympathy is neither engaged nor directed toward the Ewells.

With this as a backdrop, Bob Ewell's striking out at the Finches and all they represent becomes a highly symbolic act. The Ewells cannot, like the Cunninghams, be absorbed into the circle of Maycomb's "ordinary folk." The Ewells do not, like Tom Robinson and Calpurnia, fit into some image that Maycomb has of them. With a knife as a weapon, Bob Ewell rips through to the Finches, using the last resort of those living on the margin—violence.

"The Negroes"

Although under Jem's classification, the Negroes constitute a single group, *To Kill a Mockingbird* actually portrays two different kinds of southern Blacks: the "good" Negroes like Tom and Calpurnia, and the "bad" Negroes like Lula. Calpurnia and Tom Robinson's family are among the most sympathetic characters in the novel. They represent a certain kind of southern Black that might hope to move beyond the margins of Maycomb and under the protection of its laws. But they must play quite stereotypical roles: Calpurnia is the "good Mammy" and Tom is the disempowered "naif."

Calpurnia might be the wisest person in the novel after Atticus; yet she represents a certain kind of Black, the kind who treat white folks with traditional, if not deserved, respect. When the children enter the church with Calpurnia "the men stepped back and took off their hats;

the women crossed their arms at their waists, weekday gestures of respectful attention. They parted and made a small pathway to the church door for us."[56] At the trial, we come to understand the consequences of such deference. Tom is similarly obeisant to Mayella and it is such obeisance that leads him into trouble. If she wants him to chop up a chiffarobe for her, he is willing to do it, even after a hard day of work.[57]

Tom Robinson cannot be guilty. The physical evidence of the location of Mayella's bruises and the withered condition of Tom's arm leave no doubt that he has been unjustly accused. Yet the jury, at least officially, chooses to accept the Ewells' version of what happened. While we are sympathetic to Tom Robinson, our attention unfortunately is directed away from the tragedy of his death; instead, we seem to be led by the book's structure to focus on Atticus's goodness in defending him. If Tom had been patient[58] and allowed Atticus to speak and act for him on appeal, he might have been saved. Instead, apparently fed up with white justice, Tom takes matters into his own hands and tries to escape. He is then destroyed by agents of white law. The book seems to recommend passivity and acceptance to Blacks.[59] Tom and Calpurnia are acceptable to Maycomb as long as they speak like the whites or allow the whites to speak for them. In other words, they are acceptable as long as they know their place.

Their place is in a little settlement beyond the town dump, in "the Quarters" outside Maycomb's town limits. Scout and Jem visit there when Calpurnia takes them to church with her in their father's absence.

First Purchase African M.E. Church was in the Quarters outside the southern town limits, across the old sawmill tracks. It was an ancient paint-peeled frame building, the only church in Maycomb with a steeple and bell, called First Purchase because it was paid for from the first earnings of freed slaves. Negroes worshiped in it on Sundays and white men gambled in it on weekdays.[60]

The Blacks' dependence on the forbearance of the white citizens of Maycomb is clear from this odd arrangement. Even in their sacred space, purchased with the first money they were allowed to possess, the whites trespass with apparent impunity. In fact, the whites bring illegal activities under the protection of an unwritten law that allows them to take whatever they please from the Blacks.

The other kind of Black, the "bad" kind, is represented by Lula, "a tall Negro woman. Her weight was on one leg; she rested her left elbow in the curve of her hip, pointing at us with upturned palm. She was bullet-headed with strange almond-shaped eyes, straight nose, and an Indian-bow mouth. She seemed seven feet high."[61] Lula is what we would now call a Black separatist. She challenges Calpurnia's relationship with the Finches, which Lula correctly identifies as servant to master. When Calpurnia says that the Finch children are her company at church, Lula lays bare their inherent inequality, "Yeah, an' I reckon you's comp'ny at the Finch house durin' the week."[62] Lula objects to the children's presence in their world: "You ain't got no business bringin' white chillun here—they got their church, we got our'n. It is our church, ain't it, Miss Cal?"[63] Lula has a valid point, one that will become commonplace in a few decades, but she is rejected by the "good" Blacks of the book. They draw together to protect the children from Lula's challenge and banish Lula; the children are instructed, "Don't pay no 'tention to Lula, she's contentious. . . . She's a trouble-maker from way back, got fancy ideas an' haughty ways—we're mighty glad to have you all."[64] Lula's "fancy ideas" have to do with equality; she finds something strange in that the Blacks are not free to enter the white world, and yet the whites can not only gamble in the Black church, but white children are greeted with undue respect. Lee makes it clear that people like Lula are not what is expected in the Blacks who hope to be protected by the white law.

Yet the white law does little for Tom Robinson. The bitter truth that flies in the face of all interpretations that see triumph[65] in the book is that Tom Robinson is dead. He has been unjustly accused, found guilty in the light of clear evidence of his innocence, and killed by officers of the law. The Negroes out beyond the dump have little to celebrate and it may be that Lula is at least partly right. While the Negroes of Maycomb have a voice that is carefully channeled through the whites, Lula's strident truth is silenced.

If all books, as Wayne Booth claims, produce a practical "patterning of desires,"[66] what does *To Kill a Mockingbird* ask us "to desire and fear and deplore"?[67] The book teaches us to desire to be like Atticus—courageous in the face of our community's prejudices. But it also teaches us to fear and deplore the Ewells and Lula. The book shapes what we see and that to which we aspire,[68] and it leaves Lula and the Ewells marginalized. The narrative voice is not so much contemptuous of them as dismissive. In fact, in terms of narrative structure, they completely disappear. Lula never reappears nor is she discussed after her brief interruption in First Purchase African M. E. Church. She serves no purpose in the novel except to demonstrate that her kind are regarded even by members of her own race as troublemakers and outsiders.

Even more surprising, after Bob Ewell's death, no one raises the issue of the now-orphaned Ewell children. Burris and his many siblings are left to swear and slouch their way into a future that promises never to share in the community life of Maycomb. *To Kill a Mockingbird* invites its readers to ignore them just as Miss Caroline should have ignored Burris's taunts—no tears should be shed for the likes of the Ewells.

We readers, like the citizens of Maycomb, see what we want to see and are blind to much else. We, like Atticus, are implicated in the town's delusions as long as we read *To Kill a Mockingbird* with uncritical admiration. We misread the novel as much as the citizens of Maycomb misread their community. It may be true, as Miss Maudie claims, that Atticus's forthright defense of Tom Robinson has been "a baby-step"[69] toward a more tolerant society, but it has far, far to go.

Notes

1. *See, e.g.*, Jay Rigdon, *Atticus Finch—A Model That Inspires*, Ind. Law., June 3, 1992, at 4. "Atticus Finch had faith in the law. . . . He did not treat the law as business, or as a vehicle to further his own desire to make money. . . . Atticus Finch bled for his clients. . . . Atticus worked long hours in preparing for the case." *Id. See also* Matthew A. Hodel, *No Hollow Hearts*, 77 A.B.A. J. 68, 68 (Oct., 1991) (praising Atticus Finch as a "fine citizen, parent, and lawyer" in an article suggesting that the "best lawyers are likely to be the most principled"); William J. O'Malley, *Atticus Finch and the Family*, 164 *America* 509, 509 (May 11, 1991) ("[*To Kill a Mockingbird*] gives us a strong image of good parenting.").

2. Monroe Freedman, *Atticus Finch, Esq., R.I.P., Legal Times*, Feb. 24, 1992, at 20.

3. *Id.* at 21.

4. Monroe Freedman, *Finch: The Lawyer Mythologized, Legal Times*, May 18, 1992, at 25.

5. *See, e.g.*, Thomas L. Shaffer, *American Legal Ethics: Text, Readings, and Discussion Topics* 3-57 (1985).

6. Louise Rosenblatt, *The Reader, the Text, the Poem* 24 (1978). Rosenblatt describes an efferent transaction in this way: "As the reader responds to the printed words or symbols, his attention is directed outward . . . toward concepts to be retained, ideas to be tested, actions to be performed after the reading." *Id.*

7. Harper Lee, *To Kill a Mockingbird* 80 (25th Anniversary ed., Warner Books 1982) (1960).

8. *Id.* at 7.

9. *Id.* at 8.

10. *See, e.g.*, James Joyce, *A Portrait of the Artist as a Young Man* (Penguin Books 1964) (1966) (focusing on the hero, Stephen Dedalus). For a discussion of the tendency of the individual self to be defined in isolation, see Wayne Booth, *The Company We Keep: An Ethics of Fiction* 240-50 (1988). This may be the appropriate point for me to acknowledge my debt to Booth's book. A few years ago, the *Journal of Legal Education* asked me to review *The Company We Keep*. I have not read the same since then. Many of my conclusions in this article are directly or indirectly the result of Booth's work in *The Company We Keep*.

11. Shaffer, *supra* note 5, at 7.

12. Lee, *supra* note 7, at 93.

13. Richard Delgado, *Storytelling for Oppositionists and Others: A Plea for Narrative*, 87 Mich. L. Rev. 2411, 2412 (1989).

14. Some critics have taken note of the class distinctions depicted in *To Kill a*

Mockingbird. See, e.g., Fred Erisman, *The Romantic Regionalism of Harper Lee*, 26 Ala. Rev. 122 (1973).

15. Lee, *supra* note 7, at 229.
16. Lee, *supra* note 7, at 230.
17. Booth, *supra* note 10, at 422.
18. Lee, *supra* note 7, at 9.
19. Lee, *supra* note 7, at 81.
20. Lee, *supra* note 7, at 231.
21. Lee, *supra* note 7, at 234.
22. Lee, *supra* note 7, at 233.
23. Lee, *supra* note 7, at 235.
24. Lee, *supra* note 7, at 235.
25. Lee, *supra* note 7, at 236.
26. Lee, *supra* note 7, at 237-38.
27. Lee, *supra* note 7, at 218.
28. Lee, *supra* note 7, at 135-36.
29. Lee, *supra* note 7, at 21.
30. Lee, *supra* note 7, at 21.
31. Lee, *supra* note 7, at 24.
32. Lee, *supra* note 7, at 24.
33. Lee, *supra* note 7, at 24.
34. Lee, *supra* note 7, at 25.
35. Lee, *supra* note 7, at 25.
36. Lee, *supra* note 7, at 21.
37. Lee, *supra* note 7, at 21.
38. Lee, *supra* note 7, at 226-27.
39. Lee, *supra* note 7, at 28.
40. Lee, *supra* note 7, at 28-29.
41. Lee, *supra* note 7, at 156.
42. Lee, *supra* note 7, at 156-57.
43. Lee, *supra* note 7, at 30.
44. Lee, *supra* note 7, at 31.
45. Lee, *supra* note 7, at 30-31.
46. Lee, *supra* note 7, at 31-32.
47. Lee, *supra* note 7, at 32.
48. Lee, *supra* note 7, at 32.
49. Lee, *supra* note 7, at 32.
50. Lee, *supra* note 7, at 35.
51. Lee, *supra* note 7, at 169-70.
52. Lee, *supra* note 7, at 170.
53. Lee, *supra* note 7, at 185.
54. Lee, *supra* note 7, at 194.
55. Lee, *supra* note 7, at 197.
56. Lee, *supra* note 7, at 121.
57. Lee, *supra* note 7, at 193.

58. One is immediately reminded, of course, of Dr. Martin Luther King, Jr.'s remarks in his *Letter from Birmingham City Jail*:

For years now I have heard the word "Wait!" It rings in the ear of every Negro with a piercing familiarity. This "Wait" has almost always meant "Never." It has been a tranquilizing thalidomide, relieving the emotional stress for a moment, only to give birth to an ill-formed infant of frustration.

Martin L. King, Jr., *Letter from Birmingham City Jail* 5 (1963).

59. Freedman also objects to Tom's passivity in the novel:

According to Christian charity, Finch, a white man, could forgive Cunningham, another white man, for his ongoing and unrepentant hatred of blacks and for his attempt to murder a black. . . . I would have had an easier time of it had it been Tom Robinson or his wife doing the forgiving.

Freedman, *supra* note 2, at 25.

60. Lee, *supra* note 7, at 120.

61. Lee, *supra* note 7, at 121.

62. Lee, *supra* note 7, at 121.

63. Lee, *supra* note 7, at 121.

64. Lee, *supra* note 7, at 122.

65. *See, e.g.*, Shaffer, *supra* note 5, at 10 ("Tom Robinson loses his case and his life, but in this loss truth triumphs over racism, meaning triumphs over power.").

66. Booth, *supra* note 10, at 202.

67. Booth, *supra* note 10, at 205.

68. For a thorough discussion of how narrative shapes our sensibilities and indeed our culture, see James B. White, *Heracles' Bow* (1989) and Delgado, *supra* note 13, at 2416.

69. Lee, *supra* note 7, at 219.

"Fine Fancy Gentlemen" and "Yappy Folk":
Contending Voices in *To Kill a Mockingbird*

Theodore R. Hovet and Grace-Ann Hovet

To Kill a Mockingbird (1960) remains an important work because Harper Lee insistently undermines typical assumptions in the United States about the origins of racism. Rather than ascribing racial prejudice primarily to "poor white trash" (Newitz and Wray), Lee demonstrates how issues of gender and class intensify prejudice, silence the voices that might challenge the existing order, and greatly complicate many Americans' conception of the causes of racism and segregation.

The popularity of *To Kill a Mockingbird* is uncontestable. Even before receiving the Pulitzer Prize in 1961, it had sold 500,000 copies and had been translated into ten languages (Cain). The movie version, generally faithful to the content and spirit of the novel, garnered Academy Awards in 1962 for Gregory Peck's portrayal of Atticus Finch and for Horton Foote's script. Of novels written between 1895 and 1975 it has been the third best selling one in the nation. Even more noteworthy, in a survey by the Book-of-the-Month Club and the Library of Congress's Center for the Book, *To Kill a Mockingbird* readers listed it second only to the Bible as a book that made a "difference" in their lives (Cain) and in 1998 members of the Library Association selected it as one of the five best novels of the twentieth century (*Seattle Times*). Arthur Appleby lists it as the fifth most studied literary work in the public schools, appearing in 69% of the curricula, and points out that at the beginning of this decade it was the only work written by a woman in the top ten of those books most often used in the schools. It has even been assigned in law classes to teach legal ethics and in 1994 was the subject of a symposium on the law and a special edition of the *Alabama Law Review*. In short, its powerful critique of racism and its sophisticated use of established elements of the American literary tradition such as the "coming of age" or "initiation" formula, the American Gothic, and classic realism—in other words, its wedding of social relevance to literary aesthetics—make it both a "readerly" and a "teacherly" work. To borrow the words of Roy Hoffman, "Long Lives the Mockingbird" (31).

It also has in recent years gained increasing critical respect. Once dismissed by influential critics such as Stanley Kauffmann and Brendon Gill as sentimental, static, and intellectually dishonest (Nicholson 155, 159), *To Kill a Mockingbird* has been praised recently by Claudia Durst Johnson, Janice Radway, Dean Shackelford, and Carolyn Jones for its literary complexity, its vivid evocation of character and setting, and its powerful critique of racism and patriarchy. We fully concur with these recent critical assessments, believing that the novel and the movie are two of the finest accomplishments in mainstream American culture. We also feel that because of the work of these critics it is unnecessary to mount yet another defense of the aesthetic and intellectual quality of the novel. Instead, we want to look at the way Lee uses the voice of the narrator and the voices of other characters that contest that narration in order to better understand the way the novel links racism to gender and class oppression.

Most readers overlook the variety of contending voices in the novel because Lee's skillful use of formulas and techniques common in American literature seamlessly absorbs them into the narrative. The story told by the mature Jean Louise Finch about events that occurred before her tenth birthday employs two literary devices familiar to most readers—the "coming of age" and "beset American justice" formulas. These devices position readers to anticipate a positive narrative closure and to read over the darker strands in the story. The coming of age formula leads readers to expect that Jean Louise, then known as Scout, will respond to negative experiences and threatening events by developing an individualistic moral center than can triumph over them. This developmental paradigm, so central to American narratives, encourages readers to equate Scout's psychological and intellectual growth with progress in the South as a whole and to overlook the reality that the social structure in Maycomb remains unchanged at the end of the novel. The other familiar formula of beset American justice (i.e., the story of the lonely lawman or crime crusader such as the central figures in *High Noon* or the *Dirty Harry* series upholding justice in a community without the aid of its cowardly and treacherous citizens) plays on the reader's expectation that the hero will succeed in restoring morality and justice. Boo Radley's killing of Bob Ewell while defending Scout and Jem, Atticus's decision not to prosecute Boo, and his almost unanimous reelection to the state legislature after his unpopular defense of Tom Robinson leave readers with the satisfying feeling that good has conquered evil. As a consequence, the voices that expressed a darker view of the meaning of the events surrounding Tom Robinson and Boo Radley are generally overlooked.

Even more importantly, Lee also utilizes what Robert Shulman calls the middle-class, conversational voice that characterizes classical American realism (160). This voice—admirably articulated by Kim Stanley in the voice overlay in the movie—establishes an intimacy with the reader, regardless of his or her cultural background, and an ethos of moral authority that initially overrides internal contradictions in her narrative and softens other voices in the story that challenge her interpretation of events. In particular, Lee's use of the conventions of American regional literature obscures the diversity of viewpoints. Like Sarah Orne Jewett's *The Country of the Pointed Firs* or Harriet Beecher Stowe's *The Pearl of Orr's Island*, Lee evokes nostalgia for America's rural past: a pastoral setting (rural Alabama in the mid-1930s), vivid characterizations of provincial eccentricity (Miss Dubose or Dolphus Raymond), a cast of likeable common folk (children, African Americans, poor but proud whites), and amusing "southern incidents" such as Scout's reaction to seeing her first snowfall ("the worlds endin'"!). These elements combine to create a yearning for a seemingly lost age of innocence that diverts readers from looking too closely at the dark side of southern life embedded in the narration.

But Lee's use of the conventions of realism and regionalism is a two-edged sword. The success of American realistic fiction and its regional variations depends on convincing its readers, mostly middle-class and urban, that it provides an acquaintance with people and conditions not part of their everyday experience. This educational function of realism distinguishes it, in the minds of its advocates, from the purely entertainment function of popular literature, particularly "sensation stories," romances, and domestic sentimentality. As William Dean Howells explained, "the realist must represent the . . . person who cannot tell his or her own tale. The realist thus plays the role of translator and mediator to make such persons known to the grammatical classes" (qtd. in Kaplan 34). One may recall how Jo March in *Little Women* gives up writing sensation stories in order to portray for urban readers the realities of the small-town New England life that she knows first hand. Or one may also recall the struggle of the narrator in *Life in the Iron Mills* to give voice to the new proletariat. Lee, following very closely the goals of the great female realists of the nineteenth century like Louisa May Alcott and Rebecca Harding Davis strives to present a "realistic" portrayal of small town southern life which will make it known to readers outside the region. Such a realistic portrayal requires that a cross-section of Maycomb, Alabama, be allowed to speak their lives in the language characteristic of their race and social class. In the frequently quoted words of Atticus, the narrator has to "learn a simple trick. . . . You never really understand a person until you consider things from his point of view—until you climb into his skin and walk around in it" (32). Thus we hear not only from the white middle class but also from such people as the drug-addicted Mrs. Dubose, a figure from "the lost cause" dear to the formula of the Southern Gothic; the miscegenationist, Dolphus Raymond; and a variety of individuals from the black community. But most significantly, members of the group considered "white trash" are given the opportunity to speak. Inevitably, then, as narrative theorists like Mikhail Bakhtin have argued, the effort to create a realistic fictional world necessitates a "dialogue" among differing voices which undermines the efforts of the narrator to impose a single version of reality.

The difference among these voices is sharpened by the events occur-ring in the South as Lee was writing the novel. Published in 1960 and filmed in 1961, *To Kill a Mockingbird* appears at the moment when the nation, pushed by an aggressive civil rights campaign led by the NAACP and changing socioeconomic and political conditions (we should not forget that the Cold War made racial discrimination an in-ternational embarrassment and a potent propaganda tool for anti-American forces), was attempting to make the watershed transition from legal segregation in most of the South and socially sanctioned segregation throughout much of the nation to a commitment to racial equality in deeds as well as words. The school desegregation decision of the Supreme Court (*Brown vs. Topeka Board of Education*) ap-peared only six years before publication of the novel and the federal as-sault on racial inequality (the 1964 Civil Rights Act) was still several years in the future. In short, *To Kill a Mockingbird* was written and published amidst the most significant and conflict-ridden social change in the South since the Civil War and Reconstruction. Inevita-bly, despite its mid-1930s setting, the story told from the perspective of the 1950s voices the conflicts, tensions, and fears induced by this tran-sition.

The middle-class narrative voice in *To Kill a Mockingbird* which is so appealing to most readers articulates what would become one of the dominant arguments of southern progressives, one uncritically echoed by many northern liberals. What some might see as virulent southern racism, the narrator tries to tell us, is not characteristic of the South as a whole but was created and sustained by a backward element in the rural South represented in the novel by the Ewell clan. Unable or unwilling to employ modern agricultural practices or to educate themselves and their children in modern forms of labor, this "white trash" mistakenly blames its increasingly marginal position in society on the intrusion of African Americans who will not accept their secondary social status. As one of the whites in *To Kill a Mockingbird* puts it, "it's time some-body taught 'em a lesson, they . . . gettin' way above themselves"

(225). Moreover, Scout explains, these rural whites blame the increasing presence of African Americans on the more prosperous white leadership in the towns—"those bastards who thought they ran this town," to quote Bob Ewell (226). For this reason, the narrator would have us believe, the unjust treatment of African Americans like Tom Robinson is not the fault of the leaders of southern society like her father, the judge, and the newspaper editor. It is the product of an uneducated and irresponsible class of poor whites who use physical intimidation and mob rule to defend what little status they have left. From her vantage point in the late 1950s, the narrator of *To Kill a Mockingbird* implies that this group is an anachronism which will disappear in the wake of an emerging industrialized and urbanized "New South." The Atticus Finches will then assume their rightful leadership positions and begin creating a more just society. The narrator's strategy of placing responsibility for American intolerance and injustice on the vanishing rural poor—what we can call "the white trash scenario"—was so successful that it has become a cliché in popular culture, evident not only in *To Kill a Mockingbird* but also in films like *Easy Rider* and in prime time television programs such as *Heat of the Night* and *I'll Fly Away*.

This is not to say that the narrator and other southern apologists were completely disingenuous. The virulent racism of rural whites helped maintain Jim Crow, fueled the resistance, often violent, to the Civil Rights Movement, and fed the popularity of demagogues like Orville Faubus, Lester Maddox, and George Wallace. The attempt by southern apologists to assign this group the primary responsibility for racism in order to exonerate middle and upper-class whites, however, is a false reading of history. As C. Vann Woodward pointed out during the early stages of the southern Civil Rights Movement, American imperialism and its slogan of "the white man's burden," along with Supreme Court decisions in the 1890s supporting segregation, implicated the nation as a whole in racist policies. Despite this reality, nevertheless, the white trash scenario worked because the accused were a natural scapegoat. Mostly uneducated and without voice in the media, desperately poor and without economic influence, poor rural whites were helpless to counter the negative stereotype created by the southern apologists and perpetuated by the national media. They were demonized into "the other" by civil rights advocates and progressive southerners. "Poor whites," conclude Annalee Newitz and Matthew Wray in their analysis of white trash, "are stereotyped as virulently racist in comparison with their wealthier counterparts. As long as the poor are said to possess such traits, people can convince themselves that the poor should be cast out of mainstream society . . . " (171).

Ironically, Lee's desire to create a realistic portrayal of a southern region unmasked the strategy of the southern apologists, including her own. In order to make southern racism understandable, she not only used the techniques of realism and regionalism, but she also created a double plot, the stories surrounding Boo Radley and Tom Robinson. Several influential critics such as W. J. Stuckey and Harold Bloom maintain that the two stories are a result of artistic failure, an inability to create an organically developed narrative. But, as Claudia Johnson has demonstrated, the double plot opens the text to a more profound reading than one would expect from Lee's use of the "coming of age" or "beset American justice" formulas. Johnson points out that by placing the story of the children's reactions to "Boo," the Finch's neighbor, whom the town thinks is mentally impaired, alongside the town's response to Tom Robinson, Lee makes concrete the psychology of racism. More specifically, Scout and Jem's construction of "Boo" as a gothic monster, an "other" that embodies the mysterious outside forces that constantly threaten the known world of home and family, suggests that white southern society has also constructed the African American as an "other," a monster, who supposedly threatens the established order. Just as Scout and Jem must grow up by confronting the gothic monster of their own and the town's creation, Johnson's reading contends, so must southern society confront the racial monster that it has constructed (*Threatening Boundaries* 67-72).

Scout's struggle to come to terms with the reality behind "the other" inevitably sensitizes her to voices silenced by white patriarchy. Guided by these voices, Scout—and the attentive reader—becomes aware that racism is part of a general pattern of exclusion and oppression which must be overcome before anyone can be said to be free. *To Kill a Mockingbird*, John Burt notes, begins as a "story about race and turns into a story about class" (367).

In keeping with the white trash scenario, the adult Jean Louise Finch places the responsibility for racial injustice squarely on the shoulders of a socioeconomic group without power or voice in the South—the poor, uneducated, disease-ridden rural whites represented by Bob Ewell. He falsely accuses Tom Robinson of raping his daughter, Mayella, whom he himself has physically and sexually abused, and tries to destroy Atticus for his defense of a "nigger." At the same time, the adult narrator disassociates from these events the leadership of the town represented by her father (a respected lawyer and longtime state legislator), the judge who presides over Tom's trial, and the local newspaper editor.

But if we pay close attention to the narration as it shifts from the adult Jean Louise's omniscient point of view to the first-person account of events by the young Scout, we hear a voice whose story of experience with exclusion and oppression creates gaps and contradictions in the story that the adult is trying to tell. First of all, Scout draws attention to the fact that the points of conflict in the narrative are marked by the absence of a female presence, particularly the maternal. Mrs. Finch, Mrs. Ewell, and Mrs. Radley have died before the key events in the story. Thus there are no mothers who have participated in Boo's confinement, implicated themselves in Mayella's abuse by her father, or exonerated Atticus's failure to act more decisively in the state legislature to combat segregation and lynching. Moreover, much to Scout's indignation, women are not allowed to serve on juries in Alabama. Consequently, they are not implicated in the wrongful conviction of Tom Robinson.

Once we begin to hear this "feminine voice," as Dean Shackelford calls it, we notice that the story in *To Kill a Mockingbird* is as much about Scout's initiation into sexism as into racism. The very first summer of the story, before the events surrounding Tom Robinson take place, Scout is introduced to the male's treatment of the female as object. Dill, the eight-year-old summer visitor, "staked me out, marked me as his property . . . then he neglected me" (43). Even more painfully—a fact noted by few critics—this same summer marks the time that "Jem and I first began to part company" (56). Previously, Jem had treated her like a boy, excluding her from the despised female category, and going so far as to discourage her from acting like a girl: "Jem told me I was being a girl, that girls always imagined things, that's why other people hated them so, and if I started behaving like one I could just go off and find some to play with" (42). But as he grows older, he begins to treat Scout like the girls he despises. The division between Scout and Jem culminates when he is twelve and approaching adolescence: As the narrator notes, "Overnight it seemed, Jem had acquired an alien set of values and was trying to impose them on me: several times he went so far as to tell me what to do. After one altercation when Jem hollered, 'Its time you started bein' a girl and acting right!' I burst into tears and fled to Calpurnia" (109). The growing gender division is underscored as Jem spends "days together" with Dill in a phallic tree house and Scout seeks refuge in the womb-like porch of Miss Maudie Atkinson, a feisty woman who refuses to play the role of Southern Lady.

Jem's admonition that she should act like "a girl" is particularly galling to Scout because she is already aware that to be female in the South is to become an ambiguous icon that precludes an individual identity. On the one hand, the churches are obsessed with what Scout calls "the Impurity of Women doctrine that seemed to preoccupy all clergymen" (115). But at the same time, women are excluded from juries because "frail ladies" need to be protected "from sordid cases like Tom's" (202). This contradiction between the masculine perception of female impurity and the myth of the pure southern lady makes Scout aware that a woman has no individual identity but is an image that keeps shifting back and forth between Jezebel and Angel in the House. This unwillingness to acknowledge a personal identity for the woman is further exemplified by the town's construction of Mayella Ewell both as white trash slut and as the southern belle who is ravished by the insatiable black rapist. In short, Scout's "coming of age" or "initiation" is marked by an introduction to the sexism that is as deaf to her individual voice as it is to Tom Robinson's assertions of innocence.

Maycomb's inability or unwillingness to hear Scout's individual voice causes her to be acutely sensitive to more subtle kinds of silence generated by white patriarchy. Her saintly father, Atticus, has served in the state legislature most of his adult life and even after defending Tom Robinson is re-elected without opposition. He presumably has had and will have opportunity to voice his opposition to racial injustice. However, Scout faithfully records how the seemingly courageous liberal is plagued by a strange inability to speak its name, i.e., racism, using instead words without any clear referents like "something" or "it." For example, in trying to explain to Jem why the jury found Tom Robinson guilty, he says that the members "saw something come between them and reason. . . . There's something in our world that makes men lose their heads—they couldn't be fair if they tried" (201). The unnamed "something" is further mystified by his frequent use of "it": "Don't fool yourselves–*it's* all adding up and one of these days we're going to have to pay the bill for *it*. I hope *it's* not in you children's time" (221, emphasis added). Atticus's inability to name "the disease" (84) is symptomatic of his failure to combat racism in Maycomb and in the state legislature. When Jem tells his father that because of Tom's unjust conviction he must "go up to Montgomery and change the law," Atticus responds: "You'd be surprised how hard that'd be. I won't live to see the law changed . . . " (201). In summary, Atticus is eloquent in defending the law but is silent concerning the racism which brought Tom to trial and conviction.

The narrator also draws our attention to still another kind of silence of well-intentioned men like Atticus. Those who have only seen the movie probably are unaware that in the novel Bob Ewell's attack on Jem and Scout is motivated as much by class hatred as by the desire to avenge Atticus's defense of Tom. They certainly would not be aware that in the novel Atticus himself is implicated in this virulent classism. As reported by his daughter, he has a hopelessly inaccurate conception of the social structure of Maycomb. Despite his law practice, which makes him relatively affluent, and a long tenure in the state legislature that gives him social prestige, he identifies himself as "poor" and as a member of the humble and decent "common folk." By using this term, he hides his privileged status and positions himself to characterize people like the Ewells as uncommonly indecent. They are "animals" (33) rather than human beings crippled by generations of poverty and disease. Thus in the Maycomb envisioned by Atticus there are only two classes of whites: the decent common folk and those "yappy" or "tacky" people, as Jem calls them, who are "not our kind of folks" (204). As with his inability to do more than identify racism as "it," Atticus's response to this group is to treat them as unredeemable. Scout explains the Finch view of "white trash":

> Every town the size of Maycomb had families like the Ewells. No economic fluctuations changed their status—people like the Ewells lived as guests of the county in prosperity as well as in the depths of the depression. No truant officers could keep their numerous offspring in school; no public health officer could free them from congenital defects, various worms, and the diseases indigenous to filthy surroundings. (157)

One result of this attitude on the part of men like Atticus is to construct for these poor whites the same kind of segregated space that has been constructed for the blacks. Their poverty forces them to live only in a "dump adjacent" to the "colored quarters." Excluded from daily contact with the town, they are demonized and treated as "an exclusive society made up of Ewells" to whom the regular laws such as compulsory school attendance don't apply (33). This exclusion, of course, makes it possible to remove them metaphorically from mainstream society and to quarantine them within the space reserved for people like the Ewells. To use Teresa Godwin Phelps's apt phrasing, "there is another disease in Maycomb that Atticus does not see: the disease of marginalization, of class distinctions that lead us to bifurcate our world into 'us' and 'them'" (514).

Because of this systematic exclusion from the life of the community, Ewell's false accusation that Tom raped his daughter must be read as more complex than a simple act of racism. Ewell is also attempting to break out of the social isolation that has been imposed upon him and his clan by mainstream society in Maycomb. Atticus admits to Scout and Jem that Ewell accuses Tom in the hopes of playing upon the racism of the "respectable" people in order to raise his status in the town. In this he succeeds in so far as the white townspeople support Tom's conviction. But at the same time he fails to overcome the class structure that has held him in poverty. Atticus explains that the judge made Ewell "look like a fool" and treats Ewell "as if he were a three-legged chicken or a square egg." "He thought he'd be a hero," Atticus concludes, "but all he got for his pain . . . was, okay, we'll convict this Negro but get back to your dump" (228). As the narrator puts it, "Maycomb gave them Christmas baskets, welfare money, and the back of its hand" (176).

This comment makes clear that Scout is attaining a more realistic view of the Ewells than that propounded by her father. She is putting into practice Atticus's advice—"to climb into his skin and walk around in it." By so doing, she perceives and reports to her readers that Ewell does not see the social structure of the town in the same way as Atticus. He identifies the common people with those like himself who are held down by a wealthy white ruling class (Atticus's "common folk") who manipulate African Americans in order to keep poor whites like himself in their place. In breaking into Judge Taylor's house or attacking the Finch children, Ewell attempts to strike back at "those bastards who thought they ran this town" (226). In short, much of the injustice and violence that occurs in the novel originates in a society obsessed with class as much as race. As Jem notes, the region is not composed of decent common folk and animals, but of a hierarchy of hatred: "our kind of folks don't like the Cunninghams, the Cunninghams don't like the Ewells, and the Ewells hate and despise the colored folks" (207). Lee's novel, therefore, verifies the contention of Newitz and Wray that "as a stereotype, white calls our attention to the way that discourses of class and racial difference tend to bleed into one another, especially in the way that they pathologize and lay waste to their 'others'" (169).

Ironically, the trashy Mayella Ewell is the element in the narrative which destabilizes the hegemony of white masculine respectability. While the casual reader might view this nineteen-year-old woman as a lying slut who causes the death of an innocent African American, Scout sensitively portrays her as another victim in this sad story, but a female victim who struggles to assert her humanity despite her ignorance and the contempt of the townspeople. Not only sexually and physically abused by her father, she bears the crushing weight of the Ewells' isolation. She is so separated from human society that when the ever-polite Atticus calls her "Miss" and "mam" she accuses him of being one of the "fine fancy gentlemen" who is "mockin'" and "making fun" of her (167). When he asks her who her "friends" are, she doesn't understand the meaning of the word and again accuses him of making fun of her (169). Scout suddenly realizes "that Mayella Ewell must have been the loneliest person in the world. She was even lonelier than Boo Radley, who had not been out of the house in twenty-five years" (176).

With this complete failure of communication with the "fine fancy gentlemen," Mayella has no choice but to fall silent for the remainder of the trial (173). Scout's recognition of Mayella's victimization is made even more poignant by her insight that in spite of the isolation, poverty, and abuse there is a human spirit struggling to express itself. In a yard littered with junk, Mayella has placed "against the fence . . .

six chipped-enamel slop jars holding brilliant red geraniums, cared for as tenderly as if they belonged to Miss Maudie Atkinson . . . " (158).

The description of the geraniums in the slop jars not only asserts Mayella's humanity, it also demonstrates the way people who think of themselves as middle-class—the respectable class—use people like the Ewells to reinforce their own social identity. Men like Atticus define "decent folk" by contrasting them with the animal-like Ewells—a "*we-they* discourse," as Cynthia Ward calls it, typical of an amorphous socioeconomic group attempting to construct an identity which separates it from the masses. By the same token, the "white trash scenario" Lee is employing depends upon outsiders replicating this construction of social identity. Readers of *To Kill a Mockingbird* will exonerate the decent southern folk like the Finches, the Taylors, and the Atkinsons by identifying with them and separating themselves from the Ewell clan.

But this artificial construction of reality—this "we-they" reading— is immediately deconstructed by Lee's need and desire to be "realistic." To make "trashiness"—or "tackiness," as Jem calls it (204)—real, Lee must give the reader a convincing description of it. As soon as she does this, reality belies the efforts of the townspeople to categorize the Ewells:

> The plot of ground around the cabin looked like the playhouse of an insane child. What passed for a fence was bits of tree-limbs, broomsticks and stool shafts, all tipped with rusty hammer-heads, snaggle-toothed rake heads, shovels, axes and grubbing hoes, held on with pieces of barbed wire. Enclosed by this barricade was a dirty yard containing the remains of a Model-T Ford (on blocks), a discarded dentist's chair, an ancient icebox, plus lesser items: old shoes, worn-out table radios, picture frames, and fruit jars, under which scrawny orange chickens pecked hopefully. (157-58)

In a provocative analysis of Carolyn Chute's *The Beans of Egypt, Maine*, Cynthia Ward, after pointing to a description of the Beans' yard which is strikingly similar to Lee's depiction of the Ewells' argues that the jumble of recycled objects gathered by the "low life" Beans constitutes a "social hieroglyphic" that defies middle-class interpretation. In the case of the Ewells, the fence is a fence, yet not a fence; the dentist's chair is totally out of context; the truck is immobile. Such a yard, Ward argues, is emblematic of the way people like the Beans (or the Ewells) stymie middle-class efforts to assign them a social identity, because, exiled outside the boundaries of society, they have none. In *To Kill a Mockingbird*, the incongruous placement of geraniums in a slop jar "bewildered Maycomb" (158) because the slop jar as flower pot marks the Ewells as trash but at the same time the beautiful geraniums indicates a common humanity. Scout notes that "Mayella looked as if she tried to keep clean," which "reminded" her "of the row of red geraniums in the Ewell yard" (165). The geraniums also remind her of the flowers of the skilled town gardener, the respected Maudie Atkinson.

As these passages make clear, Lee's effort to provide a realistic portrait of a small southern town subverts her employment of the white trash scenario and destabilizes the patriarchal foundation on which it rests. In so doing, the narration liberates a medley of voices that articulate a widespread pattern of exclusion and oppression in a typical southern town. First of all, the retrospective nature of Scout's coming-of-age saga focuses on her gradual recognition of "justice beset" and offers hope that race, gender, and class barriers can be broken down. Scout's persistence in speaking directly to the poor white Walter Cunningham about his legal problems leads to the dispersal of a mob attempting to lynch Tom; her willingness to humanize "the other" (Boo) by inviting him into her own life interjects a feminine desire for inclusion that challenges a society completely controlled by the fathers who had virtually imprisoned him for his difference; her recognition of the humanity of Mayella reveals the artificiality of a class structure that would dehumanize difference. In spite of Lee's overt use of the despicable white trash scenario, her story ends up destroying that strategy and exemplifying the observation of Judith Fetterley that the best regional fiction written by women includes "the story of one previously silenced and marginalized," thereby affecting "the definition of margin and center" and "calling into question the values that produced such definitions" (24).

But like so much else in this rich novel and movie, the voices remain elusive and contradictory. In spite of the critique of patriarchy, little seems changed in Maycomb. Towards the end of the novel, Scout points out to Jem the contradiction of her teacher hating Hitler for persecuting the Jews while at the same time declaring that the conviction of Tom was justified because "it's time somebody taught 'em a lesson, they were gettin' way above themselves" (225). Rather than supporting her viewpoint, Jem, who now identifies with the adult male world, silences her, screaming, "I never wanta hear about that courthouse again, ever, ever, you hear me? You hear me? Don't you ever say one word to me about it again . . . !" (225). The reader who has adopted a critical position toward the town leaders will clearly interpret this scene as Lee's conclusion that the town is returning to the racist, classist, and sexist norms which prevailed in this typical southern community before Tom Robinson's fateful encounter with Mayella Ewell and that it will try to silence anyone who advances any viewpoint that challenges those standards. As Scout observes, "Jem had acquired an alien set of values and was trying to impose them on me" (109).

But the attentive reader will also be inspired by another factor. Despite the downward pull to conformity that the "common folk" in Maycomb exert—especially Aunt Alexandria, Jem, and Dill—the adult Jean Louise will not be silenced. Her discovery of her own voice trumpets her power as adult narrator to challenge the hegemony of community norms that oppress and exclude individuals on the basis of race, class, and gender.

From *The Southern Quarterly* 40, no. 1 (Fall, 2001), pp. 67-78. Copyright © 2001 by The University of Southern Mississippi. Reproduced with permission.

Works Cited

Alabama Law Review 45 (Winter 1994). Spec. issue. *To Kill a Mockingbird.*

Appleby, Arthur N. "Stability and Change in the High-School Canon." *English Journal* (Sept. 1992): 27-32.

Bloom, Harold, ed. *To Kill a Mockingbird.* Broomall, PA: Chelsea, 1996.

Burt, John. "Novels and Class." *Cambridge History of American Literature.* Cambridge: Cambridge UP, 1991. 367.

Cain, Brooke. "A Touchstone Figure of Decency and Respect." [Raleigh, NC] *News and Observer* 7 July 2000: 3D.

Dudar, Helen. "New Literature: Poor White Trash." *Wall Street Journal* 13 Jan. 1989: A10.

Fetterley, Judith. "'Not in the Least American': Nineteenth-Century Literary Regionalism as UnAmerican Literature." *Nineteenth Century American Women Writers: A Critical Reader.* Ed. Karen L. Kilcup. Malden, MA: Blackwell, 1998. 15-32.

Hoffman, Roy. "Long Lives the Mockingbird." *New York Times Book Review* 9 Aug. 1998: 31.

Holt, Patricia. "'White Trash' and Others." *San Francisco Chronicle* 6 June 1988: F4.

Johnson, Claudia Durst. "The Secret Courts of Men's Hearts: Code and Law in Harper Lee's *To Kill a Mockingbird.*" *Studies in American Fiction* 19.2 (1991): 129-39.

_____. *To Kill a Mockingbird: Threatening Boundaries.* New York: Twayne, 1994.

_____. *Understanding To Kill a Mockingbird: A Student Casebook to Issues, Sources, and Historical Documents.* Westport, CT: Greenwood, 1994.

Jones, Carolyn. "Atticus Finch and the Mad Dog: Harper Lee's *To Kill a Mockingbird.*" *Southern Quarterly* 34.4 (1996): 53-63.

Kaplan, Amy. *The Social Construction of American Realism.* Chicago: U of Chicago P, 1988.

Lee, Harper. *To Kill a Mockingbird.* New York: Lippincott, 1960.

Newitz, Annalee, and Matthew Wray. "What is 'White Trash'? Stereotypes and Economic Conditions of Poor Whites in the United States." *Whiteness: A Critical Reader.* Ed. Mike Hill. New York: New York UP, 1997. 168-86.

Nicholson, Colin. "Hollywood and Race: *To Kill a Mockingbird.*" *Cinema and Fiction: New Modes of Adapting, 1950-1990.* Ed. John Orr and Colin Nicholson. Edinburgh: Edinburgh UP, 1992. 151-59.

Phelps, Teresa Godwin. "The Margin of Maycomb: A Rereading of *To Kill a Mockingbird.*" *Alabama Law Review* 45 (Winter 1994): 511-33.

Radway, Janice A. *A Feeling for Books: The Book-of-the-Month Club, Literary Taste, and Middle-Class Desire.* Chapel Hill: U of North Carolina P, 1997.

Seattle Times. "Books." 24 Jan. 24 1999: M8.

Shackelford, Dean. "The Female Voice in *To Kill a Mockingbird:* Narrative Strategies in Film and Novel." *Mississippi Quarterly* 50.1 (1996-97): 101-13.

Shulman, Robert. "Realism." *Columbia History of the American Novel*. Ed. Emory Eliot. New York: Columbia UP, 1991. 160-88.

Stuckey, W. J. *The Pulitzer Prize Novel: A Critical Backward Look*. Norman: U of Oklahoma P, 1981.

Ward, Cynthia. "From the Suwanee to Egypt, There's No Place like Home." *PMLA* 115 (2000): 75-87.

Woodward, C. Vann. *The Strange Career of Jim Crow*. New York: Oxford UP, 1966.

Telling It in Black and White:
The Importance of the Africanist Presence in
*To Kill a Mockingbird*_____

Diann L. Baecker

The racial themes of Harper Lee's *To Kill a Mockingbird* are ac-knowledged by literary scholars at the same time that they discuss the novel as though it mainly concerns Boo Radley or Atticus Finch, an impression which the author herself helps to create. Because it is rou-tinely taught to high school students, the novel deserves greater scru-tiny than it has received. As with *The Adventures of Huckleberry Finn*, where the metaphor of the river is often given prominence over the is-sue of slavery in the novel, *To Kill a Mockingbird*'s place in the high school canon has been finessed by minimizing the importance of its ra-cial themes.

In her 1992 book *Playing in the Dark*, Toni Morrison suggests sev-eral areas in American literature which warrant further study. One of them is the theme of the Africanist character as an enabler, as a vehicle by which

> the American self knows itself as not enslaved, but free; not repulsive, but
> desirable; not helpless, but licensed and powerful; not history-less, but his-
> torical; not damned, but innocent; not a blind accident of evolution, but a
> progressive fulfillment of destiny. (52)

In Lee's novel of a small southern town, the Africanist presence is muted in spite of the prominence (paradoxically) of the trial in which an innocent black man stands accused of the rape of a young white woman. Nevertheless, within the novel itself the African-American characters enable the town of Maycomb, Alabama, to define itself. Viewed as part of the literary canon, at least as it is introduced to high school students, *To Kill a Mockingbird* also illustrates the way in which literature works to illustrate and define the values of a society. Some scholars have worked very hard to deny the importance of the African-American characters in the novel while they accept the portrait of a white society these characters make possible.[1] This article will attempt to foreground the role in the novel of the Africanist characters, as defined by Morrison, in the development of the identity of all the inhabitants of Maycomb County. It will also attempt to shift the focus back from such themes as the Gothic ones or the maturation of Jem, to the issue of race.

Morrison notes that until very recently American literature has been written for an exclusively white and primarily male audience, regardless of the author's race. As Morrison points out, however, the absence of Others as audience does not erase their presence within literature. She notes that there

> seems to be a more or less tacit agreement among literary scholars that, because American literature has been clearly the preserve of white male views, genius, and power, those views, genius, and power are without relationship to and removed from the overwhelming presence of black people in the United States. (5)

Morrison seeks to articulate the pervasiveness of the Africanist presence in American literature as the context within which white America defines itself. On the concept of defining as contextualization, Kenneth Burke has said that "to tell what a thing is, you place it in terms of something else. This idea of locating, or placing, is implicit in our very word for definition itself: to *define*, or *determine* a thing, is to mark its boundaries, hence to use terms that possess, implicitly at least, contextual reference" (*Grammar* 24).

By her use of the term Africanism, Morrison means not actual persons of African heritage, but rather the "denotative and connotative blackness that African peoples have come to signify" (6). Concepts of autonomy and authority (the self-made man, the pioneer) are major themes of American literature, each one "made possible by, shaped by, activated by a complex awareness and employment of a constituted Africanism" which, in its association with savagery and the brutal elements of nature, provide the foil for the American identity (Morrison 44). The Africanist presence in America is a necessary (although not sufficient) component of what it means to be an American. Since agendas for individual freedom require an atmosphere of oppression, white America has defined itself as much by that-which-it-is-not as by that-which-it-is.

This is more than a rhetorical matter since, as Burke suggests, the traditional definition of rhetoric as "persuasion" is not complete. Before we can persuade, we must first establish an identity with the audience so that the audience comes to feel that their interests are compatible with ours. Thus, at the heart of rhetoric is identification, or consubstantiality. To use Burke's example, to identify A with B is to make it consubstantial with B, that is to make it like B while remaining distinctly A. "A doctrine of consubstantiality, either explicit or implicit," Burke says, "may be necessary to any way of life" (*Rhetoric* 21). Identification implies shared characteristics, but most importantly it also implies boundaries since it is a way of *defining* and definitions involve not only what something is but what it is not. When applied to individuals, identification in rhetorical terms is thus concerned with issues of socialization and faction, issues which often have a very real, economic base (*Rhetoric* 23-34). Since identification is achieved through the acquisition of property, Burke notes that it can, not surprisingly, be a source of conflict and ultimately war. Violent imagery of war and murder "can figure as a terminology of reidentification ('transformation' or 'rebirth')" (*Rhetoric* 45). As we will see later, violence as rebirth appears significantly in *To Kill a Mockingbird*.

This process of identification, while also functioning at the individual level, works itself out at the level of whole groups of people who judge themselves better or worse than other groups, not only in terms of economic property, but also on the basis of such characteristics as skin color, gender, education, sexuality, etc. How does a society decide who has the "good" characteristics and who has the "bad" ones? That each society has such a categorical list is without doubt; any examination of political rhetoric reveals this. Mention "welfare recipient" to most people and the image which will spring to their minds is that of the "welfare queen": overweight, black, female, uneducated, slovenly, and surrounded by a passel of equally dirty, ignorant children. Louis Althusser suggests that it is the function of ideology to interpellate individuals within a society according to a preconceived ideal.

Althusser further asserts that individuals only *believe* themselves to be free subjects. It is a sacred part of American ideology that we see ourselves as self-determining, bootstrap-pulling individuals. It is part of what Burke would call the "scene" of American society. In his theory of scene-act-agent-agency-purpose, Burke describes scene as a container which fits the act of individual subjects and which motivates the action (*Grammar* 3). The relationship is a ratio, so that it is not one which acts upon another, but a dynamic pushing and pulling, so to speak. One is no more important than the other, although we may give one greater prominence in our rhetoric. American ideology tends to obscure the importance of scene in favor of the acts of individual agents. Burke notes that

> stress upon the term, agent, encourages one to be content with a very vague treatment of scene, with no mention of the political and economic factors that form a major aspect of national scenes. . . . [O]ne may deflect attention from scenic matters by situating the motives of an act in the agent. (*Grammar* 17)

This brings us back to Morrison's analysis of the Africanist Presence. Characters can function as both individuals and as part of the scene (*Grammar* 7). It is as part of the scene that the Africanist presence makes itself felt. Morrison points out how the Africanist metaphor allows us to obscure issues of class:

There is still much national solace in continuing dreams of democratic egalitarianism available by hiding class conflict, rage, and impotence in figurations of race. . . . Freedom (to move, to earn, to learn, to be allied with a powerful center, to narrate the world) can be relished more deeply in a cheek-by-jowl existence with the bound and unfree, the economically oppressed, the marginalized, the silenced. (64)

Both Burke and Althusser would say that not only can freedom be "relished" more thoroughly in the presence of the unfree, but that the presence of the unfree is absolutely essential for freedom to exist at all. Morrison calls this concept the "parasitical nature of white freedom" (57). It is here that the Africanist presence functions as enabler, in the sense of promoting the behavior of white, bourgeois America. With race operating as the overarching metaphor for our country, white Americans can reassure themselves that the problem is not class-based, that indeed, as Burke might say, it is a problem of the act of an agent, not the scene, as though the two are not inextricably linked. An important distinction to keep in mind here is that Morrison is discussing an African*ist* presence, not actual African-Americans, many of whom are just as good at distancing themselves from *them* as many white Americans are.

Turning to the rhetoric of literature, we can see where all these theories of identification, scene, and the role of the Africanist presence begin to converge. Burke writes that a "rhetorical motive is often present where it is not usually recognized, or thought to belong" (*Rhetoric* xiii). One of these places is literature. Literature both mirrors our society and fulfills a particular ideological function within it. As such it deserves close rhetorical scrutiny, particularly, and perhaps especially, those works which are standards on high school reading lists.

Parallels between *Huckleberry Finn* and *To Kill a Mockingbird* are worth noting here. On one level, Mark Twain's story of a boy, a raft, and a runaway slave resembles Lee's tale of a young girl and the town recluse whose eventual reemergence into society is facilitated by the false accusation of a black man of the rape of a white woman. Both novels have southern settings and child narrators. Both, in some ways, contain critiques of class and race. However, because of a combination of formal properties within the text and social properties in the way the novels have been placed within the literary tradition, both books illustrate the ways in which racial critiques can be minimized and made more palatable.

The critique of race is muted, in part because of the use of a child narrator. In *Huckleberry Finn* this serves to hide the ideological assumptions of the society and culture it describes. On the one hand, we believe that Huck offers us an unfiltered view of his society because he lacks the cynicism and corruption of an adult. On the other, it is easy to dismiss Huck precisely because he is a naif already marginalized and without status in society and, thus, to dismiss the critique as the oversimplifications of a child (Morrison 54). *Mockingbird* is also narrated by a young child whose view of her society is both honest and naive because she lacks the perspective of an adult. We can accept the fact that she believes the most important event of that summer is Boo's appearance, not the trial and the eventual death of Tom Robinson at the hands of prison guards, and by accepting her point of view we, too, can downplay the significance of the racial tensions described in the novel. Moreover, both books are taught as children's stories (or, more precisely, novels suitable for adolescents) although both were written for adult readers. Clearly, *Huckleberry Finn* and *To Kill a Mockingbird* are novels which adults may feel nostalgic about but which they are not meant to take seriously, being, as they are, "children's" books.

The presence of a child narrator and society's relegation of each to "children's" literature seems to have made these books less about race in the prevailing culture. Reviewers in the 1950s helped canonize *Huckleberry Finn* by ignoring the sociological and ideological implications, at best "voicing polite embarrassment" over the racial themes in the novel (Morrison 54). *Mockingbird*'s entry into the canon was similarly finessed by contemporary reviewers. Edwin Bruell brings up the comparison to Twain's novel in his review of *Mockingbird* published in 1964. He cites with approval Twain's preface in which he threatens to prosecute anyone searching for a motive, moral, or plot in the novel. Bruell tells us that he, too, has his own "private comments on theme hunting, moral seeking, and symbol chasing" in novels (659). *Mockingbird*, he tells us, is about the townspeople, not about Robinson. Here is a man who definitely envisions his audience as white, male and, at the very least, middle-class. He not only tells us that Lee "write[s] like a woman" and that Mayella Ewell is the kind of backwoods character who "rape[s] easily," but he also denies Tom Robinson his manhood, describing him repeatedly as being "bewildered," "misunderstanding," "innocent," and "harmless," adjectives frequently applied to Twain's Jim as well (659, 660). This, then, is Bruell's conception of a novel which shines a "keen scalpel on racial ills" (658).

Edgar H. Schuster, writing in 1963, also feels that too much emphasis is placed on the racial themes of the book. He complains that students "stress the race prejudice issue to the exclusion of virtually everything else" (506). Operating on the assumption that those parts which are given the most attention in a novel are the most important, he counts the pages given to the trial and concludes that they constitute only "fifteen percent of the total length of the novel" (507). In his opinion, "any interpretation that regards the whole first half of a novel merely as prologue and the last tenth as epilogue is in dire need of refinement" (506). Moreover, since the two children, in his opinion, are relatively free from any form of racial prejudice and since the issue of race is concentrated in one part of the book only, he believes that the racial issues do not even properly qualify as a "motif" (508). Schuster believes that the five primary themes of the book are Jem's maturation, the social stratification of the town, the metaphor of the mockingbird, education, and superstition (507). He gives the last two primary importance. Schuster believes that Lee's achievement lies not in the fact that she has written another novel about race prejudice, but rather that she has placed race prejudice in a perspective which allows us to see it as an aspect of a larger thing; as something that arises from phantom contacts, from fear and lack of knowledge; and finally as *something that disappears* with the kind of knowledge or "education" that one gains through learning what people are really like when you "finally see them." (511, emphasis added)

This notion that education makes racism "disappear" is a common myth. Racism is commonly ascribed to poor white trash (Flynt 213), as though those of the middle and upper classes (who possess more education) have nothing to do with it.[2] Schuster's vision of the relative unimportance of race in the novel is as unrealistic as the idea that racism disappears with education. Schuster does, however, ask an interesting question about the novel. If this book is, indeed, about race relations why, he wonders, does it devote so little time to the trial? This is a question I will come back to, but here it is worth pointing out that there is no one-to-one correspondence between a theme's importance and the number of words devoted to it.

It might be suggested that these articles are typical only of early-1960s academic scholarship which, perhaps, reflects the determination of academia to hold on to its ivory tower image in the face of the onslaught of the civil rights movement and certainly reflects the formalist stranglehold on literature at a time when the physical properties of a work—such as the number of words devoted to a particular theme—took precedence. However, one of the most recent and extensive works on *Mockingbird* also diminishes the racial theme. Claudia Durst Johnson's *To Kill a Mockingbird: Threatening Boundaries* is based on a 1991 article she wrote about the legal and extra-legal boundaries of the novel. She calls *Mockingbird* a "study of how Jem and Scout begin to perceive the complexity of social codes" and a "tale about a variety of boundaries—those of race, region, time, class, sex, tradition, and code" (98, 31). Despite its promise to explore boundaries, the book subsumes any notice of the racial themes of the novel under discussions of the legal code, the Gothic romance, or the theme of the mockingbird. When Johnson does mention race, it is generally only in passing. Like so many scholarly works before it, *Threatening Boundaries* remains more formalist criticism than social critique.[3]

If contemporary scholars sometimes minimize the importance of race in the novel, it is small wonder, considering the fact that the author does so, too. As more than one reviewer has pointed out, Lee's novel begins and ends with Boo Radley. *Mockingbird* opens with the following words by the author/narrator:

> When he was nearly thirteen, my brother Jem got his arm badly broken at the elbow. . . . When enough years had gone by to enable us to look back on them, we sometimes discussed the events leading to his accident. I maintain that the Ewells started it all, but Jem, who was four years my senior, said it started long before that. He said it began the summer Dill came to us, when Dill first gave us the idea of making Boo Radley come out. (9)

Thus, Jem's broken arm becomes the result not of the act of a racist man, but a childhood game to lure Boo Radley from his home. The trial of Tom Robinson is a significant part of the book, even if the trial itself occupies only fifteen percent of the novel. What may be more significant than the number of pages devoted to the actual trial may be the way in which Lee has constructed the novel so as to compress the issue of race into a tightly constrained portion of the book, bounded on either side by tales of Boo. The Africanist presence in this novel is simultaneously illuminated and repressed by Lee. Rather than seeing this as proof that the novel is more about Boo (or Jem or Scout or Atticus) than about race, I would suggest that Lee's efforts to contain the racial element of the novel actually highlights its significance. Moreover, Boo—who frames Lee's story—may be more closely associated with the Africanist presence in the novel than is first apparent.

In the novel Boo, a white man, is both associated with the margins and differentiated from the people who inhabit that place. He is a spook, a vampire who eats small animals and peeks in people's windows at night. He is, as Johnson has pointed out, a Gothic figure, not quite human. Never seeing the sun, he is ghostly white. There is also something grotesquely sexual about him, in the way that he stabs his father with a pair of sewing shears (a woman's tool), in the way that he is some kind of repressed child, and in the way that he lives in the womb-like darkness of his birthplace. He is part of the margins. After Jem loses his pants on the Radley fence, Scout lies in bed that night listening to the night sounds and imagining Boo at every corner:

> Every night-sound I heard from my cot on the back porch was magnified three-fold; every scratch of feet on gravel was Boo Radley seeking revenge, every passing Negro laughing in the night was Boo Radley loose and after us; insects splashing against the screen were Boo Radley's insane fingers picking the wire to pieces; the chinaberry trees were malignant, hovering, alive. (63)

Here, Boo is associated with nature, with insects and chinaberry trees, as well as with "every passing Negro," persons also more closely associated with savage nature than with the civilizing town. As noted above, marginalized groups tend to share each other's characteristics. They collectively form the context within which they are individually placed so that women, children, and racial minorities are generally considered like each other (feminine, immature, less intelligent) as well as being dirty, uncivilized, closer to nature, and any other losing end of a dichotomy. Boo's association with insects, chinaberry trees, Negroes, and, of course, madness, helps to align him near the margins. Thus, in some ways, Boo himself is part of the Africanist presence in the novel.

Yet, as much as he lives life on the boundary of society, Boo is not like the black people or even the Ewells and Cunninghams of Maycomb. In some ways his madness makes him even more of an outcast. "A Negro," we are told, "would not pass the Radley Place at night, he would cut across to the sidewalk opposite and whistle as he walked" (15). Black people and children, both positioned near the margin, believe; they understand Boo's nature.[4] Yet, when it comes to offering Boo up to the legal system as well as to the sympathy and pity of the townspeople (specifically, the townswomen who cannot be counted upon to do what the men consider to be right for Boo), the matter is taken care of in the best small town way. Boo, by virtue of being white and of a good family, is given special consideration. Just as his father was allowed to keep him home rather than seeing his son sent to jail or a reformatory after his teenage rebellion, the sheriff and Atticus decide to administer their own extra-legal justice; Bob Ewell, they decide, dies by falling on his knife, not at the hands of Boo Radley.

While Boo crosses boundaries of white and black, culture and madness, borrowing characteristics of the Africanist presence while retaining ties to the white townspeople, other members of Maycomb's community are more definite about their identity. Jem articulates the viewpoint of the townspeople by noting that

> there's four kinds of folks in the world. There's the ordinary kind like us and the neighbors, there's the kind like the Cunninghams out in the woods, the kind like the Ewells down at the dump, and the Negroes. . . . The thing about it is, our kind of folks don't like the Cunninghams, the Cunninghams don't like the Ewells, and the Ewells hate and despise the colored folks. (239)

The townspeople, as Aunt Alexandra points out, may all have "streaks"—to drink, to madness, to intermarriage—but they are not, first of all, white trash. Unlike the Cunninghams, the townspeople do not live in the woods or suffer from "entailments." Unlike the Ewells, they do not live "behind the town garbage dump in what was once a Negro cabin" (181). They do not drink up all their money so that they must be allowed to hunt out of season so their children do not go hungry. Most important, while they may marry their cousins, they do not molest their own daughters. There is nothing particularly remarkable about these facts. "[H]e's a Cunningham" is all the explanation Scout believes the new schoolteacher should require (26). Mr. Ewell's incestuous relationship with Mayella, the driving force behind her desire to make loving contact with someone else, even if that person is a black man, is mentioned only in passing in the novel. On the other hand, the "warm bittersweet smell of clean Negro" or a black chauffeur "kept in an unhealthy state of tidiness" are facts remarkable enough to be noted (128, 137). The incestuous relationship of a white trash man with his white trash daughter is a part of the novel often glossed over by scholars who probably find it unremarkable anyway, as if to say, what else can be expected from people living so close to Negroes.

Part of the manner in which the townspeople distinguish themselves from others is through language, both the ability to read and the ability to name, abilities which fall out along racial lines. Naming is especially important in distinguishing black from white. While we know Tom's last name, he is most often referred to in the novel by only his first. Calpurnia is just "Calpurnia," as is her son, Zebo. In addition to names, the mark of literacy is an important distinction which serves to cut off the townspeople from both the black residents and the poor whites. The Ewells and the Cunninghams take their children out of school after a year or two (if that long), while Scout can read before the first grade. Much is made of Calpurnia's literacy and the fact that she has "two languages," one which she uses to other black people at her church and the other which she uses at the Finch home. She has taught her son to read, also, and it is he who leads the singing in church by lining the hymns, a practice fascinating to the hyperliterate Finch children.

If the townspeople form their identities by setting themselves apart from what and who they are not, it is even more important for people like the Ewells. Poor whites in the South owned little more than the color of their skin which served to both form an identity with the class above them and to distinguish them from the black people they tried hard to keep beneath them (Flynt 212). The only way Bob Ewell is any better than his black neighbors is that, if "scrubbed with lye soap in very hot water, his skin [is] white" (182). By taking advantage of a "quiet, respectable, humble Negro," however, he comes close to losing even this distinction (216). As Atticus tells Jem, the white man who cheats a black man is trash, no matter "how fine a family he comes from" (233). Atticus's harsh judgment stems from the fact that the white man and the black man are not perceived as being equal. Taking advantage of an ignorant, humble Negro is like kicking a dog or taking candy from a child; it is capitalizing on your superior position. It is simply not done—at least not openly.

Those on the margin share not only questionable hygiene, but a more animalistic sexuality as well. For example, there is something sexual about Boo's madness. He is a child trapped in a man's body, a man who supposedly drinks the blood of animals and prowls around in the dead of night. His sexuality is frozen in adulthood. The black population of Maycomb, as well as the Ewells who live so close to them, have a much more potent sexuality, a sexuality which the townspeople with their powder and propriety try to avoid. Scout's fascination with the trial may be less related to her love of her father than to her growing awareness of her gender, a gender she shares with the powerless Mayella. In the novel, Atticus is called a nigger-lover because he defends Tom. It is extraordinary that he would take the word of a black man against a white man and that he does so forms the impetus for Bob Ewell's murderous rage. What is not treated as extraordinary in the novel is the alleged crime itself, just as the incestuous relationship of a white trash man with his white trash daughter is unremarkable. In the same sense, the brute sexuality of the black race is taken for granted. As Atticus states in his closing arguments, the Ewells are counting on the jury to understand that black men cannot be trusted around white women. In truth, it is Mayella who is literally a nigger-lover and her crime is as monstrous as Robinson's alleged one. In fact, it is the sole motivating factor for the trial.

It is Mayella who saves seven nickels over a whole year's time so that she can send all of her siblings to town for ice cream and, thus, have the house to herself when she invites Robinson in. *She* kisses *him* and, worse, is caught doing so by her father. After beating her, he goes to town and charges Robinson with rape. The novel states that Mayella's subsequent testimony in court is motivated by guilt:

> She has committed no crime, she has merely broken a rigid and time-honored code of our society, a code so severe that whoever breaks it is hounded from our midst as unfit to live with. . . . She must destroy the evidence of her offense. . . . She must put Tom Robinson away from her. Tom Robinson was her daily reminder of what she did. . . . She was white, and she tempted a Negro. She did something that in our society is unspeakable: she kissed a black man. (216)

What is speakable, what is spoken and then dismissed as irrelevant and unimportant, is that Mayella's rape has come at the hands of her father. As she tells Tom, "what her papa do to her don't count" (206). Her testimony is motivated less by shame than by fear—not of Robinson, but of her father. Atticus calls her a victim of "cruel poverty and ignorance," but what she is most clearly a victim of is incest and physical abuse. What motivates her scheme—which, again, takes her an entire year to put into practice—is the desire to be touched with love rather than violence.

It is during the trial scenes that a minor character makes his appearance who, like Boo, blurs acceptable social boundaries. The implications of his actions are much more serious, however, and he makes an appearance in the novel only to quickly recede again. Dolphus Raymond is the town scandal, always "drinkin' out of a sack" (177). He lives a scandalous life, "way down near the county line" where he resides with a "colored woman and all sorts of mixed chillun" (171-72). It is the opinion of the townspeople that these children must be "real sad" because they belong nowhere, being neither black nor white. Interestingly, while Lee offers no contradiction to the opinion that

Mayella has sinned gravely by kissing a black man, Dolphus's character is portrayed as far more sympathetic. A few pages later in the novel, he offers Dill a sip from his sack in order to settle the child's stomach and it is then that Dill and Scout learn that Dolphus is only drinking Coca-Cola. He pretends to be drunk in order to give the townspeople a reason for his behavior. Clearly it is more scandalous for a white woman to kiss a black man, than for a white man to openly live with a black woman. There are, however, other implications, not the least of which is the suggestion that this character appears and disappears so quickly because Lee finds the topic of interracial love compelling yet impossible to talk about. In addition, it is interesting to note that she carefully articulates Dolphus's status in the community. Dill observes that Raymond "doesn't look like trash" and Jem is quick to explain that he is not. In fact, "he owns all one side of the riverbank down there, and he's from a real old family to boot" (172). Like Boo, Raymond can finesse his position between borders by virtue of his unquestionable position within white society.

Lee is able to talk about issues of gender, particularly sexuality, because of the metaphorical nature of the Africanist presence in the novel. In addition to Mayella, Boo, and Dolphus Raymond, there is Atticus: he is almost Christ-like both in his devotion to what is good and true and in his virginal asexuality. He has been widowed for a number of years, but never even dates another woman. Atticus's relationship to Calpurnia is also interesting. She, too, is apparently widowed (there is a son for whom there was presumably once a father, but there is no mention of a husband). When his sister wants her fired, Atticus defends Calpurnia, noting what a big part of the family she is. While she sleeps in the kitchen when she spends the night at the Finch home, she nevertheless fulfills all the functions of a wife in 1930s Alabama—she cooks, cleans, disciplines the children, and essentially provides for the Finch family as if it were her own. Thus the Africanist presence can function as an enabling metaphor for discussing not only racial identity, but issues of gender and class as well. The process of identification made possible by the Africanist presence allows Lee's female protagonist to safely explore issues of sexuality, issues which seem to touch neither her nor her family directly. Within a larger context, it functions as the not-me which allows the rest of us—black and white, male and female—to find our relative position in society.

Formalist criticism is often valuable in itself. I do not believe any literary scholar, no matter what his/her theoretical leanings, is immune to a well-turned phrase. Scout's simple greeting—"Hey, Boo"—will always resonate for me when I think of this novel. But literature is so much more than beautiful phrases or well-crafted plots, especially when it is part of high school education. Whatever else literature can be, it remains a cultural artifact and the way we talk about a novel—or teach it—is significant. Because, as Morrison demonstrates, the Africanist presence is part of the cultural context of America, its influence can be found in American literature, even in places where we think it is not or where it has spilled over the carefully measured boundaries we have delineated for it. In spite of Schuster's assertion that the sheer number of pages devoted to a theme constitutes its importance, I would suggest that it is often the smaller things, the things we can only talk about obliquely, which are the most revealing.

From *The Southern Quarterly* 36, no. 3 (Spring, 1998), pp. 124-132. Copyright © 1998 by The University of Southern Mississippi. Reprinted by permission of The University of Southern Mississippi.

Notes

1. Compare Edwin Bruell, Edgar H. Schuster, and to a lesser extent, Claudia Durst Johnson.

2. In addition to providing a detailed, and sobering, look at poor people in Alabama, Wayne Flynt's *Poor But Proud* is also interesting for its discussion of *To Kill a Mockingbird*. In accusing Lee of giving poor whites "no respite," Flynt glosses over Bob Ewell's incestuous relationship with his daughter and the pitifulness of Mayella's attempt to establish some kind of loving contact with another human being, even if that person is black. In addition, he implies that Robinson's "accusation" of Mayella seduc-

ing him is unbelievable not only to the white jury in the novel but to white readers (214-15).

3. Johnson's most recent work is her book, *Understanding* To Kill a Mockingbird: *A Student Casebook to Issues, Sources, and Historic Documents*. In it she provides historical background for the novel, but still seems to see a critique of the ideological/sociological themes as ancillary to the formalist criticism of the novel.

4. The association of Negroes with children, both groups who exist on the margin, is further emphasized in the novel when Jem asks Miss Maudie why she doesn't get a "colored man" to work in her yard or even "Scout 'n' me" (82). In addition to the association of Negro and child, is that of Negro and nature, or Negro and animal. It has always been a little disturbing to me that Tom Robinson's name is so similar to the name of the mad dog in the novel, Tim Johnson. The two names are just enough alike that, having come to the scene where Atticus shoots the dog, I always find myself flipping back to check on the name of the Negro man Atticus is defending.

Works Cited

Althusser, Louis. "Ideology and Ideological State Apparatuses (Notes Toward an Investigation)." *Lenin and Philosophy and Other Essays*. Trans. Ben Brewster. New York: Monthly Review P, 1971.

Bruell, Edwin. "Keen Scalpel on Racial Ills." *English Journal* 53 (1964): 658-61.

Burke, Kenneth. *A Grammar of Motives*. Berkeley: U of California P, 1945.

_____. *A Rhetoric of Motives*. Berkeley: U of California P, 1950.

Flynt, Wayne. *Poor But Proud: Alabama's Poor Whites*. Tuscaloosa: U of Alabama P, 1989.

Johnson, Claudia Durst. To Kill a Mockingbird: *Threatening Boundaries*. New York: Twayne, 1994.

_____. *Understanding* To Kill a Mockingbird: *A Student Casebook to Issues, Sources, and Historic Documents*. Westport, CT: Greenwood, 1994.

Lee, Harper. *To Kill a Mockingbird*. Philadelphia: Lippincott, 1960.

Morrison, Toni. *Playing in the Dark: Whiteness and the Literary Imagination*. Cambridge: Harvard UP, 1992.

Schuster, Edgar H. "Discovering Theme and Structure in the Novel." *English Journal* 52 (1963): 506-11.

The Female Voice in *To Kill a Mockingbird*:
Narrative Strategies in Film and Novel_____

Dean Shackelford

Aunt Alexandra was fanatical on the subject of my attire. I could not possibly hope to be a lady if I wore breeches; when I said I could do nothing in a dress, she said I wasn't supposed to be doing anything that required pants. Aunt Alexandra's vision of my deportment involved playing with small stoves, tea sets, and wearing the Add-A-Pearl necklace she gave me when I was born; furthermore, I should be a ray of sunshine in my father's lonely life. I suggested that one could be a ray of sunshine in pants just as well, but Aunty said that one had to behave like a sunbeam, that I was born good but had grown progressively worse every year. She hurt my feelings and set my teeth permanently on edge, but when I asked Atticus about it, he said there were already enough sunbeams in the family and to go about my business, he didn't mind me much the way I was.[1]

This passage reveals the importance of female voice and gender in Harper Lee's popular Pulitzer Prize-winning novel, *To Kill a Mockingbird*, first published in 1960. The novel portrays a young girl's love for her father and brother and the experience of childhood during the Great Depression in a racist, segregated society which uses superficial and materialistic values to judge outsiders, including the powerful character Boo Radley.

In 1962, a successful screen version of the novel (starring Gregory Peck) appeared. However, the screenplay, written by Horton Foote, an accomplished Southern writer, abandons, for the most part, the novel's first-person narration by Scout (in the motion picture, a first-person angle of vision functions primarily to provide transitions and shifts in time and place). As a result, the film is centered more on the children's father, Atticus Finch, and the adult world in which Scout and Jem feel alien. As several commentators have noted, the film seems centered on the racial issue much more than on other, equally successful dimensions of the novel. Clearly, part of the novel's success has to do with the adult-as-child perspective. Lee, recalling her own childhood, projects the image of an adult reflecting on her past and attempting to recreate the experience through a female child's point of view.

That the film shifts perspective from the book's primary concern with the female protagonist and her perceptions to the male father figure and the adult male world is noteworthy. While trying to remain faithful to the importance of childhood and children in the novel, Foote's objective narration is interrupted only occasionally with the first-person narration of a woman, who is presumably the older, now adult Scout. However, the novel is very much about the experience of growing up as a female in a South with very narrow definitions of gender roles and acceptable behavior. Because this dimension of the novel is largely missing from the film's narrative, the film version of *To Kill a Mockingbird* may be seen as a betrayal of the novel's full feminist implications—a compromise of the novel's full power.

Granted, when a film adaptation is made, the screenwriter need not be faithful to the original text. As Robert Giddings, Keith Selby, and Chris Wensley note in their important book *Screening the Novel*, a filmmaker's approaches to adapting a literary work may range from one of almost complete faithfulness to the story to one which uses the original as an outline for a totally different work on film.[2] Foote's adaptation seems to fall somewhere in between these extremes, with the film decidedly faithful to certain aspects of the novel. His story clearly conveys the novel's general mood; it is obvious he wishes to remain close to the general subject matter of life in the South during the Great Depression and its atmosphere of racial prejudice and Jim Crow. Reflecting on the film, Harper Lee herself states, "For me, Maycomb is there, its people are there: in two short hours one lives a childhood and lives it with Atticus Finch, whose view of life was the heart of the novel."[3]

Though admittedly Atticus Finch is at the heart of the film and novel, there are some clear and notable discrepancies between the two versions that alter the unique perspective of the novel considerably—despite what Lee herself has commented. Only about 15% of the novel is devoted to Tom Robinson's rape trial, whereas in the film, the running time is more than 30% of a two-hour film. Unlike the book, the film is primarily centered on the rape trial and the racism of Maycomb which has made it possible—not surprising considering it was made during what was to become the turbulent period of the 1960s when racial issues were of interest to Hollywood and the country as a whole. Significant, though, are the reviewers and critics who believe this issue, rather than the female child's perspectives on an adult male world, is the novel's main concern and as a result admire the film for its faithfulness to the original.

Many teachers of the novel and film also emphasize this issue to the neglect of other equally important issues. In 1963 and again in the year of the film's twenty-fifth anniversary, the Education Department of Warner Books issued Joseph Mersand's study guide on the novel, one section of which is an essay subtitled "A Sociological Study in Black and White." Turning the novel into sociology, many readers miss other aspects of Lee's vision. In an early critical article, Edgar Schuster notes that the racial dimensions of the novel have been overemphasized, especially by high school students who read it, and he offers possible strategies for teaching students the novel's other central issues, which he lists as "Jem's physiological and psychological growth" (mentioning Scout's growth in this regard only briefly as if it is a side issue), the caste system of Maycomb, the title motif, education, and superstition.[4] What is so striking about Schuster's interpretation is his failure to acknowledge that the issue of Scout's gender is crucial to an understanding not only of the novel but also of Scout's identification with her father.[5] As feminists often note, male readers sometimes take female perspectives and turn them into commentaries from a male point of view. Because the novel and film center so much on Atticus, he, rather than Scout, becomes the focus.

With regard to the film, I do not mean to suggest that Foote has not attempted to make some references to Scout's problems with gender identity. When he does, however, the audience is very likely unable to make the connections as adequately as careful readers of the novel might. Of particular interest are two scenes from the film which also appear in the novel. During one of their summers with Dill, Jem insults Scout as the three of them approach the Radley home and Scout whines, fearful of what may happen. As in the novel, he tells her she is getting to be more like a girl every day, the implication being that boys are courageous and non-fearful and girls are weak and afraid (a point which is refuted when Jem's fears of Boo Radley and the dark are demonstrated). Nevertheless, what is most important in the scene is Scout's reaction. Knowing that being called a girl is an insult and that being female is valued less than being male in her small Southern town, she suddenly becomes brave in order to remain acceptable to her brother.

In another scene, as Scout passes by Mrs. Dubose's house and says "hey," she is reprimanded for poor manners unbecoming of a Southern lady. This scene occurs in both film and novel. However, in the novel Lee clarifies that the presumed insult to Mrs. Dubose originates with Mrs. Dubose's assumptions as a Southern lady, a role which Scout, in the novel especially, is reluctant to assume. The film's lack of a consistent female voice makes this scene as well as others seem unnecessary and extraneous. This is only one example of the way in which the superior narrative strategy of the novel points out the weakness of the objective, male-centered narration of the film.

One scene from the film concerning girlhood does not appear in the novel. Careful not to suggest that the Finches are churchgoers (for what reason?), as they are in the novel, Foote creates a scene which attempts to demonstrate Scout's ambivalence about being female. As Scout becomes old enough to enter school, she despises the thought of wearing a dress. When she appears from her room to eat breakfast before attending school for the first time, Jem ridicules her while Atticus, Miss Maudie, and Calpurnia admire her. Scout comments: "I still don't see why I have to wear a darn old dress."[6] A weakness of the film in this regard is that until this scene, there has been little indication that Scout strongly dislikes wearing dresses, let alone has fears of growing up as a female. The novel makes it clear that Scout prefers her overalls to wearing dresses, which is perhaps why Foote found it necessary to create this particular scene. However, the previous two crucial scenes, while faithful to the novel's general concerns with gender, create loose ends in the film which do not contribute to the success of the narration and which compromise the novel's feminist center.

The intermittent efforts to focus on the female narrator's perspective prove unsuccessful in revealing the work's feminist dimensions. As the film opens, the audience sees the hands of a small girl, presumably Scout, coloring.[7] After the credits, a woman's voice, described by Amy Lawrence as a "disembodied voice exiled from the image," is heard reflecting on her perceptions of Maycomb.[8] By introducing the audience to the social and spatial context, this first-person narrator provides a frame for the whole. The audience at this point, without having read the novel first, may not, however, recognize who the speaker is. As Scout appears playing in the yard, the viewer is left to assume that the voice-over opening the film is the female character speaking as a grown woman. The camera zooms down to reveal Scout and soon thereafter shifts to the standard objective narration of most films.

When the disembodied narrator is heard again, she reflects on Scout's views of Atticus after he insists she will have to return to school; yet, despite what her teacher says, father and daughter will continue reading each night the way they always have. Here the voice-over is designed to emphasize the heroic stature of Atticus and perhaps even to suggest that one reason for Scout's identification with him is his freedom of thought and action: "There just didn't seem to be anyone or thing Atticus couldn't explain. Though it wasn't a talent that would arouse the admiration of any of our friends. Jem and I had to admit he was very good at that but that was all he was good at, we thought" (Foote, p. 35). This intrusion becomes little more than a transition into the next scene, in which Atticus shoots the mad dog.

In the next intrusion the female voice interrupts the objective narration when, at school, Scout fights Cecil Jacobs for calling Atticus a "nigger lover." She states: "Atticus had promised me he would wear me out if he ever heard of me fightin' any more. I was far too old and too big for such childish things, and the sooner I learned to hold in, the better off everybody would be. I soon forgot . . . Cecil Jacobs made me forget" (Foote, p. 42). Here again, the first-person narration provides coherence, allowing the scene of Scout's fight with Cecil Jacobs to be shortened and placing emphasis on the relationship between Atticus and Scout. The subtext of their conversation could perhaps be viewed as a reflection of traditional views that women should not be too aggressive or physical, but this scene, coupled with earlier scenes reflecting social values, is not couched in terms of Scout's transgressive behavior as a woman-to-be. The female voice in the film is not used to demonstrate the book's concern with female identity; rather, it reinforces the male-centered society which Atticus represents and which the film is gradually moving toward in focusing on the trial of Tom Robinson.

Another instance during which the female narrator intrudes on the objective, male-centered gaze of the camera occurs when Jem and Scout discuss the presents Boo Radley leaves for them in the knothole. At this point in the film, the attempt to convey the book's female narrative center falls completely apart. Not until after the very long trial scene does the camera emphasize the children's perceptions or the female narrator's angle of vision again. Instead, the audience is in the adult male world of the courtroom, with mature male authority as the center of attention. Immediately after the trial, the film seems most concerned with Jem's reactions to the trial, Jem's recognition of the injustice of the verdict in the Tom Robinson case, and Jem's desire to accompany his father when he tells Helen Robinson that Tom has been killed. Scout is unable to observe directly the last event, and, as a result, the narration is inconsistent—by and large from the rape trial to the end of the film.

The film does, however, make use of voice-over narration twice more. In the first instance, the female narrator again provides the transition in time and place to move from the previous scene, the revelation of Tom Robinson's death to his wife, into the confrontation between Atticus and Bob Ewell. As the camera focuses on an autumn scene with Scout dressed in a white dress, Jean Louise prepares the audience for the climax, which soon follows: "By October things had settled down again. I still looked for Boo every time I went by the Radley place. This night my mind was filled with Halloween. There was to be a pageant representing our county's agricultural products. I was to be a ham. Jem said he would escort me to the school auditorium. Thus began our longest journey together" (Foote, p. 72). Following this passage is the climactic scene, when Bob Ewell attacks Scout and Jem and Boo Radley successfully rescues them.

Shortly thereafter, the camera focuses on Scout's recognition of Boo as the protector and savior of Jem and her, and for the remainder of the film, the narration, arguably for the first time, is centered entirely on Scout's perception of the adult male world. She hears Heck Tate and Atticus debate over what to do about exposing the truth that Boo has killed Ewell while defending the children. The movement of the camera and her facial expression clearly indicate that Scout sees the meaning behind the adults' desires to protect Boo from the provincial Maycomb community which has marginalized him—and this scene signifies Scout's initiation into the world of adulthood.

As the film draws to a close, Scout, still in her overalls which will not be tolerated much longer in this society, walks Boo home. For the last time the audience hears the female voice:

Neighbors bring food with death, and flowers with sickness, and little things in between. Boo was our neighbor. He gave us two soap dolls, a broken watch, and chain, a knife, and our lives. One time Atticus said you never really knew a man until you stood in his shoes and walked around in them. Just standin' on the Radley porch was enough. . . . The summer that had begun so long ago ended, another summer had taken its place, and a fall, and Boo Radley had come out. . . . I was to think of these days many times;—of Jem, and Dill and Boo Radley, and Tom Robinson . . . and Atticus. He would be in Jem's room all night. And he would be there when Jem waked up in the morning. (Foote, pp. 79-80)

The film ends when, through a window, Scout is seen climbing into Atticus's lap while he sits near Jem. The camera gradually moves left-ward away from the two characters in the window to a long shot of the house. By the end, then, the film has shifted perspective back to the fe-male voice, fully identified the narrator as the older Scout (Jean Lou-ise), and focused on the center of Scout's existence, her father (a patri-archal focus). The inconsistent emphasis on Scout and her perceptions makes the film seem disjointed.

Noting the patriarchal center of the film, Amy Lawrence suggests the possibility for a feminist reading. She argues that the disembodied narrator—as well as the author, Harper Lee, and the characters of Scout and Mayella Ewell—provides a "disjointed subjectivity" on film which is characteristic of "the experience of women in patriarchy" (p. 184). Such "disjointed subjectivity" is, however, missing from the novel, which centers on Scout's perceptions of being female in a male-dominated South. The novel's female-centered narration provides an opportunity for Lee to comment on her own childlike perceptions as well as her recognition of the problems of growing up female in the South. The feminine voice, while present in the film, receives far too little emphasis.

In the novel the narrative voice allows readers to comprehend what the film does not explain. Though some critics have attacked Lee's nar-ration as weak and suggested that the use of first person creates prob-lems with perspective because the major participant, first-person nar-rator must appear almost in all scenes, the novel's consistent use of first person makes it much clearer than the film that the reader is seeing all the events through a female child's eyes. Once the children enter the courtroom in the film, the center of attention is the adult world of Atticus Finch and the rape trial—not, as the book is able to suggest, the children's perceptions of the events which unravel before them.

Although it is clear in the film that Scout is a tomboy and that she will probably grow out of this stage in her life (witness the very feminine and Southern drawl of the female narrator, who, though not seen, conveys the image of a conventional Southern lady), the film, which does not openly challenge the perspective of white heterosexuals (male or female) nearly to the degree the novel does, does not make Scout's ambivalence about being a female in an adult male world clear enough. Because the novel's narrative vision is consistently first-person throughout and as a result focused on the older Scout's perceptions of her growing-up years, the female voice is unquestionably heard and the narration is focused on the world of Maycomb which she must inevitably enter as she matures.

Furthermore, a number of significant questions about gender are raised in the novel: Is Scout (and, by implication, all females) an outsider looking on an adult male world which she knows she will be unable to enter as she grows into womanhood? Is her identification with Atticus due not only to her love and devotion for a father but also to his maleness, a power and freedom she suspects she will not be allowed to possess within the confines of provincial Southern society? Or is her identification with Atticus due to his androgynous nature (playing the role of mother and father to her and demonstrating stereotypically feminine traits: being conciliatory, passive, tolerant, and partially rejecting the traditional masculine admiration for violence, guns, and honor)? All three of these questions may lead to possible, even complementary readings which would explain Scout's extreme identification with her father.

As in the passage quoted at the beginning of this essay, the novel focuses on Scout's tomboyishness as it relates to her developing sense of a female self. Also evident throughout the novel is Scout's devotion to her father's opinions. Atticus seems content with her the way she is;

only when others force him to do so does he concern himself with traditional stereotypes of the Southern female. Especially significant with regard to Scout's growing sense of womanhood is the novel's very important character, Aunt Alexandra, Atticus's sister, who is left out of the film entirely. Early in the novel, readers are made aware of Scout's antipathy for her aunt, who wishes to mold her into a Southern lady. Other female authority figures with whom Scout has difficulty agreeing are her first-grade teacher, Miss Fisher, and Calpurnia, the family cook, babysitter, and surrogate mother figure. When the females in authority interfere with Scout's perceptions concerning her father and their relationship, she immediately rebels, a rebellion which Atticus does not usually discourage—signifying her strong identification with male authority and her recognition that the female authority figures threaten the unique relationship which she has with her father and which empowers her as an individual.

Exactly why Scout identifies with Atticus so much may have as much to do with his own individuality and inner strength as the fact that he is a single parent and father. Since the mother of Scout and Jem is dead, Atticus has assumed the full responsibility of playing mother and father whenever possible—though admittedly he employs Calpurnia and allows Alexandra to move in with them to give the children, particularly Scout, a female role model. However, Atticus is far from a stereotypical Southern male. Despite his position as a respected male authority figure in Maycomb, he seems oblivious to traditional expectations concerning masculinity (for himself) and femininity (for Scout). The children in fact see him as rather unmanly: "When Jem and I asked him why he was so old, he said he got started late, which we felt reflected on his abilities and his masculinity" (p. 93). Jem is also upset because Atticus will not play tackle football. Mrs. Dubose criticizes Atticus for not remarrying, which is very possibly a subtle comment on his lack of virility. Later the children learn of his abilities at marksmanship, at bravery in watching the lynch mob ready to attack Tom Robinson, and at the defense of the same man. Perhaps this is Lee's way of suggesting that individuals must be allowed to develop their own sense of self without regard to rigid definitions of gender and social roles.

Scout's identification with Atticus may also be rooted in her recognition of the superficiality and limitations of being a Southern female. Mrs. Dubose once tells her: "'You should be in a dress and camisole, young lady! You'll grow up waiting on tables if somebody doesn't change your ways . . .'" (p. 106). This is one of many instances in the novel through which the first-person narrator reveals Lee's criticism of Southern women and their narrow-mindedness concerning gender roles. Even Atticus ridicules the women's attitudes. In one instance he informs Alexandra that he favors "'Southern womanhood as much as anybody, but not for preserving polite fiction at the expense of human life'" (p. 149). When Scout is "indignant" that women cannot serve on juries, Atticus jokingly says, "I guess it's to protect our frail ladies from sordid cases like Tom's. Besides . . . I doubt if we'd ever get a complete case tried—the ladies'd be interrupting to ask questions" (p. 224). This seemingly sexist passage may in fact be the opposite; having established clearly that Atticus does not take many Southern codes seriously, Lee recognizes the irony in Atticus's statement that women, including his own independent-minded daughter, are "frail."

Admittedly, few women characters in the novel are very pleasant, with the exceptions of Miss Maudie Atkinson, the Finches' neighbor, and Calpurnia. Through the first-person female voice, Southern women are ridiculed as gossips, provincials, weaklings, extremists, even racists—calling to mind the criticism of Southern manners in the fiction of Flannery O'Connor. Of Scout's superficial Aunt Alexandra, Lee writes: ". . . Aunt Alexandra was one of the last of her kind: she has river-boat, boarding-school manners; let any moral come along and she would uphold it; she was born in the objective case; she was an incurable gossip" (p. 131). Scout's feelings for Alexandra, who is concerned with family heritage, position, and conformity to traditional gender roles, do alter somewhat as she begins to see Alexandra as a woman who means well and loves her and her father, and as she begins to accept certain aspects of being a Southern female. As Jem and Dill exclude her from their games, Scout gradually learns more about the alien world of being a female through sitting on the porch with Miss Maudie and observing Calpurnia work in the kitchen, which makes her begin "to think there was more skill involved in being a girl" than she has previously thought (p. 118). Nevertheless, the book makes it clear that the adult Scout, who narrates the novel and who has presumably now assumed the feminine name Jean Louise for good, is still ambivalent at best concerning the traditional Southern lady.

Of special importance with regard to Scout's growing perceptions of herself as a female is the meeting of the missionary society women, a scene which, like Aunt Alexandra's character, is completely omitted from the film. Alexandra sees herself as a grand host. Through observing the missionary women, Scout, in Austenian fashion, is able to satirize the superficialities and prejudices of Southern women with whom she is unwilling to identify in order to become that alien being called woman. Dressed in "my pink Sunday dress, shoes, and a petticoat," Scout attends a meeting shortly after Tom Robinson's death, knowing that her aunt makes her participate as "part of . . . her campaign to teach me to be a lady" (p. 232). Commenting on the women, Scout says, "Rather nervous, I took a seat beside Miss Maudie and wondered why ladies put on their hats to go across the street. Ladies in bunches always filled me with vague apprehension and a firm desire to be elsewhere . . ." (p. 232).

As the meeting begins, the ladies ridicule Scout for frequently wearing pants and inform her that she cannot become a member of the elite, genteel group of Southern ladyhood unless she mends her ways. Miss Stephanie Crawford, the town gossip, mocks Scout by asking her if she wants to grow up to be a lawyer, a comment to which Scout, coached by Aunt Alexandra, says, "Not me, just a lady" (p. 233)—with the obvious social satire evident. Scout clearly does not want to become a lady. Suspicious, Miss Stephanie replies, "'Well, you won't get very far until you start wearing dresses more often'" (p. 233). Immediately thereafter, Lee exposes even further the provincialism and superficiality of the group's appearance of gentility, piety, and morality. Mrs. Grace Meriwether's comments on "'those poor Mruna'" who live "'in that jungle'" and need Christian salvation reflect a smug, colonialist attitude toward other races. When the women begin conversing about blacks in America, their bigotry—and Scout's disgust with it—becomes obvious.

Rather than the community of gentility and racism represented in the women of Maycomb, Scout clearly prefers the world of her father, as this passage reveals: ". . . I wondered at the world of women. . . . There was no doubt about it, I must soon enter this world, where on its surface fragrant ladies rocked slowly, fanned gently, and drank cool water" (p. 236). The female role is far too frivolous and unimportant for Scout to identify with. Furthermore, she says, "But I was more at home in my father's world. People like Mr. Heck Tate did not trap you with innocent questions to make fun of you. . . . Ladies seemed to live in faint horror of men, seemed unwilling to approve wholeheartedly of them. But I liked them. . . . [N]o matter how undelectable they were, . . . they weren't 'hypocrites'" (p. 236). This obviously idealized and childlike portrayal of men nevertheless gets at the core of Scout's conflict. In a world in which men seem to have the advantages and seem to be more fair-minded and less intolerant than women with their petty concerns and superficial dress codes, why should she conform to the notion of Southern ladyhood? Ironically, Scout, unlike the reader, is unable to recognize the effects of female powerlessness which may be largely responsible for the attitudes of Southern ladies. If they cannot control the everyday business and legal affairs of their society, they can at least impose their code of manners and morality.

To Scout, Atticus and his world represent freedom and power. Atticus is the key representative of the male power which Scout wishes to obtain even though she is growing up as a Southern female. More important, Lee demonstrates that Scout is gradually becoming a feminist in the South, for, with the use of first-person narration, she indicates that Scout/Jean Louise still maintains the ambivalence about being a Southern lady she possessed as a child. She seeks to become empowered with the freedoms the men in her society seem to possess without question and without resorting to trivial and superficial concerns such as wearing a dress and appearing genteel.

Harper Lee's fundamental criticism of gender roles for women (and to a lesser extent for men) may be evident especially in her novel's identification with outsider figures such as Tom Robinson, Mayella Ewell, and Boo Radley. Curiously enough, the outsider figures with whom the novelist identifies most are also males. Tom Robinson, the male African American who has been disempowered and annihilated by a fundamentally racist, white male society, and Boo Radley, the reclusive and eccentric neighbor about whom legends of his danger to the fragile Southern society circulate regularly, are the two "mockingbirds" of the title. Ironically, they are unable to mock society's roles for them and as a result take the consequences of living on the margins— Tom, through his death; Boo, through his return to the protection of a desolate isolated existence.

Throughout the novel, however, the female voice has emphasized Scout's growing distance from her provincial Southern society and her identification with her father, a symbol of the empowered. Like her father, Atticus, Scout, too, is unable to be a "mockingbird" of society and as a result, in coming to know Boo Radley as a real human being at novel's end, she recognizes the empowerment of being the other as she consents to remain an outsider unable to accept society's unwillingness to seek and know before it judges. And it is perhaps this element of the female voice in Harper Lee's *To Kill a Mockingbird* which most makes Horton Foote's screen adaptation largely a compromise of the novel's full power.

From *Mississippi Quarterly* 50, no. 1 (Winter, 1996/1997), pp. 101-113. Copyright © 1996 by Mississippi State University. Reprinted by permission of Mississippi State University.

Notes

1. Harper Lee, *To Kill a Mockingbird* (New York: Popular Library, 1962), pp. 85-86.

2. *Screening the Novel: The Theory and Practice of Literary Dramatization* (New York: St. Martin's Press, 1990), pp. 10-12.

3. Joseph Mersand, *Studies in the Mass Media: To Kill a Mockingbird: 25th Anniversary Brochure and Study Guide* (Urbana, Illinois: NCTE, 1963, 1988), p. 18.

4. Edgar H. Schuster, "Discovering Theme and Structure in the Novel," *English Journal*, 52 (1963), p. 507.

5. The earliest reviewers generally bypass the novel's concerns about being a young female in the South—even when they mention the work's autobiographical dimensions. Recent critics, most notably Harold Bloom and Claudia Durst Johnson, still fail to acknowledge the heavily feminist dimensions of the novel. See Harold Bloom, ed., *Harper Lee's To Kill a Mockingbird: A Contemporary Literary Views Book* (Broomall, Pennsylvania: Chelsea House, 1996). In her useful casebook on and introductory critical study of the novel, Johnson includes the gender issue but still focuses primarily on the novel's concerns about race relations in the South. See Claudia Durst Johnson, ed. *Understanding To Kill a Mockingbird: A Student Casebook to Issues, Sources, and Historic Documents* (Westport, Connecticut: Greenwood Press, 1994); and Claudia Durst Johnson, *To Kill a Mockingbird: Threatening Boundaries* (New York: Twayne, 1994). The appearance of the Bloom and Johnson books may indicate a growing interest in the novel as a serious work of literature rather than merely a canonical novel for high school students.

6. Horton Foote, *To Kill a Mockingbird*, in *Three Screenplays: To Kill a Mockingbird, Tender Mercies, and The Trip to Bountiful* (New York: Grove Press, 1989), p. 30.

7. Universal Studios, *To Kill a Mockingbird*. Directed by Robert Mulligan; produced by Alan Pakula; screenplay by Horton Foote.

8. Amy Lawrence, *Echo and Narcissus: Women's Voices in Classical Hollywood Cinema* (Berkeley: University of California Press, 1991), p. 170.

"When You Finally See Them":
The Unconquered Eye in *To Kill a Mockingbird*_____

Laurie Champion

> Standing on the bare ground—my head bathed by the blithe air, and up-
> lifted into infinite space,—all mean egotism vanishes. I become a transpar-
> ent eye-ball. I am nothing. I see all. The currents of the Universal Being cir-
> culate through me; I am part or particle of God.
>
> —Ralph Waldo Emerson

Although hitherto unacknowledged in critical studies, Harper Lee's *To Kill a Mockingbird* is primarily a story about perception, the ability to see clearly.[1] The notion of visual perception is a prevailing metaphor established through abundant references to eyes, sight, and blindness. Sight or lack of sight and modes of visual perception are further illustrated with recurring images of light and darkness. Throughout the novel, various types of eye and light imagery form a structure that supports Emersonian transcendentalism.[2] Degrees of seeing symbolize human perception or prophetic vision and reveal Emerson's notion of a "transparent eyeball." Moreover, descriptions of physical eyes and references to shades of light metaphorically denote philosophical and social concerns the novel expounds and suggest Emerson's idea that we can truly see only with an unconquered eye.

Atticus wears glasses, cannot physically see well, yet he has insight and wisdom. In several significant scenes, Atticus performs specific gestures using his glasses. When Scout and Jem wonder why Atticus is older than their friends' parents, Scout recalls, "Besides that, he wore glasses. He was nearly blind in his left eye, and said left eyes were the tribal curse of the Finches. Whenever he wanted to see something well, he turned his head and looked from his right eye" (98). Indeed, Atticus sees from the "right," visually perceptive, unconquered eye. In this sense, while Atticus possesses insight from his "right" eye, Mayella's right eye is both literally and figuratively bruised.

When Atticus shoots Tim Johnson, the rabid dog, he raises "his glasses and Calpurnia murmured, 'Sweet Jesus help him'" (104). Scout observes, "Atticus pushed his glasses to his forehead; they slipped down, and he dropped them in the street. In the silence, I heard them crack. Atticus rubbed his eyes and chin; we saw him blink hard" (104). Immediately after Atticus shoots the dog, he "stooped and picked up his glasses, ground the broken lenses to powder under his heel" (105). Scout recalls this incident twice, both times mentioning Atticus's glasses. She remembers that when the mob approached Atticus at the jail, he had "calmly fold [ed] his newspaper and push[ed] back his hat" and relates that image to "Atticus standing in the middle of an empty waiting street, pushing up his glasses" (167), the act he performs just before his glasses fall off and he shoots the raging dog. At the end of the novel, Scout walks back from escorting Boo home and remembers a montage-like summary of the summer's events, including her recollection of the time Atticus "walked into the street, dropped his glasses, and shot a dog" (294).

The repeated mention of Atticus's glasses seems a minor detail when set against the significance of Atticus shooting the dog. However, references to glasses draw attention to Atticus's poor visual sight, which because of its opposition draws attention to his acute moral perception. When one considers Atticus as acting under Emerson's idea of truly seeing, attention to Atticus's insight as opposed to his visual impairment becomes important. In fact, as Lee Brown so astutely points out, transparent eyes are physically blind. Brown convincingly argues that Emerson builds both on the traditional premise developed since Plato that the physical makeup of the eye impedes "clear transmission of the light of truth" and on the medieval tradition that asserts that "the pupils of the saints are made transparent and they can see the uncreated light directly and with a sight which reveals its essence" (127). Leonardo used optical laws to deduce "that completely transparent eyes must be blind to natural or created light (as opposed to supernatural or 'uncreated' light), for they lack a 'thick opaque instrument'—the retinal surface which lies behind the pupil of the eye. Hence, if angels are invisible to us, we are just as invisible to them" (127). Brown argues that "the Emersonian eyeball, like Leonardo's angel, lacks the interior opacity requisite for vision" (128); he concludes, "By itself, the transparent eyeball is blind; in fact, it would be 'void' rather than transparent if it were not for the oversight of a higher eye which focuses on an object (or meaning) beyond it" (135). Atticus possesses just such a transparent eye—physically blind yet able to focus on meaning beyond literal sight.

Shooting the dog relates to the broader theme the novel expounds. Because he performs this heroic deed, Scout recognizes that Atticus is not merely an old man who does not achieve anything, and she looks forward to telling her friends that her father is "the deadest shot in Maycomb County" (107). She asks Miss Maudie why Atticus never uses his shooting skill, why he never hunts. Miss Maudie explains that Atticus is "civilized in his heart. Marksmanship's a gift of God, a talent. . . . [H]e realized that God had given him an unfair advantage over most living things. I guess he decided he wouldn't shoot till he had to, and he had to today" (107). While Atticus deems it morally necessary to shoot a dog that might hurt someone, he says "it's a sin to kill a mockingbird" (98), the only act Atticus says is sinful. Although others judge that it is not immoral to shoot mockingbirds, Atticus is the self-reliant individual whose internal moral values are not contingent upon external social judgments.

Tom is the symbolic mockingbird whose plight illustrates that racial injustice is the most apparent manifestation of moral corruption in Maycomb County; thus, the novel suggests that it is also a sin, spiritually wrong, to shoot Tom and to discriminate against people. When the prison guards shoot Tom, they shoot a mockingbird metaphorically. On the other hand, shooting the rabid dog signifies the antithesis of "senseless slaughter of songbirds by hunters and children" (254). In contrast to the harmless mockingbirds, the dog "seemed dedicated to one course and motivated by an invisible force . . . his jaw opened and shut; he was alist" (103). Atticus accepts responsibility for the fates of both the dog and Tom: he seeks to destroy the dog, who threatens society's physical health, and to acquit Tom and expose and eliminate racism, a different type of social threat. In both cases, Atticus gets only one chance to abolish these threats. Tate tells Atticus that shooting the dog "is a one-shot job" (104), knowing the dog will attack the shooter if he misses. Likewise, Atticus tells Scout that "simply by the nature of the work, every lawyer gets at least one case in his lifetime that affects him personally. This one's mine, I guess" (84). Atticus successfully accomplishes his first "one-shot job" when he slays the physical threat; but when Tom is convicted, Atticus loses his one personal legal case. Atticus easily expels physical threats to Maycomb County, but eliminating philosophical social threats poses nearly impossible challenges.

When Dill runs away to the Finches' house, Aunt Rachel forgives him and allows him to stay with Jem and Scout. Shortly after "Atticus pushed up his glasses and rubbed his face," Scout says, "Dill and I decided to be civil to Jem" (152). Here, just as when Miss Maudie says that Atticus is "civilized," the word "civil" is positioned against a reference to eyesight. Immediately after Atticus pushes up his glasses, he makes a connection between Dill's crime and the crime Tom did not commit. He says, "From rape to riot to runaways" (152). Scout uses legal terms to describe Dill's offense, as though Atticus were defending a client: "After many telephone calls, much pleading on behalf of the defendant, and a long forgiving letter from his mother, it was decided that Dill could stay" (155). Dill is excused for escaping his domestic prison; yet when Tom attempts to escape custody, he is brutally shot. Atticus says, "They fired a few shots in the air, then to kill. . . . Seventeen bullet holes in him. They didn't have to shoot him that much" (248). While Dill is given mercy for an offense he indeed committed, the innocent Tom is shot cruelly, much more fiercely than the dangerous dog that Atticus shoots only once. The word "civil" has legal connotations, and the irony is that judicial laws do not reflect moral integrity. Atticus is "civilized" and Scout and Dill act "civilly" toward Jem, forgiving him for telling Atticus that Dill has run to the Finches' house. But the social system, represented as the Fifth Judicial Circuit Court, acts anything but civilly toward Tom. Judicial laws reflect rational thought, but Emerson suggests that clear vision depends not on rational thought but upon recognizing the world's transparency, a cosmic phenomenon.

During the climactic courtroom scenes, Atticus first confirms that Bob Ewell is left-handed and that Tom's left arm is mangled. After providing circumstantial evidence that Bob Ewell beat Mayella, "Atticus reached up and took off his glasses, turned his good right eye to the witness, and rained questions on her" (199). Atticus asks Mayella, "Why don't you tell the truth, child, didn't Bob Ewell beat you up?" (199). Immediately afterward, Atticus "sat down wearily and polished his glasses with his handkerchief" (200). A plea for acknowledging truth is juxtaposed against a reference to Atticus's eyesight. Unlike Atticus, Mayella may physically see clearly, as she does not wear glasses, yet she does not speak the truth.

Even though he interrogates her on the witness stand, Atticus obviously feels empathy for Mayella. When Mayella begins to cry hysterically and refuses further questioning from both defense and prosecution, Scout says that Atticus "hit her hard in a way that was not clear to me, but it gave him no pleasure to do so. He sat with his head down, and I never saw anybody glare at anyone with the hatred Mayella showed when she left the stand and walked by Atticus's table" (200). Atticus, with his poor physical eyesight and strong sense of moral decency, does not glare at Mayella or cause her unnecessary humiliation. Atticus feels compassion for Mayella, yet she despises him, "glares" at him with strong physical eyesight that is unable philosophically to see clearly.

Atticus presents his rhetorically superb closing argument, explaining that the prosecuting argument rests on the faulty assumption that blacks are more immoral than whites, then "he took off his glasses and wiped them . . ." (217). Atticus proves his argument, and the jury surely understands Atticus's speech on an intellectual level; but in Emersonian terms, the jury convicts Tom because of their inability to see truly—this ability to judge is not mental but visual. They use thought processes when they make their decision, but as Emerson observes, "Sturdy and defying though he look, [every man] has a helm which he obeys, which is, the idea after which all his facts are classified. He can only be reformed by showing him a new idea which commands his own" ("Circles" 180). Acquitting a black person does not fit into the jury's preestablished mental constructs. To assume that Tom is telling the truth and that a white girl is lying is a verdict that will not fit their belief system; therefore, they decide Tom raped Mayella because that scenario fits their preconceptions that whites are superior to blacks.

Fred Erisman suggests that when in Atticus's speech to the jury he states that people of all races perform immoral acts, he, "like the Puritans . . . assumes the flawed nature of man, but, like Emerson, he looks to the higher laws—those of the court and of the nation—that enable man to transcend his base diversity and give him the only form of equality possible in a diverse society" (132). Although Atticus appeals to the higher laws, he admits to Jem that he is "no idealist to believe firmly in the integrity of our courts and the jury system. A court is only as sound as its jury, and a jury is only as sound as the men who make it up" (218). Atticus says that he is "confident" the jury will "restore this defendant to his family"; yet he pleads, "In the name of God, do your duty" (218). Jem repeats, "In the name of God, believe him" (218). Obviously, Atticus does not depend on the higher man-made courts, for he pleads with the jury "in the name of God," a phrase that echoes the Emersonian plea for humanity to harmonize with God. Atticus teaches his children, the symbolic future generation, to be nondiscriminatory, to observe events from an innocent eye that does not seek to categorize people hierarchically. Atticus presents to the jury rational, logical arguments, but his defense fails. Even if Atticus has a glimmer of hope that he may acquit Tom through rhetoric and, therefore, begin to obliterate racism, Lee's message suggests the contrary.

Because of the sexual nature of the crime, Reverend Sykes asks Scout, Jem, and Dill if Atticus knows they are watching the trial. While "Reverend Sykes's black eyes were anxious" for Jem to answer him, Jem says that Atticus "can't see us this far away" (184). Denying Sykes's request to ask all children and women to leave the courtroom, Judge Taylor says, "People generally see what they look for . . ." (185). Reverend Sykes searches the courtroom for drama that is unsuitable for children. His concerns reflect racist attitudes, suggesting that the children should not hear about a black man raping a white woman. Contrary to Reverend Sykes, Atticus cannot see his children, and according to Judge Taylor's dictum, he cannot see his children because his transparent eye does not perceive whether or not children and women watch the trial. Atticus, however, sees truth, and that is what he attempts to prove.

Atticus asks Calpurnia to accompany him to inform Helen that Tom has been shot, and he raises "up his glasses" (249). Atticus says he told Tom he might win a court appeal, explaining that he "couldn't in truth say that we had more than a good chance. I guess Tom was tired of white men's chances and preferred to take his own" (249). Here, Atticus raises his glasses immediately prior to speaking the truth. In the courtroom scene, he pushes up his glasses after expounding truth. In both instances, allusions to Atticus's glasses, his poor physical sight, are juxtaposed against his ability to speak the truth.

References to Atticus's glasses also come when he makes minor judgments. For example, when Atticus takes Aunt Alexandra's advice and attempts to tell the children to remember their "gentle breeding" and act like wellborn citizens, Scout begins to cry. Comforting Scout, Atticus tells her to forget everything he and Aunt Alexandra have said about what it means to be a Finch. As Atticus walks toward the door Scout notices that his "eyebrows were raised, his glasses had slipped" (144-45). He recognizes that Aunt Alexandra is wrong and that he is giving his children bad advice. His glasses slip, and he loses physical sight, but he reverts to his own child-rearing methods. Throughout the novel, Atticus performs his parental role according to Emerson's dictum: "To the well-born child, all virtues are natural, and not painfully acquired. Speak to his heart, and the man becomes suddenly virtuous" ("Over-Soul" 163-64).

Allusions to eyes and sight in Tate's testimony symbolize truth in ways similar to those to Atticus's sight. As Scout first observes the trial, she notices Tate "touching his glasses during his testimony" (177). When Atticus asks Tate which one of Mayella's eyes was black on the day she was assaulted, Tate "blinked and ran his hands through his hair" (179). Realizing Mayella's right eye was black, "Mr. Tate blinked again, as if something had suddenly been made plain to him" (179). Atticus's argument rests on the certainty that Mayella's right eye, instead of her left, was black. Therefore, Tate builds Atticus's case by exposing evidence that Atticus uses to demonstrate Tom's innocence.

Eye imagery in reference to other minor characters suggests that they possess only superficial vision, lack moral perception and Emersonian clear vision. Scout observes that Mr. Gilmer, the prosecuting attorney, has "a slight cast in one of his eyes which he used to his advantage: he seemed to be looking at a person when he was actually doing nothing of the kind, thus he was hell on juries and witnesses. The jury, thinking themselves under close scrutiny, paid attention; so did the witnesses, thinking likewise" (177). Whereas Atticus uses clear vision during the trial, Mr. Gilmer relies on a gaze, a peculiar look that manipulates juries and witnesses. The jury and witnesses pay attention not because they are interested in the facts of Mayella's assault but because they fear Mr. Gilmer. They appear to listen to testimonies, but they neither hear nor see evidence that suggests Tom's innocence. Just as Mr. Gilmer only appears to see a person, the jury only appears to consider a verdict in Tom's case.

Subtle references to Aunt Alexandra's sight and overt references to Walter Cunningham's blindness suggest they also possess only superficial vision. Atticus says that Cunningham almost acquitted Tom, and Scout says that she wants to befriend Walter. Aunt Alexandra looks at

Scout "over her sewing glasses" and tells her that she should not befriend the Cunninghams because they are from a lower social class than the Finches (236). While Aunt Alexandra explains that Scout cannot befriend Walter because the Cunninghams are "trash," she "took off her glasses and stared at [Scout]" (237). Scout ponders Aunt Alexandra's habit of placing people in hierarchical social classes, recalling that Aunt Alexandra also does not want her to visit Calpurnia. With her glasses Aunt Alexandra has physical sight, but with or without her glasses she lacks Emersonian clear vision. When Scout asks Atticus why Mr. Cunningham, one of the men she had recognized amongst those who attempted to lynch Tom, would participate in a confrontation against Atticus, he replies, "Mr. Cunningham's basically a good man . . . he just has his blind spots along with the rest of us" (168). Atticus admits he also has blind spots, indicative of a person willing to acknowledge his own flaws, a sign of honor. Atticus sees in spite of self-proclaimed blind spots and physically impaired eyes that require glasses, but Aunt Alexandra and Cunningham, representative of most of the community's members, remain unable to recognize their blind spots, much less see beyond their narrow-minded views.

The theme of clear visual perception integrates with images of light and darkness to suggest that insight comes from an innocent perspective, the unconquered eye. Images of light are used to describe the children and Atticus while Atticus is standing guard over Tom to protect him from any lynching attempt. By contrast, images of darkness describe the men who intimidate Atticus. The children sneak out of the house to look for Atticus, and approaching the town square, they observe light beaming from outside the jail: "[W]e saw a solitary light burning"; "[I]n the light from its bare bulb, Atticus was sitting propped against the front door" of the jail (161). The children witness the townsmen threaten Atticus, and Scout notices a "flash of plain fear was going out of his eyes, but returned when Dill and Jem wriggled into the light" (162-63). Atticus leaves the light on while he talks to Mr. Underwood, who he discovers has witnessed the scene from his office window. Immediately before Atticus and the children leave the square, Atticus turns "off the light above the jail door" (166). The threat is gone—there is no need for literal or spiritual light. Walking home, Scout assumes Atticus scolds Jem for disobeying him, but as "they passed under a streetlight, Atticus reached out and massaged Jem's hair, his one gesture of affection" (166). Atticus and Jem stand in both literal and spiritual light when Atticus applies situational ethics to conclude Jem acted wisely when he refused to obey him.

Contrarily, Atticus's adversaries stand in the dark with only superficial vision. Scout observes "dusty cars" approaching the town square, and she describes the men who get out of the cars as "shadows, sullen-looking, sleepy-eyed" (162, 164). When the children first approach the town square and notice the light shining from outside the door, Jem says, "That's funny . . . jail doesn't have an outside light" (161). The jail has no outside light except for the light Atticus brings with him. As demonstrated in Tom's conviction, the jail also lacks spiritual light. Atticus, who brings the spiritual light with him, tries to establish Tom's innocence as he struggles against firmly fixed racism.

Near the end of the novel, images of light and references to eyes and sight signify important moral decisions. Boo carries Jem, walks under a "street light," and hands him to Atticus, while "[l]ight from our front door framed Atticus . . ." (277). The crowd moves to the front porch because the "livingroom lights were awfully strong." Scout leads Boo to the corner of the porch, "in deep shadow. Boo would feel more comfortable in the dark." Atticus sits in the swing and Tate stands beside him, "light from the livingroom windows" shining on them. Tate tries to persuade Atticus to pretend Bob Ewell fell on his own knife, stabbed himself in a drunken stupor. Atticus says, "I guess the thing to do— good Lord, I'm losing my memory. . . . Atticus pushed up his glasses" (286). Literally, Boo stands in the dark; metaphorically, he stands in the dark because he does not know what Tate and Atticus are discussing. Atticus thinks Jem stabbed Bob Ewell, "got hold of Ewell's knife somehow in the dark" (287). Atticus stands in the dark symbolically because he believes Jem stabbed Bob Ewell; Bob Ewell is described as literally standing in the dark. During this discussion, Tate asks, "Got a flashlight?" and Dr. Reynolds says, "I can ease around and turn my car lights on" (288).

Atticus argues that his children know the truth and that if he lies to protect Jem, he "couldn't meet his eye" (288). Tate counters that Scout and Jem do not know who killed Bob Ewell because it "was mighty dark out there, black as ink. It'd take somebody mighty used to the dark to make a competent witness . . ." (289). Someone accustomed to darkness literally could see Boo kill Bob Ewell; symbolically, only someone who is "in the dark" would not understand that Boo stabbed Bob Ewell to protect Jem and Scout. When Tate explains that Boo, not Jem, stabbed Bob Ewell, Atticus agrees that Tate should lie, pretend Bob Ewell stabbed himself. While Tate tells Atticus that Jem did not kill Bob Ewell, "Mr. Tate's boot hit the floorboards so hard the lights in Miss Maudie's bedroom went on. Miss Stephanie Crawford's lights went on" (289). Atticus now stands in the light both literally and symbolically and sees from a new perspective. Emerson suggests that a new perspective is essential for clear sight: "The eye is the first circle; the horizon which it forms is the second; and throughout nature this primary figure is repeated without end. . . . Our life is an apprenticeship to the truth, that around every circle another can be drawn; that there is always another dawn risen on mid-noon, and under every deep a lower deep opens" ("Circles" 179). Atticus's eye has been cleansed and space has allowed a new opening for the horizon of the eye; he has achieved a new level of Emersonian transcendence.

Scout also experiences this type of Emersonian transcendence. When Atticus assures Scout that Tate is right, that Bob Ewell killed himself, she understands fully the morality at work. To prosecute Boo would "be sort of like shootin' a mockingbird, wouldn't it?" (291), she asks. Atticus walks to the darkened corner where Boo sits, thanks him for saving his children, and Boo stands up, "light from the livingroom windows glisten[ing] on his forehead" (291). After escorting Boo home, Scout "turned to go home. Street lights winked down the street all the way to town. I had never seen our neighborhood from this angle" (293). Indeed, she sees from a new perspective, understands that Boo is not a "malevolent phantom" as described by local rumor, and infers that telling the complete truth is not always morally correct (15). Scout asks Atticus to read from *The Gray Ghost* when she gets home. She summarizes for Atticus the plot that involves children who falsely accuse a boy of breaking into a clubhouse: "An' they chased him 'n' never could catch him 'cause they didn't know what he looked like, an' Atticus, when they finally saw him, why he hadn't done any of those things . . . Atticus, he was real nice . . ." (295). Atticus answers, "Most people are, Scout, when you finally see them" (296).

Amidst images of light and darkness, Scout and Atticus use descriptions of physical sight—"see," "saw," and "look"—symbolic of the ability to see from a fresh perspective. In this case, to understand people and recognize their character strengths in spite of local rumor that implies contrary reputations. Scout recognizes that Boo is the community's "gray ghost," a description that echoes Atticus's comment to Jem that although Mr. Radley does not chain Boo to a bed literally, there are "other ways of making people into ghosts" (18).[3]

Boo is portrayed as unsophisticated and innocent, yet he is treated unjustly for a petty childhood prank committed years earlier. Because Mr. Radley keeps "Boo out of sight" (18), he remains a "phantom," ostracized by the community. Boo does not speak until the end of the novel, when he says to Scout, "Will you take me home?" Scout says, "He almost whispered it, in the voice of a child afraid of the dark" (292). According to Emerson, "We owe many valuable observations to people who are not very acute or profound, and who say nothing without effort, which we want and have long been hunting in vain. The action of the soul is oftener in that which is felt and left unsaid, than in that which is said in any conversation" ("Over-Soul" 165). While Jem lies sick in bed, Boo lightly touches his hair (the same gesture Atticus uses when he realizes Jem was correct for refusing to leave the scene of the attempted lynching) and tightens his grip on Scout's hand. His gentle gestures move Scout immensely. She recalls, "Boo was our neighbor. He gave us two soap dolls, a broken watch and chain, a pair of good-luck pennies, and our lives" (293).

It is important to remember that the novel is told from the adult Scout's point of view, as she recalls incidents that occurred during one summer of her childhood. It is, finally, this point of view, that of a child, from which the truth is seen. Erisman refers to what he perceives as Emersonian innocent vision in *To Kill a Mockingbird*: "Atticus's individualism is emphasized . . . through his awareness of the clarity of the childhood vision (suggesting Emerson's remark that 'the sun illuminates only the eye of the man, but shines into the eye and the heart of the child. The lover of nature is he . . . who has retained the spirit of infancy even into the era of manhood [*Nature* 9])'" (131). He notes that Emerson's remark is illustrative both of the mob when it leaves the scene of Tom's jail cell and of Atticus's statement, "So it took an eight-year-old child to bring 'em to their senses, didn't it?," as well as with Dolphus Raymond's recognizing the children's instinctual reaction to Tom's trial (168).

After Tom is convicted, Atticus tells Jem: "If you had been on that jury, son, and eleven other boys like you, Tom would be a free man. . . . So far nothing in your life has interfered with your reasoning process" (233). Erisman concludes, "The point could not be more obvious; in the unsophisticated vision of the child is a perception of truth that most older, tradition-bound people have lost. Atticus, like Emerson's lover of nature, has retained it . . ." (131). Jem questions Atticus, "How could they do it, how could they?" (225). Atticus answers, "I don't know, but they did it. They've done it before and they did it tonight and they'll do it again and when they do it—seems that only children weep" (225). In addition to possessing "unsophisticated vision," Jem is "looking out from his corner on such people and facts as pass by, he tries and sentences them on their merits, in the swift summary way of boys. . . . He gives an independent genuine verdict. . . . Who can thus avoid all pledges, and having observed, observe again from the same unaffected, unbiased, unbribable, unaffrighted innocence . . ." ("Self-Reliance" 29). Jem is unbiased, or "color blind." Scout and Jem dress to visit Calpurnia's church, and Calpurnia tells him that he can't wear a green tie with a blue suit. Scout laughs and says, "Jem's color blind" (128), a reference to physical sight. Jem is also metaphorically color blind, for he visits Calpurnia's church without hesitation. Lula, however, tells Calpurnia that white children should attend their own church—a discriminatory attitude juxtaposed against Jem's which enhances the viewpoints of both. By comparison, Jem's attitude is the more noble of the two. Whereas Scout jokes that Jem is color blind, Lula, who desires separate churches for whites and blacks, is certainly not.

In terms of Emersonian transcendentalism, it may at first seem plausible that like Atticus, Boo, and the children, the jury also sees clearly. Throughout his writings, Emerson privileges the unsophisticated and those who retreat to nature. Jem asks Atticus "Why don't people like us and Miss Maudie ever sit on juries? You never see anybody from Maycomb on a jury—they all come from out in the woods" (234). Emerson advocates that *entering* the woods helps one (re)gain childlike innocence and clear vision: "In the woods too, a man casts off his years, as the snake his slough, and at what period soever of life, is always a child. In the woods, is perpetual youth. . . . In the woods, we return to reason and faith. There I feel that nothing can befall me in life—no disgrace, no calamity (leaving me my eyes), which nature cannot repair" (*Nature* 10).[4] Atticus's answer to Jem's question, however, suggests that the jury lacks clear vision and is anything but self-reliant. Because it took the jury a few hours rather than a shorter time to convict Tom, Atticus feels that he has made at least a step towards eliminating racism from Maycomb County. He says that Walter Cunningham may have considered Tom's innocence: "If we'd had two of that crowd, we'd've had a hung jury. . . . There's a fair difference between a man who's going to convict and a man who's a little disturbed in his mind, isn't there? He was the only uncertainty on the whole list" (235-36). The "little disturbance" in Cunningham's mind is prompted, of course, because he would rather agree with the other members of the jury than speak from his personal moral convictions. As Emerson says, "It is easy in the world to live after the world's opinion; it is easy in solitude to live after our own; but the great man is he who in the midst of the crowd keeps with perfect sweetness the independence of solitude ("Self-Reliance" 31). Unlike Atticus, who for the sake of impartial justice places his children and himself in jeopardy, Cunningham is not willing to suffer the consequences of publicly acknowledging Tom's innocence. While both apparently understand that "for nonconformity the world whips you with its displeasure" ("Self-Reliance" 32), only Atticus is willing to defend his convictions.

Although the Ewells and those chosen for juries in Maycomb County are unsophisticated, some might even be considered "brutes," they fail to meet Emerson's requirement for people who see with an unconquered eye: "What pretty oracles nature yields us on this text in the face and behavior of children, babes and even brutes. That divided and rebel mind, that distrust of a sentiment because our arithmetic has computed the strength and means opposed to our purpose, these have not. Their mind being whole, their ego is as yet unconquered, and when we look in their faces we are disconcerted. Infancy conforms to nobody . . ." ("Self-Reliance"' 28). Unequivocally, Atticus, Boo, and the self-reliant children possess the unconquered eye—instead of allowing only selective knowledge to enter their perceptions, their sight remains true and unimpaired.

The central theme of *To Kill a Mockingbird* involves Maycomb County's inability to recognize Tom as a victim of racial bias or to "see" justice. Maycomb County residents are not metaphorically color blind, for they condemn a man because he is black. Tom's jurors understand who assaulted Mayella, but to acquit Tom they must convict Bob Ewell. Because of the racially biased justice system, the guilty Bob Ewell is spared simply because he is white. Discrimination, therefore, operates both to condemn the innocent and to acquit the guilty, and justice is served in neither case. Ultimately, Tom's conviction is due to the judgment of those who cannot understand, that "[e]very particular in nature, a leaf, a drop, a crystal, a moment of time, is related to the whole, and partakes of the perfection of the whole. Each particle is a microcosm, and faithfully renders the likeness of the world" (*Nature* 27). Emerson advocates the eye that refuses to discriminate and categorize, one that does not attempt to specify priorities. Harper Lee and Emerson championed the egalitarian eye that both leads to and derives from innocent observation, that becomes cyclical as the eye rises repeatedly to form new horizons: "The life of man is a self-evolving circle, which, from a ring imperceptibly small, rushes on all sides outwards to new and larger circles, and that without end" ("Circles" 180); "So shall we come to look at the world with new eyes. It shall answer the endless inquiry of the intellect,—What is truth? And of the affections,—What is good?" (*Nature* 44).

In *To Kill a Mockingbird* ethnicity becomes the ultimate issue that involves the light/dark and sighted/blind dichotomies. Both Tom and Bob Ewell are finally (mis)judged according to shades of light or dark, namely the color of their skin. Because they are not color blind, Maycomb County residents recognize that Tom is black and Bob Ewell is white, yet they cannot see nor understand racist social misconceptions. The more sonorous point is, in fact, that they employ only a superficial vision that sees and distinguishes color and arrives at conclusions by valuing ethnicity hierarchically. Lee does more than provide a story about the evils of racism. Through references to sight/blindness and light/darkness, she suggests that predisposed discrimination prevents clear perception and manifests itself as racial injustice. Racism cannot be eliminated by man-made laws nor intellect, she submits, but only by seeing clearly from a fresh perspective, one that cyclically leads to a cleansed eye, that again and again remains unconquered.

Notes

1. Surprisingly enough, despite its literary and commercial successes, *To Kill a Mockingbird* has received little scholarly attention. It was not until 1994 that Claudia Durst Johnson produced the first two full-length studies of the novel. Much of the criticism, Johnson notes, has been written by practicing lawyers and professors of law who are concerned with the legal ramifications of segregation or Atticus's professional ethics. The most recent criticism written from a primarily legal perspective is collected in *Symposium: To Kill a Mockingbird*, a 1994 special issue of *Alabama Law Review.*

2. Fred Erisman discusses *To Kill a Mockingbird* in terms of "an Emersonian view of Southern romanticism, suggesting that the South can move from the archaic, imported romanticism of its past toward the more reasonable, pragmatic, and native romanticism of a Ralph Waldo Emerson" (123). He concludes that the "New South," like Emerson, "spurns the past, looking instead to the reality of the present. With him, it places principled action above self-interest, willingly accepting the difficult consequences of a right decision" (128).

3. In addition to references to Boo as having clear vision, possessing a "transparent eyeball," descriptions of him as a ghost or phantom suggest that he is a transparent being, one who represents Leonardo's angels discussed earlier.

4. Significantly, this passage immediately precedes the well-known transparent eyeball passage that serves as the epigraph of this essay.

Works Cited

Brown, Lee Rust. "Emersonian Transparency." *Raritan* 9.3 (1990): 127-44.

Emerson, Ralph Waldo. *The Collected Works of Ralph Waldo Emerson*. 2 vols. Cambridge: Belknap P of Harvard UP, 1971-79.

_____. "Circles." Vol. 1. *Collected Works*. 177-90.

_____. *Nature*. Vol. 2. *Collected Works*. 7-46.

_____. "The Over-Soul." Vol. 1. *Collected Works*. 157-75.

_____. "Self-Reliance." Vol. 1. *Collected Works*. 25-51.

Erisman, Fred. "The Romantic Regionalism of Harper Lee." *Alabama Review* 26 (1973): 122-36.

Godfree, Elizabeth C., ed. *Symposium: To Kill a Mockingbird. Alabama Law Review* 45 (1994): 389-727.

Johnson, Claudia Durst. *To Kill a Mockingbird: Threatening Boundaries*. Twayne's Masterwork Studies Ser. 139. New York: Twayne, 1994.

_____. *Understanding To Kill a Mockingbird: A Student Casebook to Issues, Sources, and Documents*. Literature in Context Ser. 1. Westport, CT: Greenwood, 1994.

Lee, Harper. *To Kill a Mockingbird*. New York: Lippincott, 1960.

Harper Lee and the Destabilization of Heterosexuality

Gary Richards

Unlike Lillian Smith's fiction, which, after its initial notoriety and even infamy, quickly fell out of popular circulation, Harper Lee's *To Kill a Mockingbird* (1960) met with enthusiastic critical and popular reception upon its publication and has remained one of the nation's most pervasive texts. It was, according to the *Commonweal*'s review, "the find of the year," and Robert W. Henderson raved that Lee had written both a "compassionate, deeply moving novel, and a most persuasive plea for racial justice." Almost without exception, reviewers praised her depiction of small-town southern life. Granville Hicks noted her "insight into Southern mores," and Keith Waterhouse, writing from the other side of the Atlantic, offered that "Miss Lee does well what so many American writers do appallingly: she paints a true and lively picture of life in an American small town. And she gives freshness to a stock situation." This "freshness" arises in part, suggested Frank H. Lyell, because Lee avoids the tropes and imagery of the southern gothic. "Maycomb has its share of eccentrics and evil-doers," he admits, "but Miss Lee has not tried to satisfy the current lust for morbid, grotesque tales of Southern depravity." Perhaps recalling *Other Voices, Other Rooms* and *The House of Breath*, a reviewer for *Time* agreed with Lyell, arguing that Lee's novel includes "all of the tactile brilliance and none of the preciosity generally supposed to be standard swamp-warfare issue for Southern writers." "Novelist Lee's prose has an edge that cuts through cant," this reviewer asserted, concluding, "All in all, Scout Finch is fiction's most appealing child since Carson McCullers's Frankie got left behind at the wedding."[1]

These reviewers' criticisms were few and easily dismissed. Critics seemed intent to disregard the possibility that the narrative might be Scout's adult reflections on her childhood rather than a telling of yesterday's events. Hicks thus identified Lee's central problem as "to tell the story she wants and yet to stay within the consciousness of a child," while the hostile reviewer for the *Atlantic Monthly* deemed the narration "frankly and completely impossible." The only other real concern indicted the novel's didacticism, which most reviewers were content merely to note and then dismiss as minor. The reviewer for *Booklist*, for example, concluded, "Despite a melodramatic climax and traces of sermonizing, the characters and locale are depicted with insight and a rare blend of wit and compassion," and *Time*'s granted that, although "a faint catechistic flavor may have been inevitable," "it is faint indeed." The consensus was, as the *Commonweal*'s reviewer put it, that the "author unknown until this book appeared will not soon be forgotten."[2]

Lee was indeed not forgotten, for the novel won the Pulitzer Prize in 1961 and was soon adapted into a screenplay by Horton Foote. The resulting 1962 film starring Gregory Peck met with critical acclaim and simultaneously made Lee's narrative, albeit significantly altered, accessible to a wider audience. Since this time, the novel has been widely taught in American schools, in no small part, Eric Sundquist argues, because of its "admirable moral earnestness" and "comforting sentimentality." To him, as to early reviewers, the book offers "a merciless string of moral lessons" presented through "a model of conventional plot and character" that is nevertheless "an episodic story of wit and charm."[3] Because of this teachable didacticism, thousands of adolescents have been subjected to Lee's less-than-subtle symbolism and Atticus Finch's palatable liberal dicta to his children for social tolerance.

Despite—or perhaps because of—these popular circulations, *To Kill a Mockingbird* has been for the most part critically neglected, typically being dismissed simply as a popular novel or as children's literature. *The History of Southern Literature*, for instance, devotes but a solitary paragraph to the novel. Martha Cook briefly summarizes the plot and, at odds with Sundquist, tersely concludes, "*To Kill a Mockingbird* is most successful in its unsentimental portrayal of enlightened views on the rights of blacks." More substantial critical discussions of the novel remain few, with an ebbing to almost nothing of late. Only two notable exceptions emerge, essays by Sundquist and Claudia Johnson, the latter of which was expanded into the slim *To Kill a Mockingbird: Threatening Boundaries*. And yet these works share a primary focus of contextualizing the novel's circulations of race within larger historical ones of the novel's setting and period of composition, the mid-1930s and the mid- to late-1950s respectively. Both essays approach the novel through the Scottsboro case, the Supreme Court's ruling in *Brown v. Board of Education*, Rosa Parks's bus ride, and the desegregation of the University of Alabama, and thus keep the lens of analysis primarily that of race.[4]

This evolution of critical approaches from initial fanfare at publication to general dismissal to one informed foremost by race should by now be familiar, since such an evolution parallels the shifting approaches to *Strange Fruit* and Lillian Smith's other writing, and both trajectories of critical reception reflect southern literary studies' increased awareness and interrogations of race. As the previous chapter establishes, however, the scholarship on Smith has of late expanded to incorporate other significant critical lenses and those of gender and sexuality in particular. And, as I hope to have shown, *Strange Fruit* and *Killers of the Dream* prove themselves texts subject to such approaches. This chapter argues that *To Kill a Mockingbird* not surprisingly bears comparable richness under such scrutiny.

Just as Lee's novel shares with *Strange Fruit* a narrative structure that privileges racial tensions, with Tom Robinson's trial for miscegenistic rape and his ultimate death paralleling in importance Tracy Deen and Nonnie Anderson's interracial affair and its tragic results, so too does Lee include as significant an array of sexual otherness as does Smith. But, whereas Smith overtly addresses homoerotic desire in Laura Deen, Lee explores sexual difference more obliquely through transgressions of gender, the absence and parody of heterosexual relations, and the symbolic representation of closetedness. What nevertheless emerges in *To Kill a Mockingbird* is a destabilization of heterosexuality and normative gender that seems far more radical, because of its cultural pervasiveness, than the momentary presences of overt same-sex desire in Smith's novel. That is, whereas Smith depicts struggles of isolated lesbians within southern society understood to be as homophobic as it is racist, Lee presents this society to be, without it ever being fully conscious of the fact, already distinctively queer.

* * *

Like so much southern literary production during and after World War II, *To Kill a Mockingbird* centrally preoccupies itself with gender transitivity. These violations of normative gender manifest themselves in characters as diverse as Dill Harris, Scout Finch, Miss Maudie Atkinson, and even, to a lesser degree, Atticus Finch, as well as in a number of minor figures. Lee draws attention to such transgressive performances through their alterity to normative ones, such as those of Aunt Alexandra, and by overt communal demands for gender conformity. Lee does not, however, use these transgressions as consistent cultural shorthand for homosexual or proto-homosexual identities, as Capote and Goyen do. Unlike the effeminate Joel Knox and Boy Ganchion, whose narratives culminate in struggles to negotiate and, albeit uneasily, to accept same-sex desire, Lee's gender-transitive characters do not face such moments of crisis. Their narratives end without comparable culminations and thus suggest that she is as interested in gender transitivity when it is not indicative of same-sex desire as when it is, and she seems concerned at broadest with how rarely normative gender is *ever* performed.

Of *To Kill a Mockingbird*'s central trio of young protagonists, only Jem Finch is conventionally gendered, behaving as a southern white boy his age ostensibly ought. In contrast, Scout and Dill struggle with such behaviors and seem more comfortable in gender-transitive roles. Consider first Dill. Lee not only scripts him as effeminate but also underscores his sissiness through the contrast to Jem and his crystallizing masculinity. Although the elder boy is underweight for Maycomb's football team, he nevertheless dwarfs Dill, and even Scout stands almost a head taller. Dill is in fact so small that, when the Finches first encounter him sitting in his aunt's collard patch, "he wasn't much higher than the collards." Scout and Jem are amazed when, after guessing Dill to be four-and-a-half years old based on his size, he informs them he is almost seven. "I'm little but I'm old," Dill demands when Jem offers, "You look right puny for goin' on seven."[5]

Comparisons of Dill and Jem become overt when they offer up their individual sizes and names for inspection, and, given the cultural valorizations of masculinity, Dill fares poorly when placed alongside Jem:

> Jem brushed his hair back to get a better look. "Why don't you come over, Charles Baker Harris?" he said. "Lord, what a name."
>
> "'s not any funnier'n yours. Aunt Rachel says your name's Jeremy Atticus Finch."
>
> Jem scowled. "I'm big enough to fit mine," he said. "Your name's longer'n you are. Bet it's a foot longer."
>
> "Folks call me Dill," said Dill, struggling under the fence. (11)

At least in his own opinion, Jem physically measures up to his full name, whereas Dill, metaphorically a foot deficient, does not and is instead forced into an appropriately truncated nickname.

If Dill's prepubescent body is less than masculine in size, his dress and actions do little to counter this effeminacy. Like Capote's delicate Joel Knox, Dill dresses in clothes perceived to be sissy, wearing "blue linen shorts that buttoned to his shirt" rather than Maycomb County boys' customary overalls. Although perhaps not necessarily feminine, his actions and desires are nevertheless likewise unconventional. He is, Scout says, "a pocket Merlin, whose head teemed with eccentric plans, strange longings, and quaint fancies" (12). Foremost among these fancies is to establish contact with Maycomb's reclusive Boo Radley. After hearing Scout and Jem rehearse communal gossip of Boo, the "Radley Place fascinated Dill" and "drew him as the moon draws water" (12-13). For all the intensity of these longings, however, he is conspicuously cowardly and will go no closer to the Radleys' than the light pole at the corner, and the resulting scenario allows Lee yet another arena to establish Dill's lack of daring in contrast to Jem's bravery. Not surprisingly, it is he rather than Dill who first enters the Radleys' yard and touches the house.

It is common knowledge that, in this characterization of Dill, Lee drew heavily upon Truman Capote's effeminate childhood identity, as he readily acknowledged. In a series of interviews with Lawrence Grobel, Capote reflects on this childhood in Monroeville, Alabama, and recalls his friendship with Nelle Harper Lee and her family: "Mr. and Mrs. Lee, Harper Lee's mother and father, . . . lived very near. Harper Lee was my best friend. Did you ever read her book, *To Kill a Mockingbird*? I'm a character in that book, which takes place in the same small town in Alabama where we lived." He clearly implies Dill, whose childhood replicates Capote's so closely as sketched by biographer Gerald Clarke:

> As the years passed, the differences between him and other boys became even more pronounced: he remained small and pretty as a china doll, and his mannerisms, little things like the way he walked or held himself, started to look odd, unlike those of the other boys. Even his voice began to sound strange, peculiarly babylike and artificial, as if he had unconsciously decided that that part of him, the only part he could stop from maturing, would remain fixed in boyhood forever, reminding him of happier and less confusing times. His face and body belatedly matured, but his way of speaking never did.[6]

With Dill, Lee draws upon not only these generic effeminate mannerisms but also Capote's ubiquitous short pants, his precociousness, his string of surrogate- and stepfathers, and even his distinctive white hair that "stuck to his head like duckfluff" and formed "a cowlick in the center of his forehead" (12).

Although the lascivious photo of Capote on the dust jacket of *Other Voices, Other Rooms* still haunted readers in the 1960s, when *To Kill a Mockingbird* appeared at the beginning of the decade, this image of Capote was but a few short years away from being replaced by comparably vivid others, ones that readers of Lee's novel might, if they knew Dill's biographical basis in Capote, bring with them to the text and thus to their understanding of Dill. In 1966 Capote not only published to wild acclaim *In Cold Blood* but, to celebrate the novel's completion, also hosted the Black and White Ball at Manhattan's Plaza Hotel. The publicity of each event was phenomenal, but that of the ball in particular inundated Americans with images of Capote's over-the-top campy effeminacy. As the photo spreads in *Life* and other magazines attested, the evening was, in Capote confidante Slim Keith's terms, "the biggest and best goddamned party that anybody had ever heard of" despite being "given by a funny-looking, strange little man."[7]

Having thus captured the public eye, Capote refused to leave it. In his remaining years, as his creativity and productivity waned, he shamelessly compensated by crafting an eccentric public personality for himself, which he flaunted, such as during his recurring appearances on Johnny Carson's *The Tonight Show*. As with those persons who saw the photographs of the Black and White Ball, Carson's viewers internalized images of Capote as an unabashed aging gossipy queen or, as Kenneth Reed has characterized Capote, a "madcap social butterfly and late evening television chatterbox."[8] Thus, for Lee's readers aware of Dill's basis in Capote, these images of him circulating throughout the 1960s and 1970s extratextually reinforced Dill's effeminacy.

And yet it is not Dill's gender violations but rather Scout's that command the most stringent communal surveillance and discipline. Her extended family and community—virtually one and the same—incessantly work to force her out of her tomboyish ways and into those appropriate for a young southern girl of the 1930s. As Claudia Johnson notes, however, Maycomb faces no small task. Scout abandons her feminine, given Christian name of "Jean Louise" for an adventurous and boyish nickname, invariably chooses overalls over dresses, and demands an air rifle for Christmas rather than a doll so that she can, among other things, terrorize her cousin.[9] Only rarely does she abandon such behavior to aspire to perform feminine roles, and these aspirations usually meet with scant success. Scout recalls, for instance, her "burning ambition to grow up and twirl in the Maycomb County High School band" but notes that she develops this talent only "to where I could throw up a stick and almost catch it coming down" (105).

Just as Lee uses Jem as a foil to Dill to establish his effeminacy, so too does she present Aunt Alexandra, Atticus's sister, to force Scout's tomboyishness into sharp relief. Alexandra is the period's model of white southern femininity and casts a figure reminiscent of Alma Deen, Smith's fictionalization of the stereotypic frigid southern mother of a decade earlier. Like Alma, Alexandra subjects her body to fashion's requisite contortions so that it may be read as feminine. "She was not fat, but solid," Scout remembers of her aunt, "and she chose protective garments that drew up her bosom to giddy heights, pinched in her waist, flared out her rear, and managed to suggest that Aunt Alexandra's was once an hour-glass figure. From any angle, it was formidable" (130). Her manners and actions are comparably ladylike, and Maycomb responds to them with considerably more appreciation than Scout does: "To all parties present and participating in the life of the county, Aunt Alexandra was one of the last of her kind: she had riverboat, boarding-school manners; let any moral come along and she would uphold it; she was born in the objective case; she was an incurable gossip. . . . She was never bored, and given the slightest chance she would exercise her royal prerogative: she would arrange, advise, caution, and warn" (131). "Had I ever harbored the mystical notions about mountains that seem to obsess lawyers and judges," Scout offers when recalling her aunt, "Aunt Alexandra would have been analogous to

Mount Everest: throughout my early life, she was cold and there" (82). Yet, because of the very aspects of this personality that Scout finds so distasteful, the town welcomes Alexandra, allowing her to fit "into the world of Maycomb like a hand into a glove" (134).

Just as Aunt Alexandra ascribes to and performs proper southern white femininity, so too does she demand the same of others—and the transgressive Scout in particular. As Johnson observes, "Aunt Alexandra brings with her a system of codification and segregation of the human family according to class, race, and in Scout's case, sex."[10] Alexandra is correspondingly adamant about enforcing normative mappings of gender onto biological sex. Lee is hardly subtle in her condemnations of such strictures, manipulating readers' sympathies through both Scout's first-person narration and its rehearsals of Alexandra's seemingly endless carping about Scout's appearance and behavior. A description of Finch's Landing, where Alexandra and her husband live, allows Scout to clarify:

> Aunt Alexandra was fanatical on the subject of my attire. I could not possibly hope to be a lady if I wore breeches; when I said I could do nothing in a dress, she said I wasn't supposed to be doing things that required pants. Aunt Alexandra's vision of my deportment involved playing with small stoves, tea sets, and wearing the Add-A-Pearl necklace she gave me when I was born; furthermore, I should be a ray of sunshine in my father's lonely life. I suggested I could be a ray of sunshine in pants just as well, but Aunty said that one had to behave like a sunbeam, that I was born good but had grown progressively worse every year. (85-86)

When Alexandra moves in with the Finches for the summer of Tom Robinson's trial, she immediately launches a protracted assault on Scout: "'Put my bag in the front bedroom, Calpurnia,' was the first thing Aunt Alexandra said. 'Jean Louise, stop scratching your head,' was the second thing she said" (129).

The women of Aunt Alexandra's missionary circle are no less relentless in both providing suitable models for Scout and attacking her when she does not internalize them. On the afternoon of Alexandra's tea, Miss Stephanie Crawford pounces immediately upon Scout's entrance into the room. Cattily observing that her presence at Tom's trial has violated traditional separations of spheres, Miss Stephanie demands before the entire missionary circle, "Whatcha going to be when you grow up, Jean Louise? A lawyer?" and responds before Scout can answer, "Why shoot, I thought you wanted to be a lawyer, you've already commenced going to court" (232). When Scout mildly suggests that she wants to be "just a lady," a rebuffed Miss Stephanie shifts from cajoling to outright chastising: "Miss Stephanie eyed me suspiciously, decided that I meant no impertinence, and contented herself with, 'Well, you won't get very far until you start wearing dresses more often'" (233).

Although most readers already sympathize with Scout, Lee reinforces the dismissal of Miss Stephanie and the rest of the missionary circle's criticisms by undercutting the model of their supposedly natural southern femininity. As Scout and the women themselves realize, there is little natural about them at all. Their painstakingly crafted bodies and carefully orchestrated acts and gestures instead attempt to pass as natural or, at worst, artfully artless constructions. "The ladies were cool in fragile pastel prints," Scout remembers; "most of them were heavily powdered but unrouged; the only lipstick in the room was Tangee Natural. Cutex Natural sparkled on their fingernails, but some of the younger ladies wore Rose. They smelled heavenly" (232). As Lee emphasizes with these brand names, Alexandra and her neighbors insist on wearing only "natural" lipstick and fingernail polish and opt for powder but no rouge, since they have communally—although, from a logical standpoint, somewhat arbitrarily—agreed that the bodily alterations of powder do not call attention to and thus expose the artifice of femininity as rouge does. And yet "Tangee Natural" lipstick and "Cutex Natural" fingernail polish are not natural. They are commercially designated, appearance-altering products named to assist women in their efforts to perpetuate the illusion of expressing an inherent femininity. Thus, in that this description makes overt the women's efforts to disguise the feminizations of their bodies, Lee exposes their attempts to conceal the genesis of gender. With the revelation, the implied logical basis of Alexandra's and others' demands for Scout's femininity—that she express the natural gender with which she is born—crumbles, since readers now see the full complicity of these women in their tacit agreements to mystify the immediate cultural origins of femininity.

As this terminology suggests, with Lee's revelation of the missionary circle's conspiracy, she anticipates in fiction precisely what Judith Butler, building upon the work of other theorists and historians of gender and sexuality, has cogently argued concerning the deployment of gender. Like Lee, Butler interrogates—to dismiss as false—gender's presumed expressivity, the enactment of an interior essential gender. In simplified terms, Butler argues that, because gender is performed rather than expressed, "there is no preexisting identity by which an act or attribute might be measured." If such is indeed the case, "there would be no true or false, real or distorted acts of gender, and the postulation of a true gender identity would be revealed as a regulatory fiction." To prevent precisely this revelation, however, gender functions to eradicate signs of its performativity: "Gender is, thus, a construction that regularly conceals its genesis; the tacit collective agreement to perform, produce, and sustain discrete and polar genders as cultural fictions is obscured by the credibility of those productions—and the punishments that attend not agreeing to believe in them; the construction 'compels' our belief in its necessity and naturalness. The historical possibilities materialized through various corporeal styles are nothing other than those punitively regulated cultural fictions alternately embodied and deflected under duress."[11] To Kill a Mockingbird reveals both these concealments, as symbolized in the accoutrements of "natural" beautification, and, through the disciplinary actions and demands exercised on Scout, the punishments for disbelief in the naturalness of the performances of polarized genders. Lee's readers thus have the potential to realize just as forcefully as Butler's that white southern femininity, like any other sort, is but "a regulatory fiction."

Such observations from Butler concerning gender's performativity are not, however, the most innovative components of her argument. Both the fame and critical usefulness of *Gender Trouble* arise primarily out of Butler's articulations of how the parody of drag has the potential to expose gender performativity's reification as expressivity: "As much as drag creates a unified picture of 'woman' (what its critics often oppose), it also reveals the distinctness of those aspects of gendered experience which are falsely naturalized as a unity through the regulatory fiction of heterosexual coherence. *In imitating gender, drag implicitly reveals the imitative structure of gender itself—as well as its contingency.* . . . In place of the law of heterosexual coherence, we see sex and gender denaturalized by means of a performance which avows their distinctness and dramatizes the cultural mechanism of their fabricated unity." Butler does not, however, champion drag's parody as invariably subversive, as some critics have accused. "Parody by itself is not subversive," she offers, "and there must be a way to understand what makes certain kinds of parodic repetitions effectively disruptive, truly troubling, and which repetitions become domesticated and recirculated as instruments of cultural hegemony." Consistently tentative in her claims outside the hypothetical and conditional, Butler hazards only that a crucial element for the subversion of gender is the exposure of its repetitive structure. Yet this is the site where all gender transformation, whether ostensibly subversive or not, must originate: "The possibilities of gender transformation are to be found precisely in the arbitrary relation of such acts, in the possibility of a failure to repeat, a deformity, or a parodic repetition that exposes that phantasmatic effect of abiding identity as a politically tenuous construction." Nevertheless, in that any transformation calls into question "the abiding gendered self," any of the acts of Butler's catalogue—and not merely parodic repetitions such as drag recognized as such—has subversive potential.[12]

Lee's scene of the missionary circle's tea would seem to bolster Butler's suggestion that a failure to repeat stylized acts need not necessarily be parodic to expose the performativity of gender. In her description of the ladies' appearances, Scout notes that "Cutex Natural sparkled in their fingernails, but some of the younger ladies wore Rose." One could hardly say that, in having made this choice of fingernail polish, the younger women self-consciously parody femininity as Butler maintains drag performers to do. Indeed, these women cannot function in the same manner, since Butler understands much of drag queen's subversiveness to arise from their anatomically male bodies performing femininity. "If the anatomy of the performer is already distinct from the gender of the performer, and both of these are distinct from the gender of the performance," Butler clarifies, "then the performance suggests a dissonance not only between sex and performance, but sex and gender, and gender and performance."[13] Because the younger women at Alexandra's tea are, in contrast to drag queens, neither anatomically male nor knowingly parodic, no such valorizable dissonance of gender, sex, and performance can emerge from them if one retains the criteria of Butler's scenario. Nevertheless, these women's deviations from applying Cutex Natural to their nails draw attention to the false naturalness of the other women's bodies, whose nails sparkle as brilliantly as those painted Rose.

In addition to these women with the red fingernail polish, Scout herself disrupts the illusions of gender's expressivity in this scene. Until this point, she, like the novel's other gender-transitive characters, has loosely paralleled the drag queens of Butler's discussion, destabilizing gender through vaguely parodic performances of the "opposite" gender. Whereas the drag queens often satirically imitate femininity, Scout parodies—although far less self-consciously—masculinity, and one might argue that this parody operates with the subversiveness that Butler feels it capable. As is not the case with the scarlet-nailed ladies, because Scout's anatomy is distinct from the gender of her performances, they make public the same dissonances of corporeality as arise from drag performances. In the scene of Alexandra's tea, however, Lee gives Butler's theories an additional twist and suggests that a comparable disruption emerges when the drag artist attempts to perform the gender "correct" for his or, in this case, her anatomy. Scout follows her aunt's dictates and wears a "pink Sunday dress, shoes, and a petticoat" (231), casting a comic figure not unlike McCullers's Frankie when dressed for the wedding. Although this attire will supposedly correct Scout's gender trouble in the community's opinion, recollected images of Scout in her customary drag of overalls and her internalization of masculine acts and gestures so denaturalize the feminine clothes that communal representatives such as Miss Stephanie and even Miss Maudie can only focus on the absent overalls: "'You're mighty dressed up, Miss Jean Louise,' she said. 'Where are your britches today?'" (232). Scout's appearance in the pink dress thus becomes the equivalent of the drag queen abandoning her sequined gown and pumps to sport a tool belt and work boots or, as *La Cage aux Folles* and *The Birdcage* would have it, John Wayne's jeans, Stetson, and swagger. In these cases, the alterity of performances of normative gender to drag's pervading stylized repetitions establishes the former as, if anything, even more of a drag performance than the latter and thus, in Scout's case, ironically enables her enactment of *normative* gender to destabilize femininity.

Although Lee's readers may savor these destabilizations, they go largely unnoticed or ignored by characters within the novel, and the demands for gender conformity persist, both from the missionary society and elsewhere. Indeed, it is no one from Aunt Alexandra's circle who most dramatically antagonizes Scout. Mrs. Henry Lafayette Dubose, another of the Finches' neighbors, is fierce to the point of being unladylike herself in attempts to coerce Scout into appropriate feminine behavior. Secure in her age and infirmity Mrs. Dubose has no qualms about public outbursts, as Scout recalls: "Jem and I hated her. If she was on the porch when we passed, we would be raked by her wrathful gaze, subjected to ruthless interrogation regarding our behavior, and given a melancholy prediction on what we would amount to when we grew up, which was always nothing. We had long ago given up the idea of walking past her house on the opposite side of the street; that only made her raise her voice and let the whole neighborhood in on it." In keeping with these brazen outbursts, Mrs. Dubose rejects Alexandra's tactics of wheedling and nagging to alter Scout's behavior and instead opts for cruel shame. The old woman repeatedly resurrects the image of Atticus's dead wife to Jem and Scout, asserting that a "lovelier lady than our mother had never lived" (104) and that her children are a disgrace to her memory. When the shame of not meeting her mother's presumed expectations fails to drive Scout out of her overalls, however, Mrs. Dubose does not hesitate to employ fear: "'And *you*—' she pointed an arthritic finger at me—'what are you doing in those overalls? You should be in a dress and camisole, young lady! You'll grow up waiting on tables if somebody doesn't change your ways—a Finch waiting on tables at the O.K. Café—hah!'" (105-6).

Mrs. Dubose also allows Lee to continue yet another means of damning those persons who would enforce normative gender. Because the novel most centrally calls for an end to southern racism through the manipulation of a sympathetic African-American martyr and benign aristocratic paternalism, Lee's narrative invites readers to evaluate the racial attitudes of each of the white characters and judge them racist or not. Although at times she seeks to complicate this binarism, she marks most of the persons who demand Scout's gender conformity—Alexandra, Mrs. Dubose, and the majority of the missionary circle—as both lingering representatives of the antebellum slave-owning South and undeniable racists. While Atticus and Jack Finch abandon the Landing to pursue careers at various times in Montgomery, Nashville, and even Boston, Alexandra chooses to remain on the family's cotton plantation, surrounded by reminders of her ancestor's slave-holding and his own strictures for feminine behavior. Scout recalls both the "old cotton landing, where Finch Negroes had loaded bales and produce, unloaded blocks of ice, flour and sugar, farm equipment, and feminine apparel," and Simon Finch's unique home: "The internal arrangements of the Finch house were indicative of Simon's guilelessness and the absolute trust with which he regarded his offspring. . . . [T]he daughters' rooms could be reached only by one staircase, Welcome's room and the guest room only by another. The Daughters' Staircase was in the ground-floor bedroom of their parents, so Simon always knew the hours of his daughters' nocturnal comings and goings" (84). Via these two observations, Lee suggests how strongly she holds antebellum white southern femininity to have been contingent upon the enslavement of African Americans. It is they who bear the physical burden of unloading the feminine apparel at the landing, that which can be afforded in the first place only because of slave labor's ostensible profits. Likewise, it is this labor that allows Simon Finch to construct a house specifically designed to regulate his daughters' affairs.

Just as Alexandra has retained Simon's sexist notions of gender as represented in the Daughters' Staircase, she has also seemingly retained elements of the racism implicit to this enslavement of African Americans. For instance, she stews when Atticus decides to defend an African American accused of raping a white woman, and Scout trounces her annoying cousin only when he repeats his grandmother's characterization of her brother as a "nigger-lover" (87). Moreover, Alexandra reveals Lee's stance that white southern femininity's contingency on the debasement of African Americans persists in the 1930s. Consider the scene in which Alexandra arrives at the Finches' for the summer. Her command concerning Scout's unladylike behavior follows her initial order for Calpurnia to put away Alexandra's suitcase. As the close proximity of these commands suggests, Alexandra's authority in her dictates to Scout arises primarily out of her own feminine model, and yet this model remains valid only so long as Calpurnia or another black person frees Alexandra from unfeminine physical exertion.

Mrs. Dubose, on the other hand, is a literal artifact of the antebellum South, born just before or during the Civil War. She supposedly keeps "a CSA pistol concealed among her numerous shawls and wraps," and whiffs of earlier slave-holdings permeate her employment of African-American servants, for she retains "a Negro girl in constant attendance" yet allows Jessie little of the respect that Atticus has for Calpurnia (103-4). With these links to the stereotypic Old South and its Confederate culmination, it is not surprising that Mrs. Dubose offers opinions similarly conservative to Alexandra's concerning both race and gender. In virtually the same breath that she condemns Scout's overalls, Mrs. Dubose seethes about Atticus "lawing for niggers": "'Yes indeed, what has this world come to when a Finch goes against his raising? I'll tell you!' She put her hand to her mouth. When she drew it away, it trailed a long silver thread of saliva. 'Your father's no better than the niggers and trash he works for!'" (106).

Although Mrs. Dubose's racism is overt and vociferous, Lee even more forcefully condemns that of Alexandra's missionary circle, which is all the more distasteful because of the women's hypocritical investments in so-called Christian uplift. Grace Merriweather, "the most devout lady in Maycomb," sponsors a local program after having offered her profuse support of Christianity's shouldering of the white man's burden: "I said to him, 'Mr. Everett,' I said, 'the ladies of the Maycomb Alabama Methodist Episcopal Church South are behind you one hundred per cent.' That's what I said to him. And you know, right then and there I made a pledge in my heart. I said to myself, when I go home I'm going to give a course on the Mrunas and bring J. Grimes Everett's message to Maycomb and that's just what I'm doing" (233-34). Immediately after this comment, however, she carps about the responses of Maycomb's African Americans to Tom's trial: "[T]he cooks and field hands are just dissatisfied, but they're settling down now—they grumbled all next day after that trial," Mrs. Merriweather explains to Scout. "I tell you there's nothing more distracting than a sulky darky. Their mouths go down to here. Just ruins your day to have one of 'em in the kitchen" (234). Gertrude Farrow, "the second most devout lady in Maycomb," responds with her own complaints, maintaining, "We can educate 'em till we're blue in the face, we can try till we drop to make Christians out of 'em, but there's no lady safe in her bed these nights" (235). With this smug paternalism, fear of black male sexuality, and hypocritical racial enlightenment, Lee underscores that she, unlike Smith, does not consider southern white women less racist than their male counterparts because of an inherent female morality, and tempts readers to dismiss all that these women value and represent, including traditional white southern femininity.

With the exception of the women of the missionary circle, Lee does not, however, allow readers wholly to dismiss these racist characters and instead elicits some sympathy for Mrs. Dubose and Alexandra in particular. Part 1 closes with Atticus's articulation of Mrs. Dubose's heroism in defeating her addiction to morphine: "I wanted you to see what real courage is, instead of getting the idea that courage is a man with a gun in his hand. It's when you know you're licked before you begin but you begin anyway and you see it through no matter what. You rarely win, but sometimes you do. Mrs. Dubose won, all ninety-eight pounds of her." As Atticus suggests to Jem, despite her racism, Mrs. Dubose is "a great lady" and "the bravest person I ever knew" (116). Alexandra garners comparable sympathy in the novel's final pages. Even if she does not necessarily counter her previous racism, she is nevertheless shaken at news of Tom's death and concedes that Atticus has done the right thing, albeit to little avail in the community's eyes: "I mean this town. They're perfectly willing to let him do what they're too afraid to do themselves—it might lose 'em a nickel. They're perfectly willing to let him wreck his health doing what they're afraid to do" (239).

With this confession, Alexandra hints at the complexity of her character. She by no means replicates her brother's saintly attitudes and actions, and, even in the emotional aftermath of hearing of Tom's death, Alexandra tersely says of Atticus, "I can't say I approve of everything he does" (239). Nevertheless, she distinguishes herself from her catty guests who, rather than recognize the significance of Atticus's actions, hold them to be misguided. Yet this ambiguous relation to race has been anticipated by Alexandra's capricious relation to gender. As Scout knows all too well, Alexandra is "fanatical" that her niece appear and behave femininely. However, Alexandra allows and even fosters significant transgressions from normative masculinity in her grandson Francis. Exasperated that her husband's shiftlessness excludes the chivalry necessary to secure her position on the figurative pedestal of white southern femininity as delineated by Smith, Scott, and Jones, Alexandra inculcates in Francis behavior that is strikingly different from his grandfather's and, as a result, hardly masculine. "Grandma's a wonderful cook," Francis boasts to Scout. "She's gonna teach me how." When Scout giggles at this image, Francis counters, "Grandma says all men should learn to cook, that men oughta be careful with their wives and wait on 'em when they don't feel good" (86-87). Alexandra thus reveals her investment in white southern femininity to be so strong that she is willing to sacrifice corresponding southern masculinity so that the former's delicacy not be impinged upon. The result is that Francis Hancock, grandson of one of the novel's most outspoken gender conformists, is a gossiping sissy who slicks back his hair and, as his Christmas wish list reveals, craves the clothes of a fashionable young dandy: "a pair of knee-pants, a red leather booksack, five shirts and an untied bow tie" (85). As his sexually ambivalent name suggests, he does not have a strong masculine identity but instead, at his grandmother's urging, a Wildean penchant for foppery, one often culturally understood to designate effeminacy and, as Capote suggests, homosexuality.

Despite this active promotion of gender transitivity in Francis and hints of racial enlightenment at the novel's conclusion, Alexandra nevertheless remains too exclusively invested in traditional white southern femininity to emerge as a viable alternative to Mrs. Dubose and the women of the missionary society. Lee instead posits Miss Maudie Atkinson, arguably the novel's most sympathetic white adult female character, as the preferable model of southern womanhood for both

Scout and readers. Unlike Alexandra, Miss Maudie is not overtly distraught about the transgressive performances of gender and indeed has constructed a public identity contingent upon adroit manipulations of such performances. This is not to suggest, however, that she jettisons social conventions. When she chooses, she can rival her neighbors in her successful enactment of white southern femininity. Just as she appears on her front porch each evening freshly bathed to "reign over the street in magisterial beauty" (47), Miss Maudie can also smoothly integrate herself into that larger world "where on its surface fragrant ladies rocked slowly, fanned gently, and drank cool water" (236). She in fact maintains this role when others falter, as when she coolly orchestrates the remainder of the tea after Alexandra crumbles at news of Tom Robinson's death.

Although not conveyed in the film adaptation, Miss Maudie is, however, "a chameleon lady," and these polished feminine performances are checked by others as transgressive as any of Scout's: working "in her flower beds in an old straw hat and men's coveralls" (46), thrusting out her bridgework with a click of her tongue as a sign of friendship, nursing charred azaleas at the sacrifice of her hands, and even meditating arson. Indeed, some of the most striking imagery associated with Miss Maudie is blatantly martial, casting her in the role of biblical warrior:

> If she found a blade of nut grass in her yard it was like the Second Battle of the Marne: she swooped down upon it with a tin tub and subjected it to blasts from beneath with a poisonous substance she said was so powerful it'd kill us all if we didn't stand out of the way.
>
> "Why can't you just pull it up?" I asked, after witnessing a prolonged campaign against a blade not three inches high.
>
> "Pull it up, child, pull it up?" She picked up the limp sprout and squeezed her thumb up its tiny stalk. Microscopic grains oozed out. "Why, one sprig of nut grass can ruin a whole yard. Look here. When it comes fall this dries up and the wind blows it all over Maycomb County!" Miss Maudie's face likened such an occurrence unto an Old Testament pestilence. (47)

Minor though this battle may seem, Lee's martial imagery and Miss Maudie's transformation into a prophet of the Old Testament stand in marked contrast to her graceful offerings of dewberry tarts at Alexandra's tea. With her public image thus in constant flux between these two gender norms, the "chameleon" Miss Maudie offers the most appropriate identity for Scout and Jem's "absolute morphodite" (72) snowman to assume. Throughout its construction, the snowman evinces an uneasy coexistence of femininity and masculinity, resembling first Miss Stephanie Crawford and then Mr. Avery. This irresolution is rendered understandable only when Jem sticks Miss Maudie's sun hat on the snowman's head and thrusts her hedge clippers in the crook of its arm. Insofar as the feminine and masculine already commingle in the culturally readable Miss Maudie, the ambiguously sexed and gendered Absolute Morphodite can also be made coherently legible by giving it her personality.

Lee suggests several things with Miss Maudie's "chameleon" self-fashioning, not least of which is that she may function comparably to Scout to disrupt reified southern white femininity. With her constant alternating performances of masculinity and femininity, clad one hour in the work clothes of a manual laborer and the next in Mrs. Dubose's requisite dress and camisole, Miss Maudie undercuts the constancy with which the rest of the missionary circle express their femininity. That is, her public performances, deliberately staged for the entire neighborhood's viewing, make overt the comparable manipulations of gender that the other women wish not to be exposed as so easily mutable. Yet, because these alternations have grown predictable, Miss Maudie's performances do not disrupt with the force that, say, Scout's unexpectedly feminine presence at the tea does. As Butler acknowledges, any stylized repetition of acts—even initially transgressive and/ or subversive ones—can be domesticated through their very repetition, since such predictable recurrences promote reification. Miss Maudie's presence nevertheless suggests how token a normatively gendered performance may be and still appease such cultural strictures as Lee understands them. Because Miss Maudie periodically participates in such ostensibly gender-reifying rituals as the missionary tea, even while she understands such participation to be simple performances, her neighbors are content to allow her otherwise inexcusable transgressions of gender. Thus, whereas Butler emphasizes almost exclusively the punishments associated with a rejection of gender's necessity and naturalness, Lee not only identifies such punishments in Scout but also counters in Miss Maudie ways in which such discipline might be negotiated and avoided. One does not have to agree to believe in gender's expressivity, Lee offers, so long as one condescends to *perform* as if one does at strategically appropriate times. Indeed, as the women of the missionary circle prove, such belief is the exception rather than the rule.

Lee further promotes readers' investments in Miss Maudie and her alternatives to southern white femininity by having her harbor little of the overt racism of Alexandra, Mrs. Dubose, and the missionary circle. With the exception of Atticus, Miss Maudie emerges—even if problematically—as the novel's most racially enlightened white character, one of the "handful of people in this town who say that fair play is not marked White Only; the handful of people who say a fair trial is for everybody, not just us; the handful of people with enough humility to think, when they look at a Negro, there but for the Lord's kindness am I" (239).[14] She realizes how pervasively racism permeates Maycomb and therefore both supports and is grateful for Atticus's stirring defense of Tom Robinson: "I was sittin' there on the porch last night, waiting. I waited and waited to see you all come down the sidewalk, and as I waited I thought, Atticus Finch won't win, he can't win, but he's the only man in these parts who can keep a jury out so long in a case like that. And I thought to myself, well, we're making a step—it's just a baby-step, but it's a step" (218-19). And yet, for all her interest in the trial's outcome, Miss Maudie nevertheless refuses to participate in the spectacle. In its aftermath, however, she abandons what may be perceived of until this point as a passive role and deftly squelches the missionary circle's attack on Atticus. Lee has Miss Maudie willing to condescend to participate in the women's charade of femininity but unwilling to tolerate their racism when they attack the sole figure to assume a public—and, in Miss Maudie's opinion, truly Christian—stance for legal equality.

Just as Miss Maudie nurses little racism in comparison with her neighbors, she also holds none of Maycomb's morbid curiosity about the Radleys. When Scout rehearses the lurid tales of Boo to Miss Maudie, she tersely dismisses the gossip as "three-fourths colored folks and one-fourth Stephanie Crawford" (50) and counters by emphasizing tolerance toward Arthur's right to do as he pleases. In a tactic similar to Atticus's suggestion that, to understand a communal outsider or misfit, one must "climb into his skin and walk around in it" (34), Miss Maudie urges Scout to consider Arthur's perspective: "'Arthur Radley just stays in the house, that's all,' said Miss Maudie. 'Wouldn't you stay in the house if you didn't want to come out?'" (48). And yet Miss Maudie sympathizes with Arthur having to function within a family and community intent on controlling and demonizing him. When Scout asks if Arthur is crazy, "Miss Maudie shook her head. 'If he's not he should be by now. The things that happen to people we never really know'" (50). Miss Maudie thus proves as exemplary in her tolerance of Arthur Radley's communal otherness as she does with differences of gender and race and emerges to readers precisely as Scout has characterized: "the best lady I know" (49).

Miss Maudie's male counterpart is, of course, Atticus Finch, the novel's almost sainted hero. He not only displays the same ostensibly enlightened attitudes as Miss Maudie but also, via privilege conferred on him by masculine spheres, works publicly for social equality and tolerance. His defense of Tom Robinson is the most significant of these efforts, but Atticus also proves himself equally determined to accord Arthur Radley some degree of communal respect. When he catches Scout, Jem, and Dill "busily playing Chapter XXV, Book II of One Man's Family" (44), their improvised production of the Radleys' fabled saga, Atticus immediately halts the performance, just as he later interrupts the children's attempt to leave a note for Boo. "Son," Atticus says to Jem in perhaps the harshest tones Lee ever allows her hero, "I'm going to tell you something and tell you one time: stop tormenting that man" (53).

Given that Atticus shares these attitudes with Miss Maudie, it is not surprising that he also is both tolerant of gender nonconformity and, in the opinion of his family and community, something less than masculine himself. His heroism, like that of Mrs. Dubose, is not contingent upon being "a man with a gun in his hand." Quite the contrary, Atticus avoids stereotypically male violence to resolve conflict and uses a gun only when forced, as in the case of the rabid dog. Thus, just as Miss Maudie adroitly deploys her femininity, so too does Atticus strategically choose when a masculine performance is in order, content in the meantime to forgo such behavior. "He did not do the things our schoolmates' fathers did," Scout recalls; "he never went hunting, he did not play poker or fish or drink or smoke. He sat in the living room and read" (94). Indeed, Atticus's failure to engage in such activities causes considerable anxiety in his children. "[T]here was nothing Jem or I could say about him when our classmates said, 'My father—,'" Scout confesses. Instead, having internalized the community's rigidly binaristic understandings of gender, she and Jem feel this failure "reflected upon his abilities and manliness" (93).

No matter how reassuringly different from the rest of Maycomb in either their ethics or performances of gender, Atticus and Miss Maudie are nevertheless problematic characters. With the capacity for manifold tolerances located within solitary figures such as these, Lee seems to posit an identity inherently resistant to any oppression of any cultural difference. That is, she suggests that all tolerances are congruent, that is, if one is tolerant of racial otherness, one will of course be equally tolerant of gendered otherness and even that difference that can only be speculated about, as in the case of Boo Radley. In contrast to this understanding, tolerance might more appropriately be considered similar to oppression as Sedgwick has theorized it. As cited earlier, she reminds that "it was the long, painful realization, *not* that all oppressions are congruent, but that they are *differently* structured and so must intersect in complex embodiments." Just as each oppression is thus "likely to be in a uniquely indicative relation to certain distinctive nodes of cultural organization," so too is each tolerance likely to reflect a potentially singular organization.[15] Therefore, despite certain similarities, tolerance of racial otherness is not the same as tolerance of gendered otherness, yet Lee's characters tend to obfuscate these differences and thus leave readers with an oversimplified representation of social mechanisms and interactions.

Regardless of this oversimplification, what emerges from Lee's novel is a portrait of a southern community in which performances of normative gender are surprisingly the exceptions rather than the rule. Not only is the narrator in whom readers so heavily invest a tomboy, but the two most sympathetic adult white characters are figures who defy normative gender roles and instead perform "appropriately" only to strategic ends. Those characters who do subscribe to these roles are hardly sympathetic and racist almost without exception. Moreover, in Lee's handling of them, these same characters unwittingly reveal the constructedness of gender that they seek to conceal and, in the case of Alexandra, even foster overt transgressions. Maycomb is thus, for all its demands for gender conformity, an arena of dizzyingly varied gender performances.

* * *

Although perhaps not at first apparent, just as *To Kill a Mockingbird* is a novel permeated with valorized gender transitivity, it is also remarkably deplete of heterosexuality as conventionally represented through traditional marriage. As Claudia Johnson reminds, unmarried people—widows and widowers, spinsters and bachelors—fill the Finches' neighborhood: Atticus, Miss Maudie, Miss Stephanie, Miss

Rachel, Miss Caroline, Mrs. Dubose, Mr. Avery, and both of the Radley sons, Nathan and Arthur. One is, in fact, hard-pressed to name a character besides Tom Robinson who both figures centrally in the novel and is within a stable marriage. And yet Tom's marriage seems readable as primarily part of Lee's heavy-handed characterization of him as "a quiet, respectable, humble Negro" (207) who heads a harmonious nuclear family of "clean-living folks" (80) and thus contrasts to the incestuous widowed Bob Ewell. If anything, to shore up how differently Tom and Helen live from the Ewells in their dump, Lee succumbs to stereotypes of African Americans when she sketches crowds of black children playing marbles in the Robinsons' front yard and the little girl standing picturesquely in the cabin's door: "Dill said her hair was a wad of tiny stiff pigtails, each ending in a bright bow. She grinned from ear to ear and walked toward our father, but she was too small to navigate the steps. Dill said Atticus went to her, took off his hat, and offered her his finger. She grabbed it and he eased her down the steps" (242). Indeed, such images are only slightly removed from those of happy plantation darkies that permeate earlier southern literature.

Neither the immediate Finch household nor its larger familial connections offer such a warm portrait of connubial life. Scout explains that Atticus is a widower, his wife having died only a few years into the marriage: "She was a Graham from Montgomery; Atticus met her when he was first elected to the state legislature. He was middle-aged then, she was fifteen years his junior. Jem was the product of their first year of marriage; four years later I was born, and two years later our mother died from a sudden heart attack" (10). That Atticus, already late to marry by Maycomb's standards, allows so many years to elapse without remarrying is something of a travesty in communal opinion. Amid her demands that Scout begin wearing dresses and that Atticus stop defending "niggers," Mrs. Dubose repeatedly offers that "it was quite a pity that our father had not remarried after our mother's death" (104). Despite these communal injunctions, however, Atticus shows no signs of taking another wife and instead seems content to function as the sole parent to his children.

Unlike Atticus, his younger brother, John Hale Finch, never marries and, although somewhat casually, evinces a phobia of reproduction. "I shall never marry," Jack wearily confesses to his brother after mishandling Scout's conflict with Francis. "I might have children" (91). Indeed, Lee offers in Jack a character readable as gay by persons understanding sexuality within a rigid binarism of heterosexuality and homosexuality and thus assuming an absence of the former to designate the presence of the latter. Moreover, Jack's life parallels those of Goyen's gay Folner and Smith's lesbian Laura, and all three characters seem fictional counterparts to queer persons discussed by historians such as George Chauncey, John D'Emilio, and Allan Bérubé. Like so many of these persons at mid-century, Jack is an aspiring professional who leaves familial constraints to study and live in a large urban area and thereby minimize small-town life. After finishing medical studies in Boston, Jack returns not to Maycomb but rather to Nashville and visits his family in Alabama only once a year at Christmas. He remains a bachelor at almost forty and has as his only acknowledged companion a much-doted-upon cat. When, during one of his visits, Jack offers to show snapshots of Rose Aylmer, Scout explains that the cat is "a beautiful yellow female Uncle Jack said was one of the few women he could stand permanently" (83). But even if Lee does not intend Jack to be read as gay, and readers do not understand him as such, he nevertheless stands as yet another character whom Lee chooses to have uninvolved in heterosexual marriage during the course of the novel.

Jack further disrupts communal heteronormativity with his parody of its courtship. Scout recalls the performance he gives with the help of Miss Maudie:

We saw Uncle Jack every Christmas, and every Christmas he yelled across the street for Miss Maudie to come marry him. Miss Maudie would yell back, "Call a little louder, Jack Finch, and they'll hear you at the post office, I haven't heard you yet!" Jem and I thought this a strange way to ask for a lady's hand in marriage, but then Uncle Jack was rather strange. He said he was trying to get Miss Maudie's goat, that he had been trying unsuccessfully for forty years, that he was the last person in the world Miss Maudie would think about marrying but the first person she thought about teasing, and the best defense to her was spirited offense, all of which we understood clearly. (48)

Regardless of Jack's asserted reasons for instigating these exchanges, they ultimately function to spoof heterosexuality by wrenching its rites of courtship from their usual contexts. Much like Scout during her performance of femininity at Alexandra's tea, Jack and Maudie are ostensibly behaving as their community expects, enacting through appropriately gendered roles the rituals to culminate in heterosexual marriage. Jack plays the role of the aggressive male suitor, while Maudie that of his coy mistress. Yet, just as Scout's customarily transgressive behavior renders her normative performances disruptive, Jack and Maudie's usual silences in expressing heterosexual desire denaturalize their displays of heterosexuality and reveal them to be artificial. Unlike Scout, however, Jack and Maudie are fully conscious of this revelation and artfully stage it in the public arena to create even more of a spectacle.

Such a performance would not be nearly so significant if Lee tempered it with normative enactments of heterosexual desire, ones that reveal such rituals to unfold as they supposedly ought in set cultural scripts. Instead of doing this, however, Lee offers a series of parodies, ones that, although not self-consciously satiric, nevertheless function to establish heterosexuality as existing in the novel primarily in comic deviations from its fictional norm. The first of these parodic heterosexual pairings appears in Miss Caroline's traumatic discovery of Burris Ewell's head lice. When her scream arrests the attention of the entire class of children, the chivalric Little Chuck Little emerges to rescue and console her:

Little Chuck grinned broadly. "There ain't no need to fear a cootie, ma'am. Ain't you ever seen one? Now don't you be afraid, you just go back to your desk and teach us some more."

Little Chuck Little was another member of the population who didn't know where his next meal was coming from, but he was a born gentleman. He put his hand under her elbow and led Miss Caroline to the front of the room. "Now don't you fret, ma'am," he said. "There ain't no need to fear a cootie. I'll just fetch you some cool water." (30)

Lee strengthens Little Chuck's chivalry when Burris defies Miss Caroline's questions about his hygiene, family, and school attendance. "Little Chuck Little got to his feet," Scout recalls. "'Let him go, ma'am,' he said. 'He's a mean one, a hard-down mean one. He's liable to start somethin', and there's some little folks here.'" Unlike the questionably masculine Atticus, Little Chuck is quite willing to opt for violence, doing so despite his diminutive size: "[W]hen Burris Ewell turned toward him, Little Chuck's right hand went to his pocket. 'Watch your step, Burris,' he said. 'I'd soon's kill you as look at you. Now go home'" (32). The hero ultimately triumphs, and the damsel, although emotionally shaken, as is befitting her more delicate sex, is saved.

Like Jack and Maudie, Little Chuck and Miss Caroline thus enact sex-appropriate roles. Lee undercuts these performances, however, with the situational irony that arises between the ideal of heterosexual chivalry and the reality of the classroom's scenario. The foes from whom Lee's hero must protect the damsel are neither a dragon nor a rival knight but rather a nomadic head louse and a surly prepubescent first grader. For that matter, the hero is no aristocratically virile Lancelot. Little Chuck Little is only a step above common white trash, far from adult, and, as Lee emphasizes with his name, ridiculously small. As a result, she presents readers not with a reifying performance of heterosexual chivalry but rather with a quasi-sexualized relationship comically deviant in its transgressions of differences in class and age and thus unable to be sexually enacted.

Lee comparably undercuts chivalric courtship in Jem's ritualized visits to Mrs. Dubose. Although these afternoons of reading to her are supposedly penance for the destruction of her camellias, the visits replicate the mythic suitor's persistent wooing of his beloved with stirring pronouncements of affection. Jem composes no sonnets for his partner, but Lee nevertheless keeps him firmly within romantic expression, having him read to Mrs. Dubose from *Ivanhoe*, a novel emblematic of the romanticization of heterosexual courtship. Just as Jem is no Petrarch or Sidney, however, Mrs. Dubose is neither Laura nor Stella: "She was horrible. Her face was the color of a dirty pillowcase, and the corners of her mouth glistened with wet, which inched like a glacier down the deep grooves enclosing her chin. Old-age liver spots dotted her cheeks, and her pale eyes had black pinpoint pupils. Her hands were knobby, and the cuticles were grown up over her fingernails. Her bottom plate was not in, and her upper lip protruded; from time to time she would draw her nether lip to her upper plate and carry her chin with it. This made the wet move faster" (111). Lee thus reverses the asymmetries of the relationship between Little Chuck and Miss Caroline. Although hovering at puberty, Jem is a male suitor of a socially appropriate age to enter into such a ritual, but Mrs. Dubose is, in contrast, a grotesquely old female beloved. The end result, however, is much the same, in that readers encounter yet another image of implied transgressive heterosexuality.

Although with Dill's proposal of marriage and Scout's acceptance, this pair enacts heterosexual rituals further than any of the three couples discussed so far, much the same destabilizing humor emerges from the two. As Scout recalls, Dill "asked me earlier in the summer to marry him, then he promptly forgot about it. He staked me out, marked as his property, said I was the only girl he would ever love, then he neglected me" (46). Like Little Chuck Little, Scout and Dill are too young by societal standards to engage in the heterosexual acts that usually accompany marriage. Their woeful ignorance of these acts' intricacies and results emerges in a discussion of babies' origins, where neither child is too clear on the process. Moreover, in that Scout and Dill are both gender transitive, they present a pairing as superficially disconcerting as Capote's Joel Knox and Idabel Thompkins. In each case, the genders are ostensibly transposed, and the woman rather than the man disciplines wandering affections through violence. When Dill chooses homosocial interactions with Jem rather than pseudoheterosexual ones with Scout, she forgoes feminine tears and coaxing and instead "beat him up twice but it did no good, he only grew closer to Jem" (46).

Lee concludes the novel with a final nonnormative heterosexual pairing, that of Scout and Boo Radley. After he saves Scout and Jem from the malevolent Bob Ewell, the shy Boo is in the awkward situation of himself needing to be seen safely home, and Scout kindly assists him:

> "Will you take me home?"
>
> He almost whispered it, in the voice of a child afraid of the dark.
>
> I put my foot on the top step and stopped. I would lead him through our house, but I would never lead him home.
>
> "Mr. Arthur, bend your arm down here, like that. That's right, sir."
>
> I slipped my hand into the crook of his arm.
>
> He had to stoop a little to accommodate me, but if Miss Stephanie Crawford was watching from her upstairs window, she would see Arthur Radley escorting me down the sidewalk, as any gentleman would do. (281)

As with the other parodic images of heterosexual courtship, this one is marked by socially disruptive elements such as an incongruity of ages, an inverted incongruity in levels of maturity, and, at least with Scout, transgressions of gender norms. This image, however, crucially differs from those that precede it. Whereas the pairings of Little Chuck and Miss Caroline, Jem and Mrs. Dubose, and Dill and Scout are each unself-conscious in its parody of heterosexuality, and the performances of Uncle Jack and Miss Maudie are deliberately satiric so as to expose those characters' distance from heterosexuality, Scout intentionally orchestrates her interactions with Boo to replicate the contours of a heterosexual relationship. She has, in essence, learned the lessons taught by Miss Maudie. Just as she purchases a certain amount of freedom by periodically appeasing the neighborhood through her performances of femininity at the missionary teas, Scout potentially negotiates a comparable freedom for Boo when she crafts the illusion of his normative heterosexuality. That is, although Boo may continue to transgress communal norms by eschewing a public existence, that community is more apt to accord him this transgression because he performs "correctly" during his brief foray into the public arena. Although this image includes disruptive elements, it nevertheless comes closer to fulfilling communal expectations of Boo's appropriate sexual behavior than the rumors of macabre voyeurism circulating in the absence of observed sexual performances.

As these delineated differences suggest, Lee's parodies of heterosexuality are not identically structured, nor do they work to exactly the same ends. These pairings nevertheless remain parallel in that they fill the text's relative void of normative heterosexuality. Moreover, despite the lack of sexual desire and the often comic or horrific elements in these parodies, they frequently provide far more gratification than the novel's actual marriages. Scout recalls, for instance, her closeness with Dill and the sadness she feels in his absence. "[S]ummer was the swiftness with which Dill would reach up and kiss me when Jem was not looking, the longings we sometimes felt each other feel," Scout remembers. "With him, life was routine; without him, life was unbearable. I stayed miserable for two days" (118). In the novel's final pages she comparably notes the gratification provided by the relationship with Boo Radley and her anxiety about her lack of reciprocation: "We never put back into the tree what we took out of it: we had given him nothing, and it made me sad" (281). Even Jem's horrendous interactions with Mrs. Dubose prove extraordinarily meaningful to him, and part 1 significantly closes with him, having heard Atticus's explanations of Mrs. Dubose's situation, symbolically recanting his hatred. Readers' final image is of Jem meditatively fingering the perfect snow-on-the-mountain camellia she sends him so as to die "beholden to nothing and nobody" (116).

In contrast to the meaningful bonds arising within these relationships scripted as parodies of heterosexual courtships, when Lee does on rare occasion depict marriage, the union seems unenviable. Consider that of Alexandra. One of the novel's least sympathetic characters, she is also married to a virtual nonentity. Scout recalls Uncle Jimmy as "a taciturn man who spent most of his time lying in a hammock by the river wondering if his trot-lines were full" (9) and only reluctantly amends her recollections of Christmases at Finch's Landing to mention him: "I should include Uncle Jimmy, Aunt Alexandra's husband, but as he never spoke a word to me in my life except to say, 'Get off that fence,' once, I never saw any reason to take notice of him" (81). His relationship with Alexandra seems so strained that her protracted visit to the Finches seems a welcomed respite from a less-than-pleasant marriage, a respite not unlike that sketched by Kate Chopin for Clarisse Laballière at the conclusion of "The Storm." Of Alexandra's own childbearing within marriage, Scout explains, "Long ago, in a burst of friendliness, Aunty and Uncle Jimmy produced a son named Henry, who left home as soon as was humanly possible, married, and produced Francis" (81-82). The elder Hancocks' marriage thus seems emotionally and sexually unfulfilling, and, unlike Tom Robinson's children, Henry regards his parents' household as something to escape and then avoid, only a convenient place to deposit his son while he and his wife "pursued their own pleasures" (82).

Although generations of Finches before Atticus and his siblings have married with greater frequency and presumably more gratification, they nevertheless often transgress the boundaries of normative heterosexuality. As Atticus gently reminds his sister, the Finches have something of a penchant for mild incest: "Once, when Aunty assured us that Miss Stephanie Crawford's tendency to mind other people's business was hereditary, Atticus said, 'Sister, when you stop to think about it, our generation's practically the first in the Finch family not to marry its cousins. Would you say the Finches have an Incestuous Streak?'" Alexandra's reply is a cryptic affirmation and denial: "[N]o, that's where we got our small hands and feet" (132). She claims her ancestors' transgressive acts so long as they result in bodies culturally understood as refined, but she implicitly denies that such acts are truly incestuous, presumably because they are not confined within the nuclear family and are therefore socially valid and even welcomed by most nineteenth-century standards. Alexandra's dismissal notwithstanding, Atticus's accusations seem, in hindsight, to designate all the more transgressive acts when readers encounter the novel's only other suggestion of incest, that between Bob Ewell and his daughter Mayella. Although the relationships between sexual participants are markedly different, Lee nevertheless prompts readers to map back onto Alexandra's ancestors the very acts that Atticus publicly condemns.

Just as Lee offers heterosexuality represented through marriage as either absent, unfulfilling, or culturally transgressive in each of these scenarios, so too does she characterize the sexual interactions that come under scrutiny at Tom Robinson's trial in a similar manner. As Atticus proves to no avail, Tom's rape of Mayella Ewell, arguably the novel's central heterosexual act, is a fiction. The sexual interactions that occur between the two are, nevertheless, simultaneously unfulfilling and culturally transgressive insofar as they are miscegenistic. Indeed, this manifestation of heterosexuality is far more transgressive within a southern context than Tracy Deen and Nonnie Anderson's interracial affair in *Strange Fruit*. Rather than have a white man instigate a sexual relationship with a black woman, as Smith does, Lee chooses to have a white woman seduce a black man. As Atticus explains to the jury, Mayella thus violates one of the mid-twentieth-century South's strongest taboos: "She was white, and she tempted a Negro. She did something that in our society is unspeakable: she kissed a black man. Not an old Uncle, but a strong young Negro man" (206). Because of these social strictures, the interaction is hardly fulfilling. Mayella's sexual gratification ceases immediately upon her father's murderous presence, and the hesitant Tom Robinson meets with an end as gruesome as that of Richard Wright's comparably tempted Chris Sims.

Sexuality thus emerges in *To Kill a Mockingbird* in much the same way that gender does: normative expressions are rare, whereas transgressive ones abound, often manifesting in the novel's most sympathetic characters. Although Lee's community sets up enduring heterosexual marriages as the norm, they are almost nonexistent and, with the one exception of Tom and Helen Robinson, never gratifying. Images of transgressive heterosexuality fare somewhat better in Lee's handling but are usually contingent upon the relative presence or absences of sexual desire. In its presence arise, on the one hand, incestuous relationships that either beget elitist whites or accompany the domestic violence of white trash and, on the other hand, interracial relationships that invariably lead to humiliation and death for African Americans. In contrast, the absence of sexual desire in heterosexual relationships often promotes liaisons that are simultaneously disruptive parodies of heterosexuality and mutually gratifying. Moreover, each of the sympathetic white characters engages in neither heterosexual marriage nor transgressive heterosexuality during the novel. And, although this absence of marriage does not necessarily designate a character such as Atticus, Jack, or Miss Maudie to be nonheterosexual or even homosexual, Lee nevertheless offers in Jack a character easily understandable as such to readers who have internalized the absoluteness of a heterosexual/homosexual binarism. Scout and Jem are therefore coming into adulthood not within an utterly conventional "tired old town" (9), as emphasized in Horton Foote's screenplay, but rather within a community whose instabilities of gender and sexuality mark it as, in the broadest sense, queer.

* * *

Although southern community as Lee imagines it is thus, as a whole, pervasively queer in its circulations of gender and sexuality, she nevertheless conspicuously creates individuals who emerge as outsiders within this social matrix. Indeed, as the title indicates, the novel's most pervasive and unsubtle symbolism concerns itself with communal negotiations of these outsiders and their alterity to others. The valorized mockingbird becomes the all-too-readable symbol of the innocent Tom Robinson, shot seventeen times by a white guard while attempting to escape imprisonment. In fact, with heavy-handedness justifying Sundquist's critique of the novel, Lee has Braxton Underwood's editorial overtly expose and then explain the symbol: "Mr. Underwood simply figured that it was a sin to kill cripples, be they standing, sitting, or escaping. He likened Tom's death to the senseless slaughter of songbirds by hunters and children, and Maycomb thought he was trying to write an editorial poetical enough to be reprinted in *The Montgomery Advertiser*" (243). Unlike Underwood's editorial, however, Lee's novel more broadly identifies Tom's crucial otherness as his race rather than his physical handicap. Thus, when readers map the defining attributes of the mockingbird onto Tom, who seems to represent all African Americans in Lee's figurations, he emerges as the harmless victim of empowered whites' destructive racial discrimination.

Tom Robinson is not, however, the only figure that the mockingbird symbolizes. With somewhat greater subtlety, Lee uses the bird to represent the equally innocent Boo Radley, who, like the mockingbirds that Atticus saves from Scout's and Jem's rifles, ultimately escapes meaningless slaughter. To expose Boo's heroism and thus bring him to public attention, Scout realizes, would "be sort of like shootin' a mockingbird, wouldn't it?" (279). Despite sharing this symbol with Tom, however, Boo crucially differs in that it is not the color of his skin that dictates his status of cultural outsider. But rather than grounding Boo's communal alienation in an identifiable alternative to race, Lee instead offers only damning speculative rumors about him and his identity, and he remains with few exceptions within the confines of his dilapidated house until the novel's closing chapters. With this figure and his unique relationship to the community, Lee thus shifts her focus away from white southern responses to racial otherness and instead presents a scenario that obliquely—if not always coherently—parallels ones crucially informed by sexual otherness. That is, because Lee surrounds Boo with so many of the silences and absences that structure the frequent closetedness of same-sex desire, she invites readers to speculate that Boo's reclusiveness is comparable to closeted sexuality and thus explore what bearing this literal representation of closetedness might have on an understanding of the figurative. Such a consideration of this parallel in turn invites a reading of the mockingbird to represent persons negotiating same-sex desire as well as social recluses and African Americans.[16]

To assert that Lee's representation invites such a reading is not, however, to argue that Boo is gay. Although the structure of reclusiveness as Lee presents it may strongly resemble that of the closet, they are not the same. Indeed, fissures almost immediately begin to surface if one approaches Boo as directly representative of a closeted gay or lesbian individual. Perhaps foremost, Lee never establishes the transgressive elements of Boo's identity to be anything other than reclusiveness. Although this may at first seem closely akin to closetedness, reclusiveness can be a social deviancy in and of itself rather than a silencing or secreting of deviancy, as closetedness is. The more appropriate comparison of reclusiveness to actual homosexuality, however, reveals how differently these two components of identity are structured and thus how Lee's potential metaphor for a closeted gay individual is somewhat tenuous. Homosexual acts can usually be kept hidden while an individual circulates with relative freedom within a community, whereas a recluse is most forcefully marked by the very desire *to be* hidden, to avoid *any* communal circulations. In short, a homosexual's closet is figurative; a recluse's is literal. By giving Boo a reclusive rather than an identifiably homosexual identity, Lee creates a situation in which he, in effect, cannot come out of the closet, for coming out would erase the transgressive element of his identity.

Although this fissure between Lee's representation of reclusiveness and the actualities of closeted gayness suggests the uniqueness of the gay closet, her depiction's employability as a symbol or parallel to closetedness nevertheless should not be invalidated. In other ways, Boo's reclusiveness does remind readers of closetedness, insofar as it can be essentialized, and the trajectory of his life loosely replicates one of the most pervasive and cherished narratives of coming out. Consider first the parallels between a closeted gay person whose sexuality is not an open secret and Boo as he initially appears—or, more correctly, does not appear—in the novel. Absence is a—if not *the*—crucially defining factor for each. Just as Boo is physically absent within his community, definitive knowledge of a gay person's sexual identity is comparably absent in some or all others' understandings of him or her. As a result, these identities are constituted largely by rumor, conjecture, or otherwise indirect knowledge. A closeted person's hidden sexuality provides his or her community little basis for a more accurate understanding of his or her particular queerness, and he or she is thus usually left to exist within a communal space permeated with, at best, homophilia confirmed through knowledge of others' gay identities or, at worst, homophobia bolstered by derogatory images of homosexuality.

Although sequestered within his house, Boo nevertheless exists within similar currents imposing upon him an identity in his absence. There are those townspeople, such as Atticus and Miss Maudie, who base their opinions of Boo on his youth and, although they have not seen him in years, studiously attempt to squelch gossip. "I remember Arthur Radley when he was a boy," Miss Maudie reflects. "He always spoke nicely to me, no matter what folks said he did. Spoke as nicely as he knew how" (50). On the other hand, the majority of Maycomb thrives on rumors, elaborating on them to create a horrific monster. Jem's thorough internalization of these images, gleaned from "bits and scraps of gossip and neighborhood legend" (44), for instance, allows him to give a full response to Dill's request for a description of Boo: "Boo was about six-and-a-half feet tall, judging from his tracks; he dined on raw squirrels and any cats he could catch, that's why his hands were bloodstained—if you ate an animal raw, you could never wash the blood off. There was a long jagged scar that ran across his face; what teeth he had were yellow and rotten; his eyes popped, and he drooled most of the time" (17). Maycomb's gossip thus demonizes Boo in his absence as savagely as homophobic discourse can.

Jem's description of the imagined Boo also reveals Lee's understanding that popular imagination has a pronounced need to script a transgressive individual as knowable through his or her very body. As a result, Jem conspicuously includes Boo's bloodstained hands as indelible markers of his lack of civility and other deviant behavior. Such presumptions about a transgressive body have also long existed in popular imaginings of homosexuals. The most recurring presumption, of course, is of gender transitivity, but others involve the ostensible effects of same-sex acts on the gay or lesbian body. During World War II, for instance, military physicians reasoned for the detection of gay men during clinical examinations, since sexual activity would have invariably and permanently distended their rectums and made their throats capable of accepting tongue depressors without display of gag reflexes.[17]

These popular images of Boo further parallel homophobic understandings of gays and lesbians in that both script transgressive individuals as disrupting familial unity and ensuring parental fear, anxiety, and embarrassment. Jem, Scout, and Dill revise their "melancholy little drama" of the Radleys' lives to include precisely this. Scout recalls Mrs. Radley's characterization in particular: "Mrs. Radley had been beautiful until she married Mr. Radley and lost all her money. She also lost most of her teeth, her hair, and her right forefinger (Dill's contribution. Boo bit it off one night when he couldn't find any cats and squirrels to eat.); she sat in the living room and cried most of the time, while Boo slowly whittled away all the furniture" (44). In the children's imaginations, Boo's deviancy is so devastating to his family that its members become unfit to function within greater society. Boo's mother can only mourn that which she had lost in her son, even as he continues to destroy the actual house.

Such sentiments parallel those sometimes shown by parents when they learn of their children's gayness. Sedgwick reflects on precisely this when she writes, "I've heard of many people who claim they'd as soon their children were dead as gay. What it took me a long time to believe is that these people are saying no more than the truth."[18] These feelings have historically arisen in no small part because the prevailing and often overlapping ideologies of most twentieth-century social institutions—military, legal, religious, and medical—have labeled homosexuality deviant. A gay or lesbian person was—and sometimes still is—thus often simultaneously treasonous, criminal, sinful, and psychologically disturbed, left without legitimate space in any of these institutions. Not insignificantly, these simultaneous stigmatizations are precisely what Lee rehearses in the communal gossip of Boo. At various moments, he emerges within these narratives as criminal, sinful, mentally ill, or all three. If neighborhood legend is to be believed, Boo's first transgressions are indeed vaguely criminal. As a teenager, he becomes involved with "the wrong crowd," "the nearest thing to a gang ever seen in Maycomb" (14). Mr. Radley's response to his son's transgressions is swift and exacting, and, even if the specifics remain unknown, there is the suggestion that Mr. Radley's punishments are so extreme that Boo is permanently traumatized. After these events, "[t]he doors of the Radley house were closed on weekdays as well as Sundays, and Mr. Radley's boy was not seen again for fifteen years" (15). Despite there being no proof of further illegal behavior, Boo nevertheless becomes within popular imagination "a malevolent phantom" responsible for a range of criminal activities. "Any stealthy small crimes committed in Maycomb were his work," Scout recalls. "Once the town was terrorized by a series of morbid nocturnal events: people's chickens and household pets were found mutilated; although the culprit was Crazy Addie, who eventually drowned himself in Barker's Eddy, people still looked at the Radley Place, unwilling to discard their initial suspicions" (13).

Just as Boo breaks the law but neither to the extent nor with the malevolence that his community wishes, so too does he presumably sin, if only according to the strictures of his father's conservative religion. Miss Maudie explains to Scout that Mr. Radley's religious preferences are not those of Maycomb's stolid Baptists and Methodists but rather the biblical fundamentalism of "a foot-washing Baptist" who believes "anything that's pleasure is a sin" and "take[s] the Bible literally" (49). Indeed, because of these sectarian differences, the Radleys hardly deign to interact with their fellow townspeople. "They did not go to church, Maycomb's principal recreation, but worshiped at home," Scout offers. "Mrs. Radley seldom if ever crossed the street for a mid-morning coffee break with her neighbors, and certainly never joined a missionary circle" (13). Nevertheless, no one presumes the family— and Mr. Radley in particular—to lack either religious conviction or devotion: "Miss Stephanie Crawford said he was so upright he took the word of God as his only law, and we believed her, because Mr. Radley's posture was ramrod straight" (16).

Lee leaves little doubt, however, as to how readers are to accept this figure. Scout's memories reveal that Lee's biblical patriarch displays all the warmth and friendliness of Faulkner's Simon McEachern: "He was a thin leathery man with colorless eyes, so colorless they did not reflect light. His cheekbones were sharp and his mouth was wide, with a thin upper lip and a full lower lip. . . . He never spoke to us. When he passed we would look at the ground and say, 'Good morning, sir,' and he would cough in reply" (16). Moreover, Lee has characters that readers presume to be trustworthy damn Mr. Radley and, by extension, his coercive fundamentalist Christianity. Calpurnia, for example, offers one of her rare comments on "the ways of white people" to curse Mr. Radley's corpse as "the meanest man ever God blew breath into" (16-17). Miss Maudie is somewhat more temperate in her explanations of the Radleys, but she too implicitly critiques the effects of Mr. Radley's religious fanaticism: "'You are too young to understand it,' she said, 'but sometimes the Bible in the hand of one man is worse than a whiskey bottle in the hand of—oh, of your father.'" "There are just some kind of men who—who're so busy worrying about the next world they've never learned to live in this one," Miss Maudie concludes, "and you can look down the street and see the results" (49-50).

As with so much of Boo's story, Miss Maudie leaves unsaid the specifics of these results; however, Miss Stephanie Crawford elaborates on the facts of Boo's narrative to suggest a logical series of causes and effects. Angered by his son's minor infractions of the law, Mr. Radley ensures "that Arthur gave no further trouble" (15), and Boo disappears. The community hypothesizes that Mr. Radley exerts the patriarchal authority invested in him by Scripture to discipline Boo's rebelliousness so excessively that Jem, amplifying communal gossip, judges "that Mr. Radley kept him chained to the bed most of the time" (16). Even Miss Maudie mournfully replies to Scout's inquiry if Boo is crazy, "If he's not he should be by now. The things that happen to people we never really know. What happens in houses behind closed doors, what secrets—" (50). Given the effectiveness and perhaps even excessiveness of this unspecified discipline suggested by Boo's physical absence, a rebellion against this patriarchal authority seems not only understandable but also expected.

Yet, within both familial and communal responses, Boo's reaction to his father's oppression is figured as proof of mental instability. The very placidity and methodicalness with which Boo supposedly interrupts work on his scrapbook to stab his father in the leg with a pair of scissors bespeak his insanity as well as hint at Lee's appropriation of an unresolved Freudian Oedipal conflict. According to Miss Stephanie's polished version of the tale, "As Mr. Radley passed by, Boo drove the scissors into his parent's leg, pulled them out, wiped them on his pants, and resumed his activities" (15). His mother immediately presumes utter insanity in her son and runs "screaming into the street that Arthur was killing them all," and Maycomb as a whole "suggested that a season in Tuscaloosa might be helpful to Boo." Even Mr. Radley concedes that, although "Boo wasn't crazy, he was high-strung at times" (15).

If Lee suggests with this identity, triply damned by crime, sin, and insanity, that Boo's family and community play a significant role in the imposition and, after Mr. Radley's death, self-imposition of the closet, she also depicts the community as equally, if perhaps somewhat paradoxically, preoccupied with making Boo come out of that space. Even as Jem, Scout, and Dill participate in the elaborations on the closet-bolstering rumors, the children are also fascinated with Boo and plot scheme after scheme to lure him into communal interactions and thus supposedly to learn his true identity. "Wonder what he does in there," Dill murmurs before suggesting, "Let's try to make him come out . . . I'd like to see what he looks like" (17). Such a paradoxical response to deviant identity was and, according to Sedgwick, continues to be a staple reaction to homosexuality: "To the fine antennae of public attention the freshness of every drama of (especially involuntary) gay uncovering seems if anything heightened in surprise and delectability, rather than staled, by the increasingly intense atmosphere of public articulations of and about the love that is famous for daring not speak its name."[19] That is, as discourses proliferate around homosexuality, whether homophobic or homophilic, there persists and even increases a fascination with deviant sexuality being made knowable in public arenas.

To Kill a Mockingbird culminates with this knowability of the deviant when Boo literally comes out to rescue Scout and Jem from Bob Ewell, and the final chapters of the novel explore personal and anticipated communal responses to this knowability. Lee's narrative dictates these responses, however, by less than subtly establishing Boo as thoroughly sympathetic despite his cultural otherness. Just as she scripts Tom Robinson as quiet and respectable, she creates in Boo a figure epitomizing self-sacrifice and heroism. Each of his previous interactions with the children has been a gesture of friendliness and consideration: leaving intriguing trinkets in an oak tree as tokens of affection, providing a quilt for the shivering Scout as she watches Miss Maudie's house burn, and mending Jem's ripped pants. Boo's ultimate gifts, however, are Scout and Jem's very lives, as Atticus recognizes. Thus, whereas Tom eventually proves as innocent as Harriet Beecher Stowe's martyr with the same name, Boo, a protector of children as innocent as Little Eva, proves as heroic as the Christian knight to whom his name Arthur alludes.

If Boo's actions are thus antithetical to those attributed to him by gossip, so too is his body at variance with images circulating in popular imagination. Instead of a drooling, bloodstained oaf, Scout encounters a man easily mistakable for an unknown ordinary townsperson. As she surveys Jem's bedroom in the aftermath of the encounter with Bob Ewell, but before she knows Boo's identity, Scout notes the presence of the children's rescuer and finds him immediately readable as benign: "The man who brought Jem in was standing in a corner, leaning against the wall. He was some countryman I did not know. He had probably been at the pageant, and was in the vicinity when it happened. He must have heard our screams and come running" (268). He wears the most ordinary of clothes for Maycomb—khaki pants and a denim shirt—and, despite a paleness unsettling in a community of sunburned farmers, verges on being thoroughly generic in Scout's initial notice of him.

Even after Scout learns who this figure is, however, she finds Boo to be anything but the monster of communal gossip. She no longer fears his house and even pauses to savor the view from its porch when she escorts him home. The walk comes close to fulfilling the visions made possible by the maturity she gains during the summer of Tom's trial: "I imagined how it would be: when it happened, he'd just be sitting in the swing when I came along. 'Hidy do, Mr. Arthur,' I would say, as if I had said it every afternoon of my life. 'Evening, Jean Louise,' he would say, as if he had said it every afternoon of my life, 'right pretty spell we're having, isn't it?' 'Yes, sir, right pretty,' I would say, and go on" (245). The novel's final didactic lines underscore this sympathetic character even further. Although Scout drowsily refers to the events of *The Gray Ghost* as Atticus puts her to bed, she might as well be discussing Boo:

> He guided me to the bed and sat me down. He lifted my legs and put me under the cover.
> "An' they chased him 'n' never could catch him 'cause they didn't know what he looked like, an' Atticus, when they finally saw him, why he hadn't done any of those things . . . Atticus, he was real nice. . . ."
> His hands were under my chin, pulling up the cover, tucking it around me.
> "Most people are, Scout, when you finally see them." (283-84)

Like the wronged Stoner's Boy whom Scout recalls in *The Gray Ghost*, Boo is an innocent victim of social accusations. When Scout finally meets him and can judge his identity for herself rather than rely on malicious rumors, he strikes her not as a freakish demon but instead as simply "real nice."

In its generic form, this narrative is one often championed as the ideal for the advancement of social tolerance. The cultural outsider is known only in the abstract and accordingly demonized for his or her rumored differences until prolonged or heroic interactions establish reassuring commonalties for the cultural insider and ultimately ensure acceptance. Within gay communities this narrative is particularly familiar, since one of the most consistently promoted courses of action is coming out. Gay persons, the valorized narrative goes, must confront society to demythify homosexuality and thus allow others to understand same-sex desire more accurately, with the ultimate goal being acceptance or at least tolerance of homosexuals. In fact, the narrative usually figures the closet as a site of fear, cowardice, and self-loathing, and persons who remain within this space often stand accused of retarding and even jeopardizing the tolerance fostered by persons who have already come out.

The terms of this acceptance and/or tolerance, however, mark one of the most divisive splits within these communities. At one end of the conventional spectrum are those persons who hold gayness to be radically different from a usually—and inaccurately—homogenized straightness and urge acceptance of this alterity. At the other end of this spectrum are those who emphasize perceived commonalties between heterosexual and homosexual persons, downplaying differences between the two and within each to stress gays and lesbians' "normalcy" when compared to, again, homogenized straight persons. Despite minor differences, this rhetoric implies all persons are first and foremost human and deserve to be treated as such.

Like most persons with culturally minoritized identities, gays and lesbians struggle with these negotiations of difference and sameness, debating the personal and political efficacy of not only these extremes but also the more complex and more common intervening stances. But, as historian John D'Emilio has suggested, such debates did not emerge only when the Stonewall riots electrified gay and lesbian communities in 1969. At precisely the moment when Lee was completing *To Kill a Mockingbird*, a crucial handful of American homosexuals were engaged in one of the most significant rounds of these debates. Nascent homosexual communities such as those considered in George Chauncey's work experienced tremendous growth that frequently solidified a group identity during and immediately after World War II. With this emergent identity, D'Emilio argues, came the struggle for its public acknowledgment. Early advocates for this recognition, such as those persons organizing the Mattachine Society in 1951, tended toward political radicalness, often bringing with them Communist affiliations and usually characterizing their efforts as working toward militant "homosexual emancipation." It is perhaps not surprising, however, that in this era of Joseph McCarthy's Communist paranoia, the probings of the House's Un-American Activities Committee, Dwight Eisenhower's seemingly benign presidency, and the return to prewar cultural and familial normalcy with a vengeance, comparable conservatism also crucially affected emerging gay activism. Indeed, by the mid-1950s the leadership of these organizations dramatically shifted from its radical instigators, such as Harry Hay and Charles Rowland, to persons such as Marilyn Rieger and Kenneth Burns and constituted what D'Emilio terms a retreat into respectability.

The political strategy advocated by Rieger, Burns, and others like them, that which eventually came to characterize much of gay activism until Stonewall, directly countered the strategy of the Mattachine's original and early organizers. Whereas Hay and Rowland considered gays and lesbians a minority with its own unique culture, Rieger and Burns denied such a status. "We know we are the same," Rieger argued at the 1953 Mattachine convention, "no different from anyone else. Our only difference is an unimportant one to the heterosexual society, *unless we make it important.*" According to this logic, homosexuals should therefore come out and prove their utter normalcy to gain equality. "[B]y declaring ourselves, by integrating," Rieger continued, "not as homosexuals, but as people, as men and women whose homosexuality is irrelevant to our ideals, our principles, our hopes and aspirations," would activists "rid the world of its misconceptions of homosexuality and homosexuals." By mid-century, Rowland and Hay had been forced to cede their positions of leadership, and Rieger's rhetoric was the standard. The *Mattachine Review* and the *Ladder,* respective mouthpieces for the Mattachine Society and the exclusively female but comparably conservative Daughters of Bilitis, urged readers to prove through their dress and activity that they were "average people in all other respects outside of our private sexual inclinations." The Daughters of Bilitis in particular cautioned lesbians against wearing pants, keeping their hair short, and frequenting bars, plaintively suggesting that they do "a little 'policing' on their own."[20]

Although this strategy faced significant challenges before Stonewall, especially in the 1960s, presented through contrasting models for political action offered by the civil rights movement,[21] this conservatism nevertheless remained pervasive in gay communities and their activism throughout the 1950s, when Lee was writing *To Kill a Mock-*

ingbird. Indeed, she ultimately resolves the novel's negotiations of closetedness in a manner comparable to this political strategy. Like gay activists of the day, Lee condemns the closet as a site of darkness, death, and decay. "The house was low," Scout recalls of the Radleys' home, and "was once white with a deep front porch and green shutters, but had long ago darkened to the color of the slate-gray yard around it. Rain-rotted shingles drooped over the eaves of the veranda; oak trees kept the sun away. The remains of a picket drunkenly guarded the front yard—a 'swept' yard that was never swept—where johnson grass and rabbit-tobacco grew in abundance" (13). Yet, when the cultural outsider who has been forced into this space decides to come out, he reveals himself to be no flamboyant Randolph or Folner but instead precisely what Marilyn Rieger expected of gays and lesbians: practically "no different from anyone else" and warmly embraced by an accepting community.

Like Rieger, however, Lee does not completely eradicate all differences in Boo. Although Scout may at first take his body to be that of an ordinary farmer, it nevertheless reveals subtle differences, most noticeably in its paleness. "His face was as white as his hands, but for a shadow on his jutting chin," Scout recalls from her one interaction with Boo. "His cheeks were thin to hollowness; his mouth was wide; there were shallow, almost delicate indentations at his temples, and his gray eyes were so colorless I thought he was blind. His hair was dead and thin, almost feathery on top of his head" (273). Moreover, Boo is painfully inept in navigating unfamiliar spaces. "Every move he made was uncertain, as if he were not sure his hands and feet could make proper contact with the things he touched" (279-80), Scout remembers.

As Lee figures these differences, though, they do not alienate Boo from others but rather endear him to them. Upon seeing Boo's understandable difficulties in negotiating crowds and strange environs, Scout derives satisfaction in both helping Boo and living out her imagination's interactions: "'Won't you have a seat, Mr. Arthur? This rocking-chair's nice and comfortable.' My small fantasy about him was alive again: he would be sitting on the porch . . . right pretty spell we're having, isn't it, Mr. Arthur? Yes, a right pretty spell. Feeling slightly unreal, I led him to the chair farthest from Atticus and Mr. Tate. It was in deep shadow. Boo would feel more comfortable in the dark" (274-75). As in the imaginations of Rieger and other conservative gay activists of the 1950s, where mainstream culture would willingly help gays and lesbians function in society once they proved their normalcy was not forfeited by differing sexual desires, when Scout can ascribe to Boo a sympathetic identity, she is more than generous in assisting him during his foray into public space.

Heart-tugging though Lee's final pages may be, they nevertheless present potentially disturbing images when Scout offers this assistance to Boo. He is cast almost as helpless, unable to negotiate even the simplest of actions, such as stroking Jem's hair or climbing steps. When one reads this help potentially to symbolize heterosexual society's response to uncloseted gays and lesbians, it suggests a disconcerting balance of power. Just as Boo is wholly reliant on Scout, in this reading, homosexuals are exclusively dependent on heterosexuals' acceptance to function outside the closet. Lee's plot even imagines this acceptance as so overwhelming that the closet may have to be reinstated as a haven from heterosexuals' attention. Heck Tate is adamant that Bob Ewell dies by accidentally falling on his knife so that Boo Radley can escape not so much being brought to trial but the communal adoration of him as a hero. Attuned to the fickleness of popular response, Tate realizes that the very people who have disseminated the rumors about Boo will, upon hearing of his exploits, disregard his heretofore emphasized differences and virtually smother him with acceptance. As a result, Tate thus effectively erases all traces of Boo's coming out, leaving them to exist only in Scout's memories.

With these final images Lee once again reveals how radically her novel differs from those of Capote and Smith if one entertains this specific reading of Boo's closetedness. Unlike *Other Voices, Other Rooms* and *Strange Fruit*, in which homosexuality is markedly at variance with cultural norms and gay or lesbian individuals face overwhelming forces of homophobia, *To Kill a Mockingbird* ultimately imagines southern community to be already queer and permeated with transgressions of gender and sexuality. The implications are that, within this community, so long as a transgressive person is not too excessively or multiply different from those around him or her, and thus in harmony with the general cultural queerness, an acknowledgment of sexual otherness brings exaggerated acceptance rather than communal disfavor. This acceptance is so pervasive that it threatens to eradicate the very elements of identity necessitating the closet in the first place and therefore indirectly bolsters this space as a site of refuge. Thus, like the gay activists organizing across the United States at precisely the moment that Lee was composing her novel, she presents a community in which, once difference has been dismissed as minor and similarity acknowledged as already existing, no more innocent mockingbirds need ever be killed, no more African Americans need ever face racism, and, if only figuratively, no more gays and lesbians need ever face homophobia.

Notes

1. Review of *To Kill a Mockingbird*, by Harper Lee, *Commonweal* 9 (December 1960): 289; Robert W. Henderson, review of *To Kill a Mockingbird*, by Harper Lee, *Library Journal* (15 May 1960): 1937; Granville Hicks, "Three at the Outset," review of *To Kill a Mockingbird*, by Harper Lee, *Saturday Review* 23 (July 1960): 15; Keith Waterhouse, review of *To Kill a Mockingbird*, by Harper Lee, *New Statesman* (15 October 1960): 580; Frank H. Lyell, "One-Taxi Town," review of *To Kill a Mockingbird*, by Harper Lee, *New York Times Book Review* (10 July 1960): 5; and "About Life and Little Girls," review of *To Kill a Mockingbird*, by Harper Lee, *Time* (1 August 1960): 70-71.

2. Hicks, "Three at the Outset," 15; "Summer Reading," review of *To Kill a Mock-*

ingbird, by Harper Lee, *Atlantic Monthly* 206 (August 1960): 98; review of *To Kill a Mockingbird*, by Harper Lee, *Booklist* 57 (1 September 1960): 23; and "About Life and Little Girls," 70; review of *To Kill a Mockingbird*, *Commonweal*, 289.

3. Eric J. Sundquist, "Blues for Atticus Finch: Scottsboro, *Brown*, and Harper Lee," in *The South as an American Problem*, 182, 183, 186, 187.

4. Cook, "Old Ways," 529. See Sundquist, "Blues for Atticus Finch," 181-209; Claudia Durst Johnson, "The Secret Courts of Men's Hearts: Code and Law in Harper Lee's *To Kill a Mockingbird*," *Studies in American Fiction* 19 (Autumn 1991): 129-39; and Claudia Durst Johnson, *To Kill a Mockingbird: Threatening Boundaries* (New York: Twayne, 1994).

5. Harper Lee, *To Kill a Mockingbird* (1960; reprint, New York: Fawcett, 1962), 11, hereafter cited in the text by page number.

6. Grobel, *Conversations with Capote*, 53; and Clarke, *Capote: A Biography*, 42.

7. Clarke, *Capote: A Biography*, 389. See also Amy Fine Collins, "A Night to Remember," *Vanity Fair* 431 (July 1996): 120-39.

8. Kenneth T. Reed, *Truman Capote* (Boston: Twayne, 1981), 15-16. See also Clarke, *Capote: A Biography*, 410-15.

9. See Johnson, "The Secret Courts of Men's Hearts," 131, 134-38.

10. Ibid., 136.

11. Judith Butler, *Gender Trouble: Feminism and the Subversion of Identity* (New York: Routledge, 1990), 140-41.

12. Ibid., 137-38, 139, 141.

13. Ibid., 137.

14. For a discussion of Lee's conservative representations of racial equality, see Sundquist, "Blues for Atticus Finch," 181-209.

15. Sedgwick, *Epistemology of the Closet*, 33.

16. For a brief discussion of closetedness not specific to gayness, see Sedgwick, *Epistemology of the Closet*, 72.

17. See Allan Bérubé, *Coming Out under Fire: The History of Gay Men and Women in World War Two* (1990; reprint, New York: Penguin, 1991), 8-33, 149-74.

18. Eve Kosofsky Sedgwick, *Tendencies* (Durham, N.C.: Duke Univ. Press, 1993), 2.

19. Sedgwick, *Epistemology of the Closet*, 67.

20. John D'Emilio, *Sexual Politics, Sexual Communities: The Making of a Homosexual Minority in the United States, 1940-1970* (Chicago: Univ. of Chicago Press, 1983), 79, 113. See also Martin Duberman, *Stonewall* (New York: Plume, 1983), 174.

21. See D'Emilio, *Sexual Politics, Sexual Communities*, 129-149; and Duberman, *Stonewall*, 73-166.

RESOURCES

Chronology of Harper Lee's Life_____

1926	Nelle Harper Lee is born in Monroeville, Alabama, on April 28 to Amasa Coleman Lee and Frances Cunningham Finch Lee.
1944-1945	Lee attends Huntingdon College.
1945-1949	Lee attends the University of Alabama and participates in a study abroad program at Oxford University. During this time, she contributes pieces to the university newspaper and edits the humor magazine the *Rammer Jammer*. She leaves the university without completing her degree.
1949-1956	Lee moves to New York City and works for Eastern Air Lines and British Overseas Airways as a reservation clerk. She begins writing short stories.
1956	Around Thanksgiving Lee presents five short stories to a New York literary agent who encourages her. On Christmas Day two friends give her their Christmas present, a note reading "You have one year off from your job to write whatever you please. Merry Christmas."
1959	Lee completes the manuscript of *To Kill a Mockingbird* during the summer. In December, she joins Truman Capote as he travels on assignment from *The New Yorker* to Garden City, Kansas, to research the murders of the Clutter family. Capote eventually expands the article into *In Cold Blood*.
1960	Lee travels back and forth between New York and Kansas as she corrects the galleys for her novel and attends the trial of Richard Hickock and Perry Edward Smith, the two men accused of murdering the Clutter family. *To Kill a Mockingbird* is published on July 11.
1961	*To Kill a Mockingbird* wins the Pulitzer Prize for Fiction.
1962	*To Kill a Mockingbird* is adapted into an Academy Award-winning screenplay starring Gregory Peck.

| 1966 | President Lyndon B. Johnson names Lee to the National Council on the Arts. |
| 2007 | President George W. Bush presents Lee with the Presidential Medal of Freedom, and Lee is inducted into the American Academy of Arts and Letters. |

Works by Harper Lee

Fiction

To Kill a Mockingbird, 1960

Nonfiction

"Love—In Other Words," 1961
"Christmas to Me," 1961
"When Children Discover America," 1965

Bibliography

Armstrong, Richard. "On *To Kill a Mockingbird*." *Film Journal* 1, no. 11 (January, 2005).

Asimov, Michael. "When Lawyers Were Heroes." *University of San Francisco Law Review* 30 (Summer, 1996):1131-1138

Baecker, Diann L. "Telling It in Black and White: The Importance of the Africanist Presence in *To Kill a Mockingbird*." *Southern Quarterly* 36, no. 3 (Spring, 1998): 124-132.

Cauthen, Cramer R., and Donald G. Alpin. "The Gift Refused: The Southern Lawyer in *TKM, The Client* and *Cape Fear.*" *Studies in Popular Culture* 19, no. 2 (October, 1996): 257-275

Champion, Laurie. "'When You Finally See Them': The Unconquered Eye in *To Kill a Mockingbird*." *Southern Quarterly* 37, no. 2 (Winter, 1999): 127-136.

Chura, Patrick. "Prolepsis and Anachronism: Emmett Till and the Historicity of *To Kill a Mockingbird.*" *Southern Literary Journal* 32, no. 2 (Spring, 2000): 1-26.

Dare, Tim. "Lawyers, Ethics, and *To Kill a Mockingbird*." *Philosophy and Literature* 25, no. 1 (April, 2001): 127-141.

Dave, R. A. "*To Kill a Mockingbird:* Harper Lee's Tragic Vision." In *Indian Studies in American Fiction,* edited by M. K. Naik, S. K. Desai, and S. Mokashi-Punekar. Dharwar: Karnatak University and The Macmillan Company of India, 1974, pp. 311-324.

Erisman, Fred. "The Romantic Regionalism of Harper Lee." *The Alabama Review* 26, no. 2 (April, 1973): 122-136.

Freedman, Monroe H. "Atticus Finch, Esq., R.I.P." *Legal Times* (February 24, 1992).

Holcomb, Mark. "*To Kill a Mockingbird*." *Film Quarterly* 55, no. 4 (Summer, 2002): 34-40.

Hovet, Theodore R., and Grace-Ann Hovet. "'Fine Fancy Gentlemen' and 'Yappy Folk': Contending Voices in *To Kill a Mockingbird*." *Southern Quarterly* 40, no. 1 (Fall, 2001): 67-78.

Going, William T. "*Store* and *Mockingbird:* Two Pulitzer Novels about Alabama." In *Essays on Alabama Literature.* Tuscaloosa: University of Alabama Press, 1975, pp. 9-31.

_____. "Truman Capote: Harper Lee's Fictional Portrait of the Artist as an Alabama Child." *Alabama Review* 42, no. 2 (1989): 136-149.

Johnson, Claudia Durst. *"To Kill a Mockingbird": Threatening Boundaries.* New York: Twayne, 1994.

_____. *Understanding "To Kill a Mockingbird": A Student Casebook to Issues, Sources, and Historical Documents.* Westport, Conn.: Greenwood, 1994.

Jolley, Susan Arpajian. "Integrating Poetry and *To Kill a Mockingbird.*" *English Journal* 92, no. 2 (November, 2002): 34-40.

Jones, Carolyn. "Atticus Finch and the Mad Dog: Harper Lee's *To Kill a Mockingbird.*" *Southern Quarterly* 34, no. 4 (Summer, 1996): 53-63.

Metress, Christopher. "The Rise and Fall of Atticus Finch." *The Chattahoochee Review* 24, no. 1 (Fall, 2003): 95-102.

Nicholson, Colin. "Hollywood and Race: *To Kill a Mockingbird.*" In *Cinema and Fiction: New Modes of Adapting,* edited by John Orr and Colin Nicholson. Edinburgh: Edinburgh University Press, 1992, pp. 151-159.

Petry, Alice Hall, ed. *On Harper Lee: Essays and Reflections.* Knoxville: University of Tennessee Press, 2007.

Remler, Nancy Lawson, and Hugh Lawson. "Situating Atticus in the Zone: A Lawyer and His Daughter Read Harper Lee's *To Kill a Mockingbird.*" In *Literature and Law,* edited by Michael J. Meyer. Amsterdam, Netherlands: Rodopi, 2004, pp. 207-217.

Richards, Gary. "Harper Lee and the Destabilization of Heterosexuality." In *Lovers and Beloveds: Sexual Otherness in Southern Fiction, 1936-1961.* Baton Rouge: Louisiana State University Press, 2005, pp. 117-157.

Shackelford, Dean. "The Female Voice in *To Kill a Mockingbird:* Narrative Strategies in Film and Novel." *Mississippi Quarterly* 50, no. 1 (Winter, 1996-1997): 101-113.

Shields, Charles J. *Mockingbird: A Portrait of Harper Lee.* New York: Henry Holt and Company, 2006.

Sundquist, Eric J. "Blues for Atticus Finch: Scottsboro, *Brown,* and Harper Lee." In *The South as an American Problem,* edited by Larry J. Griffin and Don H. Doyle. Athens: University of Georgia Press, 1995, pp. 181-209.

CRITICAL
INSIGHTS

About the Editor_____

Don Noble has been the host of the Emmy-nominated Alabama Public Television literary interview show *Bookmark* since 1988. Since 2002 his weekly reviews of fiction and nonfiction, mainly Southern, have been broadcast on Alabama Public Radio. His most recent edited books are *A State of Laughter: Comic Fiction from Alabama* (2008), *Climbing Mt. Cheaha: Emerging Alabama Writers* (2004), and *Zelda and Scott/Scott and Zelda: Essays on the Fitzgeralds' Life, Work, and Times* (2005). He is also the editor of *Hemingway: A Revaluation* (1983), *The Steinbeck Question: New Essays in Criticism* (1993), *The Rising South* (1976; with Joab L. Thomas), and *A Century Hence* (1977; by George Tucker). His reviews, essays, and interviews have appeared in numerous periodicals over the past forty years, and he has written introductions to several books, most recently a reissue of William Cobb's *Coming of Age at the Y* (2008). He serves on the board of directors of the Alabama Humanities Foundation and is an honorary lifetime member of the Alabama Writers' Forum. Noble holds a B.A. and an M.A. from SUNY-Albany. After receiving a Ph.D. from University of North Carolina, Chapel Hill, Noble joined the English Department at the University of Alabama in 1969 and is now Professor Emeritus of English and Adjunct Professor of Journalism. Noble has been a Senior Fulbright Lecturer in the former Yugoslavia (1983-1984) and Romania (1991-1992) and has been on the faculty and was the director of the Alabama in Oxford Program and director of the Alabama in Ireland Program. He has been inducted into the international scholars society Phi Beta Delta. In 2000, Noble received the Eugene Current-Garcia Award for Alabama's Distinguished Literary Scholar. With Brent Davis, he received a regional Emmy in 1996 for Excellence in Screenwriting for the documentary *I'm in the Truth Business: William Bradford Huie.*

About *The Paris Review*_____

The Paris Review is America's preeminent literary quarterly, dedicated to discovering and publishing the best new voices in fiction, nonfiction, and poetry. The magazine was founded in Paris in 1953 by the young American writers Peter Matthiessen and Doc Humes, and edited there and in New York for its first fifty years by George Plimpton. Over the decades, the *Review* has introduced readers to the earliest writings of Jack Kerouac, Philip Roth, T. C. Boyle, V. S. Naipaul, Ha Jin, Jay McInerney, and Mona Simpson, and published numerous now classic works, including Roth's *Goodbye, Columbus*, Donald Barthelme's *Alice*, Jim Carroll's *Basketball Diaries*, and selections from Samuel Beckett's *Molloy* (his first publication in English). The first chapter of Jeffrey Eugenides's *The Virgin Suicides* appeared in the *Review*'s pages, as well as stories by Edward P. Jones, Rick Moody, David Foster Wallace, Denis Johnson, Jim Shepard, Jim Crace, Lorrie Moore, Jeanette Winterson, and Ann Patchett.

The Paris Review's renowned Writers at Work series of interviews, whose early installments include legendary conversations with E. M. Forster, William Faulkner, and Ernest Hemingway, is one of the landmarks of world literature. The interviews received a George Polk award and were nominated for a Pulitzer Prize. Among the more than three hundred interviewees are Robert Frost, Marianne Moore, W. H. Auden, Elizabeth Bishop, Susan Sontag, and Toni Morrison. Recent issues feature conversations with Salman Rushdie, Joan Didion, Stephen King, Norman Mailer, Kazuo Ishiguro and Umberto Eco. (A complete list of the interviews is available at www.theparisreview.org). In November 2008, Picador will publish the third of a four-volume series of anthologies of *Paris Review* interviews. The first two volumes have received acclaim. *The New York Times* called the Writers at Work series "the most remarkable and extensive interviewing project we possess."

The Paris Review is edited by Philip Gourevitch, who was named to the post in 2005, following the death of George Plimpton two years earlier. Under Gourevitch's leadership, the magazine's international distribution has expanded, paid subscriptions have risen 150 percent, and newsstand distribution has doubled. A new editorial team has published fiction by Andre Aciman, Damon Galgut, Mohsin Hamid, Gish Jen, Richard Price, Said Sayrafiezadeh and Alistair Morgan. Poetry editors Charles Simic, Meghan O'Rourke and Dan Chiasson have selected works by Billy Collins, Jesse Ball, Mary Jo Bang, Sharon Olds, and Mary Karr. Writing published in the magazine has been anthologized in *Best American Short Stories* 2006, 2007 and 2008, *Best American Poetry*, *Best Creative Non-Fiction*, the Pushcart Prize anthology, and *O. Henry Prize Stories*.

The magazine presents two annual awards. The Hadada Award for lifelong contribution to literature has recently been given to William Styron, Joan Didion, Norman Mailer and Peter Matthiessen in 2008. The Plimpton Prize for Fiction given to a new voice in fiction brought to national attention in the pages of *The Paris Review* was presented in 2007 to Benjamin Percy and to Jesse Ball in 2008.

The Paris Review won the 2007 National Magazine Award in photojournalism and the *Los Angeles Times* recently called *The Paris Review* "an American treasure with true international reach."

Since 1999 *The Paris Review* has been published by The Paris Review Foundation, Inc., a not-for-profit 501(c)(3) organization.

The Paris Review is available in digital form to libraries worldwide in selected academic databases exclusively from EBSCO Publishing. Libraries can contact EBSCO at 1-800-653-2726 for details. For more information on *The Paris Review* or to subscribe, please visit: www.theparisreview.org.

Contributors

Don Noble has been the host of the Emmy-nominated Alabama Public Television literary interview show *Bookmark* since 1988. His most recent edited books are *A State of Laughter: Comic Fiction from Alabama* (2008), *Climbing Mt. Cheaha: Emerging Alabama Writers* (2004), and *Zelda and Scott/Scott and Zelda: Essays on the Fitzgeralds' Life, Work and Times* (2005). He is also the editor of *Hemingway: A Revaluation* (1983), *The Steinbeck Question: New Essays in Criticism* (1993), *The Rising South* (with Joab L. Thomas; 1976), and *A Century Hence* (by George Tucker; 1977).

Edythe M. McGovern was a university English professor for more than thirty years. She published several books, including *The Not So Simple Neil Simon* and *They're Never Too Young for Books*, along with several articles on Southern authors such as Tennessee Williams.

Sasha Weiss is on the editorial staff of *The New York Review of Books*.

Nancy Grisham Anderson is an Associate Professor of English at Auburn University. Her work has appeared in *The Southern Quarterly, Mosaic, Alabama Review*, and *College English*. She has edited a number of volumes and written extensively on Lella Warren. Her books include *Wrestling with God: The Meditations of Richard Marius* (2006), *Reading Faulkner: Introductions to the First Thirteen Novels* (2006), and *The Writer's Audience: A Reader for Composition* (1991).

Gurdip Panesar earned his M.A. and Ph.D. degrees in English Literature from the University of Glasgow, Scotland. Dr. Panesar has contributed various entries to recent literary reference works and is at present teaching in the Department of Adult Education at the University of Glasgow.

Neil Heims is a writer and teacher living in Paris. His books include *Reading the Diary of Anne Frank* (2005), *Allen Ginsburg* (2005), and *J. R. R. Tolkien* (2004). He has also contributed numerous articles for literary publications including essays on William Blake, John Milton, William Shakespeare, and Arthur Miller.

Matthew J. Bolton is an English teacher and the academic dean of Loyola School in New York City. Bolton earned his Ph.D. in English literature in 2005 from the Graduate Center of the City University of New York, where he wrote his dissertation on Robert Browning and T. S. Eliot. He received the T. S. Eliot Society's Fathman Young Scholar Award for work related to his dissertation. In addition to his doctorate, Bolton holds master's degrees in teaching and in educational administration from Fordham University. His research and writing center on connections between Victorian and Modernist literature.

Christopher Metress is Professor of English at Samford University. His essays have appeared in *Contemporary Southern Writers* (1998), *Critical Essays on Peter Taylor* (1993), and *Reading Erskine Caldwell* (2006); and he is the editor of *The Critical Response to Dashiell Hammett* (1995), *The Lynching of Emmett Till: A Documen-*

tary Narrative (2002), and *Emmett Till in Literary Memory and Imagination* (2007). His work has also appeared in *South Atlantic Quarterly, Southern Review, African-American Review,* and *Studies in the Novel.*

Tim Dare is a Senior Lecturer and Head of the Philosophy Department at the University of Auckland. His work has appeared in scholarly journals such as *Oxford Journal of Legal Studies, Bioethics,* and *Philosophy and Literature,* and he has been a contributor to *Ethical Challenges to Legal Practice and Education* (1998), *Judicial Power, Democracy and Legal Positivism* (2000), and *Litigating Rights: Perspectives from Domestic and International Law* (2002).

Thomas L. Shaffer is the Robert and Marion Short Professor Emeritus of Law at the University of Notre Dame Law School. He is the author of almost three hundred publications on law and related fields. He has been a visiting professor of law at the University of California at Los Angeles, the University of Virginia, Washington & Lee University, Boston College Law School, and the University of Maine.

Carolyn Jones, who now writes as Carolyn J. Medine, is Associate Professor of Religion and African American Studies at the University of Georgia. She has written a number of articles on Toni Morrison, Harper Lee, and other Southern and African American women writers.

Teresa Godwin Phelps is Professor of Law at American University Washington College of Law. She is the author of *Shattered Voices: Language, Violence, and the Work of Truth Commissions* (2004) and contributed an article to *Transforming Unjust Structures: The Capability Approach* (2006). She has also published in *Notre Dame Law Review* and *Legal Studies Forum.*

Theodore R. Hovet is Professor Emeritus of English at the University of Northern Iowa. He is the author of *The Master Narrative: Harriet Beecher Stowe's Subversive Story of Master and Slave in "Uncle Tom's Cabin" and "Dred,"* and his work has appeared in *The Journal of Religion, American Transcendental Quarterly,* and *Southern Quarterly.*

Grace-Ann Hovet was Professor Emeritus at the University of Northern Iowa. She cofounded the university's Women's Studies program in 1976, and her work has appeared in *Legacy, Black American Literature Forum,* and *Southern Quarterly.*

Diann L. Baecker is Assistant Professor of English at Virginia State University. Her writing has appeared in *Composition Forum, College Teaching,* and *Southern Quarterly.*

Dean Shackelford was Associate Professor and Director of Undergraduate Studies in English at Southeast Missouri State University until his death in 2003. His articles on Southern writers such as Harper Lee, Mark Twain, Tennessee Williams, and Flannery O'Connor have appeared in *Mississippi Quarterly* and *South Atlantic Review.*

Laurie Champion is Professor of English at San Diego State University, Imperial Valley. She is the editor or coeditor of numerous critical collections, including *Unfin-*

ished Masterpiece: The Harlem Renaissance Fiction of Anita Scott Coleman (2008), *Contemporary American Women Fiction Writers: An A-to-Z Guide* (2002), and *American Women Writers, 1900-1945: A Bio-Bibliographical Critical Sourcebook* (2000). Among other journals, her work has appeared in *Southern Literary Journal*, *Studies in Short Fiction*, *Explicator*, and *Southern Quarterly*.

Gary Richards is Associate Professor of English at the University of New Orleans. He is the author of *Lovers and Beloveds: Sexual Otherness in Southern Fiction, 1936-1961* (2005), and one of his essays was selected for inclusion in *Beth Henley: A Casebook* (2002). He has also been published in *Southern Quarterly* and *Mississippi Quarterly*.

Acknowledgments_____

"Harper Lee," by Edythe M. McGovern. From *Critical Survey of Long Fiction*. 2d rev. ed. Volume 4. Edited by Carl Rollyson. Copyright © 2000 by Salem Press, Inc. Reprinted with permission of Salem Press.

"The *Paris Review* Perspective," by Sasha Weiss. Copyright © 2008 by Sasha Weiss. Special appreciation goes to Christopher Cox and Nathaniel Rich, editors for *The Paris Review*.

"The Rise and Fall of Atticus Finch," by Christopher Metress. From *Chattahoochee Review* 24, no. 1 (Fall, 2003), pp. 95-102. Copyright © 2003 by Christopher Metress. Reprinted by permission of Christopher Metress.

"Lawyers, Ethics, and *To Kill a Mockingbird*," by Tim Dare. From *Philosophy and Literature* 25, no. 1 (2001), pp. 127-141. Copyright © 2001 by The Johns Hopkins University Press. Reprinted with permission of The Johns Hopkins University Press.

"Growing up Good in Maycomb," by Thomas L. Shaffer. From *Alabama Law Review* 45 (1994), pp. 531-561. Copyright © 1994 by the Board of Trustees of the University of Alabama School of Law and Thomas L. Shaffer. Reprinted by permission of the *Alabama Law Review* and Thomas L. Shaffer.

"Atticus Finch and the Mad Dog: Harper Lee's *To Kill a Mockingbird*," by Carolyn Jones. From *The Southern Quarterly* 34, no. 4 (Summer, 1996), pp. 53-63. Copyright © 1996 by The University of Southern Mississippi. Reprinted by permission of The University of Southern Mississippi.

"The Margins of Maycomb: A Rereading of *To Kill a Mockingbird*," by Teresa Godwin Phelps. From *Alabama Law Review* 45 (1994), pp. 511-530. Copyright © 1994 by the Board of Trustees of the University of Alabama School of Law and Teresa Godwin Phelps. Reprinted by permission of the *Alabama Law Review* and Teresa Godwin Phelps.

"'Fine Fancy Gentlemen' and 'Yappy Folk': Contending Voices in *To Kill a Mockingbird*," by Theodore R. Hovet and Grace-Ann Hovet. From *The Southern Quarterly* 40 (Fall, 2001), pp. 67-78. Copyright © 2001 by The University of Southern Mississippi. Reprinted by permission of The University of Southern Mississippi.

"Telling It in Black and White: The Importance of the Africanist Presence in *To Kill a Mockingbird*," by Diann L. Baecker. From *The Southern Quarterly* 36, no. 3 (Spring, 1998), pp. 124-132. Copyright © 1998 by The University of Southern Mississippi. Reprinted by permission of The University of Southern Mississippi.

"The Female Voice in *To Kill a Mockingbird:* Narrative Strategies in Film and Novel," by Dean Shackelford. From *Mississippi Quarterly* 50, no. 1 (Winter, 1996/1997), pp. 101-113. Copyright © 1996 by Mississippi State University. Reprinted by permission of Mississippi State University.

"'When You Finally See Them': The Unconquered Eye in *To Kill a Mockingbird*,"

Index

222; fears, 159, 225; imagination, 42, 77, 292; injury, 14, 16, 34, 50, 75, 158, 166; innocence, 98, 153, 210, 250; masculinity, 258; maturation of, 6, 46, 48, 51, 60, 74, 145, 158, 206, 211, 224, 288; and the trial, 68, 129, 159, 242-243

Finch, Scout (character); adult point of view, 48, 52, 55, 145, 161-162, 223, 228, 233, 249, 254; alienation, 222, 230; childhood, 11, 16, 46, 52, 75, 145, 254; compassion, 43, 125, 152; and faith, 123, 125; fears, 225-226; friendship with Cunningham, 173-174; imagination, 77, 131, 146, 301; innocence, 96, 153; maturation of, 6, 46, 48, 74, 85, 96, 116, 120, 145, 161, 188, 193, 196, 201, 224, 231, 248, 288; narrative, 11, 16, 33, 42, 50, 53-54, 57, 62, 75, 96, 149, 158, 163, 165, 210, 213, 222-223, 226, 229, 234, 254, 262; Southern lady role, 112, 115, 121, 225, 262-263, 274; and the trial, 17, 45, 62, 68, 125, 157, 163, 217, 244; views of Atticus, 59, 226, 231, 277, 279

Flynt, Wayne, 35, 93

Foote, Horton, 10, 23, 119, 134, 138, 187, 222, 224, 235, 255, 288

Forster, E. M., 61

Freedman, Monroe, 87, 89, 92, 94, 101, 165, 186

Freud, Sigmund, 295

Gay and lesbian. *See* Homosexuality

Giddings, Robert, 223

Gill, Brendon, 188

Gilmer, Horace (character), 61, 244; abuse of Tom Robinson, 123, 128

Go Down, Moses (Faulkner), 80

Going, William T., 28

Gothic themes, 11, 73, 76-77, 193, 206, 213-214

Great Depression, 55, 222-223

Grobel, Lawrence, 259

Hancock, Alexandra Finch (character); advice of, 170, 233, 243; female role model, 12, 58, 231, 261-263, 269; husband, 262, 286; manners, 116, 232; missionary ladies, 6, 47, 113, 116, 168; opinions of, 70, 262, 270; racism, 268, 275; views on class, 173, 244

Harper Lee (Madden), 29

Harris, Dill (character), 21, 145, 160, 166, 240, 258; effeminate, 257-258; imagination, 42, 77, 292, 296; inspiration for, 10, 15-16, 34, 258-260; summers with, 68, 112, 120, 195, 225

Haverford, Rachel (character), 240

Hay, Harry, 300

Heck Tate. *See* Tate, Heck

Helen Robinson. *See* Robinson, Helen

Henderson, Robert W., 254

Hicks, Granville, 254

Hoff, Timothy, 89

Hoffman, Roy, 188

Hohoff, Tay, 22, 32

Homosexuality, 257, 280, 288, 290-293, 296, 298-300, 302

Horace Gilmer. *See* Gilmer, Horace

Hovet, Grace-Ann, 47

Hovet, Theodore R., 47

Howells, William Dean, 190

I Am Scout (Shields), 29

In Cold Blood (Capote), 10, 32, 35, 260

Intruder in the Dust (Faulkner), 92

Ivey, Caroline, 86

Wallace, George, 192

Walter Cunningham. *See* Cunningham, Walter

Ward, Cynthia, 200-201

Waterhouse, Keith, 254

Wensley, Chris, 223

We're Right, They're Wrong (Carville), 86

Wiesel, Elie, 112

Williams, Richard, 10

Woodward, C. Vann, 192

Wray, Matthew, 187, 193, 199

Wright, Richard, 288

Zebo (character), 216